PAPERBACK WRITERS

PAPERBACK WRITERS
The History of the Beatles in Print

Bill Harry

Virgin Books

First published in Great Britain in 1984 by Virgin Books
Ltd., 61-63 Portobello Road, W11 3DD

Copyright © 1984 by Bill Harry

ISBN 0 86369 021 1

Printed in Great Britain by Richard Clay Ltd
(The Chaucer Press), Suffolk.

Typeset by Keyline Graphics, London.

Designed by Jack Palmer.

Production services by Book Consultants
Cambridge

Distributed by Arrow Books.

CONTENTS

Introduction 9

The Beatles Bibliography 11

For Beatle Bookworms 77

The British Music Books 87

The Beatles Monthly 93

Beatle Magazines 115

The Comic Book Beatles 129

The World of Beatlezines 135

The Beatles in Europe 169

The Beatles as Living Legends.. 175

Index.. 181

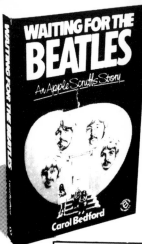

TO DINAH KELLY

The author would like to thank Sean O'Mahony of *Beatles Monthly* and the many other publishers who granted permission to use reproductions of covers to illustrate the reviews. For invaluable help, information and encouragement: Helen and Ian Drummond; Joel Glazier; Liz and Jim Hughes; Steve Philips; Eugene Beers and Gareth Davis; Jacques Volcouve; Bill King; Mark Wallgren; Rosario Grasso; Marsha Ewing; Charles Rosenay; Roger Akehurst; Ray Coleman; all at Beatles Unlimited; Carl Dunkley; Chris Daniels; David Dunn; Barb Fenick; Doylene Kindsvater; Penny Lane; Spencer Leigh; Pat Simmons; Andy Hayes and Tom Schultheiss.

BY BILL HARRY

EX-MERSEYBEATS

I dropped in to see THE GRIFF PARRY 5 practising one afternoon at The Blue Angel and bumped into DAVE ELIAS and FRANK SLOANE. Both Dave and Frank were formerly members of THE MERSEYBEATS and are currently with a group called THE NOCTURNES.

The only original founder-member of THE MERSEYBEATS in the current hit-parading group is TONY CRANE, so THE NOCTURNES can claim to have the majority of original Merseybeats members. Said DAVE ELIAS :

"TONY CRANE, BILLY KINSLEY, FRANK SLOANE and I first got together under the name THE MAVERICKS. Our first booking was at Rankin Boys Club in Sheil Road and then we played at St. Peter's Club, Seel Street and the YMCA, Mount Pleasant.

"Later, we graduated to the major Beat venues and appeared at Aintree Institute, where BOB WOOLER compèred, prior to his job at The Cavern. Bob told us that our name wasn't 'punchy' enough, so we decided to call ourselves THE PACIFICS.

"That name only lasted one week, before we changed again to THE MERSEYBEATS.

THE MOJOS—with former member ADRIAN LORD (fourth from left).

"So, in one week in 1961 we performed under three different names."

FORMER MOJO

It's a surprising thing, but almost every Mersey group to make the big time has had changes in personnel.

You know of the changes in THE BEATLES, and ARTHUR McMAHON was the former pianist with GERRY & THE PACE-MAKERS ; BRIAN REDMAN the former drummer with THE FOURMOST, and so on . . .

But did you know that ADRIAN WILKINSON was a founder-member of THE MOJOS?

Adrian, who uses the stage name ADRIAN LORD, began with THE MOJOS when they formed under the name THE NOMADS. Together with STU SLATER, he was the main songwriter in the group.

Adrian, who was replaced by guitarist NICKY CROUCH, is currently with a very dynamic R & B group, THE MASTER-SOUNDS.

And talking of The Mastersounds, that group has a member, MAL JEFFERSON, who looks very like DON ANDREW of THE REMO FOUR.

But that's not surprising really, for Mal is Don's brother and he changed his name because he didn't want to cash in on his brother's fame.

MRS. BRUM BEAT

I'm looking forward to meeting MRS. MARY REGAN who has six ballrooms in Birmingham and ten Brum groups in her stable including THE REDCAPS, THE MODS, THE MOUNTAIN KINGS, DAVE LACEY & THE CORVETTES, THE BLUE STARS, THE BRUM BEATS,

THE KAVERN FOUR and THE STRANGERS.

An animal lover, Mrs. Regan has 22 cats, 2 Alsatian dogs, 2 pet birds and an estate in Ireland with 250 head of cattle.

Born in Cork, Mrs. Regan has a son GERARD (17) and a daughter CARMEL (20). Carmel, too, seems to have the business in her blood for she also manages a Beat group. Mrs. Regan is a former schoolmistress

THE GIRLS

There have always been numerous girl vocalists on the Liverpool scene and it is not surprising that one of them, CILLA BLACK, has made the big-time.

IRENE GREEN has joined THE FOUR DIMENSIONS.

Decca recording artist BERYL MARSDEN is still without a regular backing group ; MYRA GRAYSON and BEVERLY FRASER provide vocal harmony for THE KARAC-TERS.

TED KNIBBS'S new discovery is 15-year-old VICKY CHEETHAM. Former vocalist with THE DOMINATORS, JACKIE MARTIN has commenced a solo career.

THE THREE BELLS record for Pye and have provided vocal backing for DUANE EDDY at Hamburg's Star Club.

THE CHARMERS are a vocal duo . . . and there are numerous others. The girls are always welcome on the scene . . . and good luck to them all.

But when you come to think of it, quite a few Liverpudlian girl entertainers are doing very well. There's THE VERNONS GIRLS, LYN CORNELL, THE BREAKAWAYS, LITA ROZA and THE LADYBIRDS.

THE MERSEYBEATS—one of Liverpool's top groups!

MARILYN 27-6-64

7

One of the author's earlier ventures into print, from the teen magazine Marilyn 27 June 1964.

THE BEATLES BIBLIOGRAPHY

INTRODUCTION

The number of books about the Beatles finally passed the magic figure of 200 in 1983, revealing that there have been almost twice as many books about the Fab Four published in the first three years of the eighties as in the entire decade of the sixties. So why is there an increasing thirst for information about the Beatles these days, more than at a time when the group was constantly in the public eye? Perhaps the teenagers who buy a large proportion of these Beatle books, and who weren't even born when the Beatles held sway, feel frustrated with their own decade and look back to the sixties as something of a golden age. Whatever the reason, there seems to be no sign of the boom in Beatle books abating for the present and there are still a large number of books in the pipeline.

The early sixties' books were more or less fan-type publications, collections of photographs with rather silly captions, or light-hearted biographies. Over the years, various types of Beatle books became popular. There were the photographic collections (Parkinson/Hoffmann/Freeman/Vollmer); the discographies (*Illustrated Record/All Together Now/Long and Winding Road/Beatles for the Record*); the biographies (Hunter Davies/Anthony Scaduto/Philip Norman); the "insider" books (Allan Williams/Richard Di Lello/Derek Taylor); the tour books (*In the Footsteps of the Beatles/The Beatles' England/Lots of Liverpool/Follow the Merseybeat Road*); books on a specific aspect of the Beatles' career (*The Beatles at the Beeb/The Beatles Down Under*); the collectors' publications (*The Beatles: A Collection/Collecting the Beatles*); the almanacs (*A Day in the Life/The Illustrated Diary*); and the interview books (*Lennon Remembers/Paul McCartney in His Own Words/The Lennon Tapes*). Following John's death there was a spate of books about him, which revived interest in the Beatles. There are also the "kiss and tell" books, detested by genuine Beatle fans, which set out to detail the more sensational and titillating parts of the lives of individual Beatles. These – by such authors as Peter Brown, May Pang, John Green and Fred Seaman – bring their authors large advances.

At the time of writing, more and more Beatle books are planned, including my own forthcoming filmography, to be published by Virgin as part of their Beatles Library, and my Lennon encyclopedia, *The Book of Lennon,* to be published by Aurum Press. Derek Taylor has been putting the finishing touches to his new autobiography *Fifty Years Adrift (In an Open-Necked Shirt),* to be published in an expensive limited edition by Genesis Publications and in a similar style to George's *I, Me, Mine.* Derek even went to Hawaii to finish preparing the book, accompanied by George Harrison who has been helping him in the venture.

Journalist Chris Welch has been working on *McCartney: The Definitive Biography*, to be issued in Britain by Proteus Books. Former *Melody Maker* editor Ray Coleman will have his two-volume work on John published by Sidgwick & Jackson. The first volume, *John Winston Lennon 1940-1966*, was issued in May 1984, and the second volume, *John Ono Lennon 1966-1980*, will be issued in September.

Yoko Ono is hard at work on a book, tentatively titled "A Widow's Tale"; and Cynthia Lennon is rumoured to be working on at least two books, one comprising drawings of the Beatles, the other perhaps a more revealing account of her turbulent marriage to John. Another Beatles' history, *The Long & Winding Road*, has been penned by Bob Cepicon and Walleed Ali.

On the "kiss and tell" front, Simon & Schuster will be issuing *Living With Lennon* by Fred Seaman, the former aide to John and Yoko who was arrested and taken to court for stealing various items from the Lennon apartments in the Dakota building. Fans await with horror the Albert Goldman biography of John Lennon, fearing it will tear their hero to shreds in the way that the author's previous book crucified Elvis. Jon Weiner has been working on a book concerning the background to the FBI's hounding of John in the early seventies, having spent a great deal of time researching official documents. It was published in May 1984 by Random House in America under the title *Come Together: John Lennon in His Time.*

Pierian Press will continue their excellent series of Beatle books and have obtained the rights to reprint several previously published works. Their new book in the pipeline is *The End of the Beatles?*, the final book in the trilogy of discographical information by Harry Castleman and Wally Podrazik.

Aceville, a British company, intends to issue 2,000 copies of a limited edition of a Beatle diary and Plexus will be issuing *Beatle!*, the Pete Best autobiography co-written with showbusiness journalist Pat Doncaster.

Pat Delaney, former doorman at Liverpool's Cavern Club, has been working on a book called *The Best of Cellars*; Terry Doran, a former Beatles' aide, is working on his biography, as is Dick Rowe, the Decca A&R man who turned down the opportunity of signing the Beatles. Gerry Bernstein, wife of Sid Bernstein, has a working title of "The Man Who Brought the Beatles to America" for the book about her husband Johnny Guitar, former member of Rory Storm and the Hurricanes, is to compile a book from the meticulous diaries he kept at the time; and Jimmy Nicol who deputised for Ringo on the Beatles world tour, is also writing an autobiography.

Deans International are to publish a large format, 160-page book in the autumn of 1984 which will be available exclusively from W. H. Smith in Britain. Entitled *The Beatles* it has been penned by rock journalist John Tobler, and traces the history of the group and the solo careers of the four. There is a discography as well as 160 black-and-white and 80 colour shots. It will also be published in America, Canada, Australia and New Zealand.

The late Mal Evans completed a manuscript before his death, as did John's father, Alfred, although I have no information as to whether they will ever by published in book form. Several fans are also involved in writing about their heroes, including Steve Philips who is penning a book on Ringo.

I suspect that this is just the tip of the iceberg, and hope that I will have the opportunity to add to these entries in future editions of this book. In the meantime, I will admit that I have not been overly critical in my reviews. As a bookworm, I admire anyone who writes a book and readily sympathise with their efforts. There are, of course, a handful of books which are utterly dire but, in the main, Beatle fans will collect almost anything in print about their idols – and it is a readership which is constantly growing.

Most of the books contain inaccuracies, and the errors in some cases are considerable. Tom Schultheiss provides an excellent introduction covering this specific point in his book *A Day in the Life*. Detailed information regarding the various inaccuracies in Beatle books are to be found in fanzines such as *Beatlefan, With a Little Help From My Friends, The Write Thing, Beatles Unlimited* and *Beatles Now.*

And yet, despite the publication of over 200 books, there are still aspects of the Beatles' lives and careers waiting to be uncovered – authors will be busily investigating them in the years to come.

My star system speaks for itself:

★ ★ ★ ★ ★	: Essential reading.
★ ★ ★ ★	: Essential reading
★ ★ ★	: Highly recommended
★ ★	: Fair
★	: Poor

Bill Harry
London
March 1984

THE BEATLES BIBLIOGRAPHY

THE TRUE STORY
OF
THE BEATLES

by
Billy Shepherd

•

Illustrated by BOB GIBSON

THE TRUE STORY OF THE BEATLES
Billy Shepherd. Beat Publications Ltd, 1964

Unique in being the first published book about the Fab Four, issued – appropriately – by the publishers of *Beatles Monthly*. Brian Epstein gave his blessing to the project, and Peter Jones, editor of *Record Mirror*, penned the manuscript. Jones (who used the pseudonym Billy Shepherd for his *Beatles Monthly* articles) was the first journalist from a southern music paper to interview the group; he later admitted that he had not been unduly impressed by their ability to establish themselves as a major name. Following the release of 'Love Me Do', however, he promoted them regularly in his paper.

Jones was perfectly aware of the Beatles' rowdiness and of their love affairs, but he chose to exclude this aspect from his writing. Biographical paperbacks at this time were more or less extended press hand-outs.

I remember Brian Epstein being pleased about the book as he placed it in a prominent position on his desk. The cover sports four portrait photographs, in colour; the interior contains over 30 black-and-white photographs and a series of illustrations by artist Bob Gibson (who also contributed to *Beatles Monthly*).

The True Story is rich in anecdotal material from the pre-1963 period; moreover, Jones was able to include many personal quotes from the Beatles, taken from the numerous interviews he

conducted both for *Record Mirror* and *Beatles Monthly*. Admittedly, Jones took the essence of a quote and transcribed it in what he considered correct English, rather than capturing exactly the original conversation. As a result the book contains some rather stilted dialogue. Thus we have Paul: "John propositioned me. He told me that he thought the group could do nicely and that anyway it was a lot of fun. He didn't talk about the possibility of turning professional. It was me, I think, who realised that skiffle could easily lead to some useful pocket money so that we'd be able to date the girls and maybe get a few clothes for ourselves."

But the book is an accurate account of the Beatles in the days shortly before their first American trip. It has been out of print for many years, although the publisher, Sean O'Mahony, is now considering re-issuing it. A Dutch edition, *Wij Zijn de Beatles,* was issued in Holland the same year by Het Spectrum Publishers. ★★★

ALL ABOUT THE BEATLES
Edward De Blasio. MacFadden-Bartell, 1964

One of the first American paperbacks on the market. A slim volume containing a selection of photographs of the Fab Four – including shots of their appearance on *The Ed Sullivan Show.* The 50 cent publication has the smiling quartet on the cover, with the blurb: "Here it is – The Beatle Book! – crammed with facts, figures and fotos on the most fabulous foursome in show business!"

THE BEATLES UP TO DATE
Uncredited. Lancer Books, 1964

Another 50 cent book, rush-released to cash in on the new pop phenomenon, and crammed with photographs of the Beatles, Gerry & the Pacemakers, the Dave Clarke Five, and the Searchers. Also a selection of pictures from *A Hard Day's Night.* The Beatles are featured on the cover, crouching round a tombstone-shaped design on which is written the names of the other bands mentioned in the book.

THE BEATLE BOOK
Uncredited. Lancer Books, 1964

Another "Lancer Special" paperback rush-released to cash in on the Beatles' spectacular impact in America. The cover blurb proclaims "All the facts – everything you want to know! Their lives. . . their loves. . . their music." There are almost 100 Dezo-Hoffmann photographs – one is a fold-out poster, described as a "triple-sized autographed picture."

HERE COME THE BEATLES
Charles Hamblett. Four Square Books, 1964

Illustrated with over 100 photographs, the book's 128 pages contain the minimum of text. Crammed with trivia, the standard of writing is banal; most horrendous are the corny phrases that appear in the balloons protruding from the Beatles' mouths in numerous pictures: "The fans pay to see us, let them enjoy themselves." "OK, kids. What would you like us to play for you?" "In our book, fans are the gear" and "Teenagers are the greatest ever." Other, more dreadful ones include: "Shmayrab the A-rab Lennon says: 'What gives with these British Beatles? We got plenty of scorpions back there in the desert.' " "Sitting on top of the world. Mind if we call on *you* one day for a cuppa?" and "Is, Beatles. Collect heap many trophies. Send elephant heap plenty jelly babies."

And as if this inane dialogue were not enough, there are photographs of Brigitte Bardot, a hula girl, Malcolm Muggeridge and Peter Sellers, Tarzan, Robert Morley and Marlon Brando uttering such insipid phrases as: "Like I said, man, there's 'method' in their madness." One of the poems in the book reads:

We three Beatles of Liverpool are
John in a taxi, Paul in a car,
George on a scooter bipping his hooter,
Following Ringo Starr.

Four Square Books, an imprint that no longer exists, was one of the first of the British paperback houses to take an interest in the pop scene: they had previously published books on Cliff Richard & the Shadows and Adam Faith, in addition to Phil Buckle's *Top Twenty*. Hamblett himself is described in a blurb as being "one of the world's most widely read show business writers."

OUT OF THE MOUTHS OF BEATLES
Adam Blessing. Dell Books, 1964

Another book with ridiculous captions pouring from the lips of the Fab Four. The comments in this instance are pertinent to American politics of the time. The 64-page book features Ringo on the cover – a stetson on his head, a cigarette in his mouth – with the words: "Hey, Mr Sinatra, guess who we got in the trunk of our car?" emitting from his mouth.

BEATLES LTD
Robert Freeman. George Newnes, 1964

Robert Freeman, the photographer-designer who became one of the Beatles' favourite photographers in London, has collected a number of his best shots of the Fab Four to present in book form. ★★★★

RINGO'S PHOTO ALBUM
Ringo Starr. Jamie Publishers, 1964

Strictly speaking it's a magazine: a 64-page publication with a colour cover and 75 interior photographs – candid shots of the group with their wives and girlfriends – taken by Ringo himself. Ringo also contributes an introductory letter. It is an unusual item, and it is surprising that it has never been issued subsequently. It would make a handsome book. ★★★★

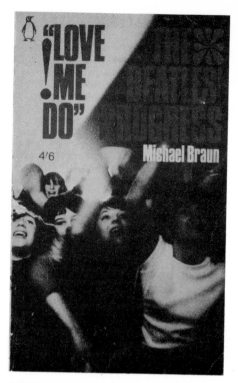

LOVE ME DO: THE BEATLES PROGRESS
Michael Braun. Penguin Books, 1964

The first, intelligent, scholarly attempt to explain "Beatlemania". New Yorker Braun had written for American publications such as the *Saturday Evening Post, Esquire* and *Playboy*, and for such British "heavies" as *The Sunday Times* and the *Spectator*. He writes more for the discerning reader than for the fan, and provides an acute and humorous observation of the group's lifestyle, as well as a detailed description of their travels.

Braun travels with the Beatles throughout England – Lincoln, Leicester, Liverpool and London – then on to Paris, New York and Washington. As the blurb states: "Michael Braun makes no claim to be an anthropologist, a sociologist, or a musicologist, he considers this book to be simply an observer's report on a phenomenon as it evolved."

The book is rich in anecdotal material and contains well chosen quotations from the Press in each of the countries the group travelled through.

The atmosphere of the Beatles' life on the road has probably never been more accurately conveyed than in this engrossing paperback, illustrated with 24 photographs. ★★★★★

A HARD DAY'S NIGHT
John Burke. Pan Books (Britain),
Dell Books (United States), 1964

A straightforward novelisation of the Beatles'
debut film. John Burke, a British writer, specialised in translating screenplays into paperback
novels; the book, based on Alun Owen's script, is
a readable version of the story. Owen, a "Liver-
pool-Welshman" and leading British TV drama-
tist, spent some time with the Beatles, and
successfully captured their exuberance and wit
in his script.

The story is a simple one: the group arrive in
London to record a television show, accompanied by Paul's grandfather, John McCartney (portrayed in the movie by actor Wilfrid Brambell),
who causes them to become involved in a
number of incidents. The story is relatively
unexciting, without the visuals and music, but the
book makes a pleasant souvenir of the movie; it is
illustrated with 12 stills from the film. ★★★

A CELLARFUL OF NOISE
Brian Epstein. Souvenir Press, 1964

In a short prologue, a boy walks into Nems record
store in Liverpool and asks for a Beatles' record –
the date is 28 October 1961. Derek Taylor (Brian
Epstein's personal assistant, who ghosted this
book for him) presents the reputed event that
led to Brian Epstein's discovery of the Beatles
in a dramatic fashion — but did the incident

occur? Dozens of fans visited Nems in the wake
of the heavy publicity the record received in
Mersey Beat. Epstein, however, was already
aware both of the record and of the Beatles: he
had been writing for *Mersey Beat* for several
months.

Derek Taylor's approach is a biased one,
giving a totally inaccurate view of the Mersey
scene. Certainly – throughout his management
both of the Beatles and of other Mersey acts –
Epstein brought the Mersey scene into the
national limelight. But from reading this book one
would think that Epstein was paramount in the
creation of this scene; he wasn't – it was already
thriving, and had been for some years, when he
first stumbled upon it. Even the story of his
discovery of Cilla Black is totally inaccurate.

Unfortunately, there has never been an impar-
tial work assessing Epstein's life. Yet this one
contains a great deal of biographical detail –
omitting, of course, the sensationalism that appeared in books of the eighties (which dwelt at
length on his homosexuality).

Credit must be given to Epstein's dedicated
belief that the Beatles were something special.
As he predicts in this book: "One day they will be
greater than Presley."

In the final analysis, what the book lacks is
depth, proving nothing more than an extended
press hand-out. Derek Taylor was well placed to
provide a great deal of insight into the world of
the Beatles: the wheeling and dealing, the struggle to the top, the heartaches as well as the
triumphs. As it stands, the book merely makes
reasonable light reading.

A Cellarful of Noise was published in America
in 1964 by Doubleday and in paperback by
Pyramid Books. New English Library published
the paperback edition in Britain in October 1965
and reprinted it in December 1981. ★★★★

THE BEATLES
Norman Parkinson and Maureen Cleave.
Hutchinson, 1964

Norman Parkinson, one of Britain's foremost
photographers – whose work can be found in
such publications as *Vogue* – took the series of
shots that form the basis of this 32-page book.
These photographs of the Fab Four were later
displayed at an exhibition devoted to Parkinson's
work at the National Portrait Gallery in 1981. The
notes were written by Maureen Cleave, then a
leading columnist with London's *Evening Standard* and the first journalist to feature the Beatles in
a national paper. ★★★★

THE BEATLES QUIZ BOOK
Jack House. William Collins & Sons Ltd, 1964

Published in the UK only, this slim (32-page)
volume comprises photographs and drawings
that illustrate a series of questions and answers
concerning the Fab Four. ★★

Love Letters to the BEATLES

selected by Bill Adler · drawings by Osborn

LOVE LETTERS TO THE BEATLES
Selected by Bill Adler. Putnam & Sons, 1964

Hardback book with drawings by the artist Osborn; the cover features an Osborn cartoon of a female fan leaning on the edge of an envelope. There is a photograph of the Beatles on the back cover. Adler selected his material from a collection of more than a quarter of a million letters, written by American fans and stored in a New York warehouse. The hardbound edition was published by Longmans Canada Ltd, and a 60p paperback version was issued in Britain. ★ ★

DEAR BEATLES
Selected by Bill Adler. Grosset & Dunlap, 1964

Adler makes further use of the American fan letters to assemble a second collection of missives sent to the Fab Four.
★ ★

IN HIS OWN WRITE
John Lennon. Jonathan Cape, 1964

The book of the year! Naturally, a volume penned by a member of the Beatles was hot property. It became an immediate best seller in Britain and the United States and was translated into French; it greatly improved the image of the Fab Four as creative people and gave a great deal of personal satisfaction to John. His first published work had appeared in *Mersey Beat* in July 1961; and this series of columns, called "Beatcomber", was virtually a test run for *In His Own Write*. The Liverpool fans loved "Beatcomber"; and John included a number of the stories from the column in the book: "Liddypool", "I Remember Arnold" and "On Safairy With Whide Hunter".

John appeared on several TV and radio shows to discuss his work and, in April 1964, was invited to a prestigious Foyle's Literary Luncheon to honour the book. John, who was recovering from a late-night clubbing spree, had not been informed that he was expected to make a speech. He stood up, mumbled a few words, then sat down. The audience appeared disgruntled until Brian Epstein saved the situation by giving a short speech of his own.

The popularity of the Beatles themselves may have tended to cloud the fact that the book contains some of the most inventive nonsense verse of the twentieth century, inviting comparisons with Lewis Carroll, Edward Lear and Ogden Nash. John's drawings, wittily complementing the text, also contain their own sparks of brilliance.

Photographer Robert Freeman designed the book; and Paul McCartney wrote the introduction, describing the first occasion when he met the fat schoolboy who was drunk. Beatle fans will point out the "Sad Michael" story on page 35 and the sentence "He'd had a hard day's night that day, for Michael was a Cocky Watchtower" to anyone who remains unclear as to the origin of their first film title.

Other stories in the book include: "Partly Dave"; "No Flies on Frank"; "Good Dog Nigel"; "At the Denis"; "The Fat Growth on Eric Hearble"; "The Wrestling Dog"; "I Wandered"; "A Letter"; "Scene Three Act One"; "Treasure Ivan"; "All Abord Speeching"; "The Fingletoad Resort of Teddyviscious"; "Alec Speaking"; "You Might Well Arsk"; "Nicely Nicely Clive"; "Neville Club"; "The Moldy Moldy Man"; "I Sat Belonely"; "Henry and Harry"; "Deaf Ted, Danoota, (and Me)"; "A Surprise for Little Bobby"; "Halbut Returb"; "Unhappy Frank"; "On This Churly Morn" and "Victor Triumphs Again and Mrs Weatherby Learns a Lesson".

I remember, having received an advance copy of the book, reading it on stage at the Blue Angel club, with Allan Williams, to a crowded audience of close friends of the Beatles. Also there were some of the Liverpool poets, Roger McGough, Adrian Henri and Brian Patten, who became successful and published a book together called *The Mersey Sound.* John's work was also the work of a poet; he relished words and was able to make them sing. When read aloud, his work betrays another influence: that of Stanley Unwin, a British humorist who became famous on radio and TV for recitations during which he would speak in a form of nonsense that could nevertheless be understood by the listener. They used to call it "fractured English".

The American edition of the book was published by Simon & Schuster, who also published the French translation, *En Flagrante Delire.* Penguin Books in Britain brought out the paperback version in 1980. ★★★★★

HELP!
Random House, 1965

A hardbound volume published in co-operation with United Artists. A handsome souvenir of their second film, it includes 30 pages of song lyrics, many stills from the film as well as location shots taken during the actual filming. An Eastern religious sect sets off in pursuit of Ringo, who has unwittingly marked himself as the fanatics' next sacrifice by wearing their secret ring. The other Beatles, realising Ringo's plight, unsuccessfully attempt to remove the offending article before fleeing to the Bahamas (by way of Austria). The Fab Four, the fanatics and a Scotland Yard Inspector finally confront one another in the sun-drenched Caribbean. ★★★

HELP!
Al Hine. Dell Books, 1965

Straightforward novelisation of their second film, with several pages of stills. It is based on the actual Marc Behm script; the cover sports the famous shot of each of the Fabs in a semaphore pose spelling out the letters H.E.L.P. The book was published in Britain as a paperback by Mayflower Books, and in Holland under the title *Help, Red de Beatles.* ★★★

JOHN LENNON
HIS FIRST BOOK
IN HIS OWN WRITE

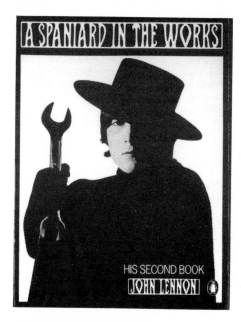

A SPANIARD IN THE WORKS
HIS SECOND BOOK
JOHN LENNON

A SPANIARD IN THE WORKS
John Lennon. Jonathan Cape, 1965

If anything, John's drawings are even more inventive than those in his first best-seller, though some of the stories in this book tend to be over-long. The title is a "fracturisation" of the phrase "a spanner in the works", and the picture on the cover shows him with both a spanner and a Spaniard's hat and cloak.

The title story concerns one Jesus El Pifco who sets off to work in Scotland and falls in love with a girl called Spastic Sporran. In the sentence "the honeymoon was don short", he is probably giving a plug to the then *Daily Mirror* showbiz columnist Don Short; "The Fat Budgie" is a poem about a bird called Jeffrey (John donated the original drawing to charity); "Snore Wife and Some Several Drawfs" is the old fairy story Lennonised; "The Singularge Experience of Miss Annie Duffield" contains lots of name checks – Ellifitzgerald, Eric Morley, Harrybellafonte, Alexguiness and Valentine Dyall – and "The Faulty Bagnose" is a poem in the "Jabberwocky" vein. The other stories are: "We Must Not Forget. . . The General Erection"; "Benjamin Distasteful"; "The Wumberlog (Or the Magic Dog)", "Araminta Ditch"; "Cassandle"; "The National Health Cow"; "Readers Lettuce"; "Silly Norman"; "Mr Boris Morris"; "Bernice's Sheep"; "Last Will and Testicle"; "Our Dad" and "I Believe, Boot. . ."

It was said that John began work on a third book in the series, but lost interest ★★★★★

COMMUNISM, HYPNOTISM, AND THE BEATLES
The Reverend David A.Noebel.
Christian Crusade, 1965

This could only be an American book! Bible-belt fanaticism going over the top again, just as it did when John made his famous comments about Christ in the Maureen Cleave interview. Noebel contends that the Beatles have been manipulated by politicians wishing to subvert the youth of America and develop a future generation of mindless puppets, ripe for a take-over by the Communists. The fact that certain American religious fanatics could believe such guff and take it seriously is frightening in itself. We were not to hear the last of Noebel!

THE PENGUIN JOHN LENNON
John Lennon. Penguin Books, 1966

Penguin was Britain's most prestigious paperback publishing house in the mid sixties. They published a few editions of this collection of John's works from his first two books (one of the covers features him sporting several pairs of spectacles, another portrays him as Superman). Penguin also published the collection in Australia. ★★★★★

UP THE BEATLES' FAMILY TREE
Cecil R.Humphrey-Smith, Michael G.Heenan, Jennifer Mount. Achievements Ltd, 1966

Slim but informative volume, produced by the "centre for heraldic and genealogical research and art-work." As the title suggests, it details the family trees of each of the Fab Four, with full-page drawings by John Bainbridge.

"Lennon is as Irish as they come," write the authors as they trace John's ancestry, mentioning that his great great grandfather was Charles Gildea. Gildea is another Irish name, adapted from the Gaelic words meaning "servant of God".

Paul's ancestors also sported Irish names such as Danher and Mohin, although the name McCartney has only been known in Ireland for a few centuries. A branch of the Scottish clan Mackintosh, the McCartneys settled in Ulster in the early seventeenth century and became the principal family in Belfast.

There is also an Irish connection to be found far back in Ringo's family tree, with an ancestor called Conroy: "It is an anglicised form of the name of several Irish sects, of Galway, Leix and Dublin."

Nor is George to be left out; we learn of an ancestor of his called French: "French is a name found largely in Ireland and the ancestors of George Harrison's grandfather may also have been among the Irish immigrants of the nineteenth century." ★★★★

JOHN LENNON. IN HIS OWN WRITE & A SPANIARD IN THE WORKS
Signet Books, 1967

John's two books in one volume. The cover features a surrealistic photograph of John wearing two pairs of spectacles with eyes drawn on them – one pair rests on his forehead, the other on his cheeks. ★★★★★

A drawing by John Lennon from his A Spaniard in the Works.
Reproduced by kind permission of Jonathan Cape Ltd.

John Lennon's illustration for "Deaf Ted, Danoota and Me" from In His Own Write.
Reproduced by kind permission of Jonathan Cape Ltd.

THE WRITING BEATLE: JOHN LENNON
Signet Books, 1967

Another Signet paperback of John's two books, the American equivalent of *The Penguin John Lennon*. The cover drawing features him standing on a plinth. He wields a giant-sized pen in place of a guitar. The slogan on the plinth announces: "Was five dollars, now ninety-five cents. Don't ask why! Buy!" ★★★★★

MURRAY THE K TELLS IT LIKE IT IS, BABY
Murray Kaufman. Holt, Rinehart & Winston, 1966

Autobiography of New York DJ Murray the K, who gained international fame when he took advantage of Beatlemania at the time of the Fab Four's first appearance in America in February 1964. Murray, from the radio station WINS, secured an introduction to the Beatles at their hotel, conducted radio interviews with them, took them out night-clubbing and even followed them down to Miami. This book includes his reminiscences about various bands, though the Beatles remain the stars. George Harrison contributed the introduction. Sadly, Murray died of cancer in 1982. ★★★

THE BEATLES:
THE AUTHORISED BIOGRAPHY
Hunter Davies. Heinemann, 1968

The first Beatles' book to become a best-seller. Hunter Davies, a writer on *The Sunday Times*, had originally contacted Paul with the idea of writing an authorised biography. Initially, he had envisaged a two-volume work. Once the project was underway he found he had to obtain copy approval from Brian Epstein and the Beatles; the finished work has been emasculated to a certain extent by these restrictions. John described it as "Bullshit!", commenting on the book in a *Rolling Stone* interview ". . . no home truths are written, my Auntie knocked all the truth bits from my childhood and my Mother out and I allowed it, which was my cop out, etc., etc. There was nothing about the orgies and the shit that happened on tour, and I wanted a real book to come out, but we all had wives and didn't want to hurt their feelings."

Sporting a cover by Alan Aldridge and containing over 40 photographs, the book is both a readable history and the most thoroughly researched document on the Beatles at the time. Davies has updated his text in subsequent editions.

Davies presents a cosy picture of the Beatles' lives. On a visit to the Lennons in Weybridge, he paints a picture of domesticity: John and Cyn discuss Julian's schooling, household food bills and pets. Paul is still lovey-dovey with actress Jane Asher, Ringo and Maureen are living in conjugal bliss rearing babies, and George and Pattie reside in a "Sunday supplement" bungalow in Esher.

The book captures the days before the storm clouds gathered in the Beatles' lives, and their story is told in a pleasant and civilised style. Davies adds a Beatle discography and an appendix on "The Beatles Finances". He states: "Annually, their gross income. . . from all sources and through all their companies, must come to at least £1,000,000." Pocket-money by today's standards!

The book was published in America by McGraw-Hill and a paperback version issued by Dell Books. ★★★★

THE BEATLES: THE REAL STORY
Julius Fast. Putnam & Sons, 1968

When the grapevine spilled the information that a full-scale Beatles' biography was being written by Hunter Davies, American publishers decided to rush-release their own books on the Fab Four. This particular one was a straightforward "cutting job", researched from press cuttings rather than interviews with the group and their circle. It includes numerous photographs.

The book has an intriguing cover – a painting of the Fabs in period costume, portrayed in the style of eighteenth-century painting. There are 16 pages of illustrations. Also published as a paperback by Berkley Medallion Books. ★★

THE BEATLES
Anthony Scaduto. Signet Books, 1968

Another US book rush-released to cash in on the publicity surrounding Hunter Davies' official biography, this time only issued in paperback. The writer's subsequent biographies of Mick Jagger and Bob Dylan were more popular. ★★

THE BEATLES: A STUDY IN SEX, DRUGS, AND REVOLUTION
The Reverend David A.Noebel.
Christian Crusade, 1968

Another emotional tract from Noebel, appealing to the rigid minds who believed that music was the Devil's work.

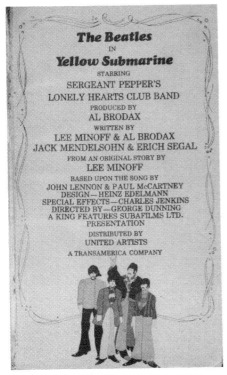

THE BEATLES IN YELLOW SUBMARINE
Max Wilk. Signet Books, 1968

A lavishly illustrated book with full colour on almost every page, utilising the marvellous drawings from the movie itself and thus providing a memorable souvenir of *The Yellow Submarine*. Because of the number of illustrations and the extent of the book (restricted to the usual 128-page paperback length of the time), the story has been condensed, dispensing with some of the film's more interesting images, such as that of the Frankenstein monster turning into John, but it should appeal to both children and adults. Pepperland is threatened by the repressive Blue Meanies. A character called Old Fred is dispatched in a Yellow Submarine by Pepperland's Lord Mayor to get help. Fred arrives in Liverpool and employs the aid of the Beatles. They set off, passing through a sea of holes, a sea of consumer products, a sea of music, a sea of time and a sea of monsters, gaining an extra passenger – the Nowhere Man – and finally arriving back in Pepperland. Here, in the guise of Sgt. Pepper's Lonely Hearts Club Band, they make music, thereby transforming the country, defeating the Blue Meanies and proving that love conquers all.

The book also contains a section of would-be humorous notes – written by someone who unfortunately lacks Lennon's comic verve.

The paperback was also issued in Britain by the New English Library. ★★★

THE YELLOW SUBMARINE GIFT BOOK
World Distributors, 1968

This large-sized, hardbound book of lavish colour illustrations from the film was issued by a firm in Manchester, England. The cover features drawings of the Yellow Submarine, the Beatles, Old Fred, the Lord Mayor and the Head Blue Meanie. ★★★

THE BEATLES: WORDS WITHOUT MUSIC
Rick Friedman. Grosset & Dunlap, 1968

In this paperback, editor Friedman has collected numerous quotes about the Beatles and from the Beatles. The forerunner of *The Beatles in Their Own Words*, dozens of photographs illustrate the text. The introduction is by Joe O'Brien, and the cover blurb states: "John, Paul, George and Ringo sound off about love and war, drugs and God, the Stones, the Maharishi and much more in this cheeky kaleidoscope of quotes and photos." ★★

THE BEATLES BOOK
Edited by Edward E.Davis.
Cowles Educational Corporation, 1968

An impressive cover features four of Richard Avedon's photographic portraits in a psychedelic style. The 14 articles and essays concern the Beatles' story and are by such eminent contributors as William F.Buckley, Timothy Leary and Ned Rorem. Only published in hardback. ★★

IN HIS OWN WRITE: THE LENNON PLAY
Adrienne Kennedy, Victor Spinetti, John Lennon.
Jonathan Cape, 1968

American author Adrienne Kennedy decided to write a play based on John's two books, and was put in touch with Victor Spinetti who told her that John's permission would be required before she could go ahead. John was consulted and the project was approved by Sir Laurence Olivier. Spinetti and Adrienne Kennedy then co-wrote the play, adapting some of the ideas contained in the books to portray a character called Me and the development of Me's opinions. The play, produced by Spinetti, was presented in June 1968. The book is the script of the play and was issued in a hardbound edition. The cover features the left-hand side of a bespectacled face, presumably John's, with a comic mouth painted over it and the title and author's names written in white script at the side. The American edition was published by Simon & Schuster. ★★★

THE BEATLES ILLUSTRATED LYRICS
Edited by Alan Adridge.
Macdonald Unit 75, 1969

A visual feast of photographs and inventive illustrations to the lyrics of more than 100 songs, this handsome package was conceived by Alan Aldridge. Many of the picture captions were written by Ray Connolly. Over 45 artists contributed to the work, including several internationally-known figures such as David Hockney, David Bailey, Ronald Searle and Tomi Ungerer. In addition, there is a selection of fan art received by the editor in response to an advertising campaign.

The illustrations cover many styles and moods including the erotic ("Lovely Rita"), the surreal ("Magical Mystery Tour"), the ribald ("Sexy Sadie"), the wistful ("Dear Prudence"), the saucy ("Day Tripper"), the sensual ("She Loves You"), and the coy ("Paperback Writer").

The idea was very favourably received, with the result that a second compilation was published. This volume was issued in America by Delacorte Press and in a cheaper edition by Dell. It was reissued in Britain with its companion volume in 1980 by Macdonald. ★★★★

THE BEATLES GET BACK
Photographs: Ethan Russell.
Text: Jonathan Cott, David Dalton.
Apple Publishing, 1970

Yet another Beatle innovation – a luxuriously printed souvenir book, contained in the same package as the *Let It Be* album. Designed by John Kosh, it is an expensively produced and visually delightful publication. Paul comments in the book: "This is a documentary of how the Beatles work." He was referring to the film they were making at that time, but he could equally well have been describing the book itself. In particular, Russell's photographs –244 colour and 26 black and white – are a vivid portrayal of the Beatles at work.

The photos capture the bleakness of Twickenham Studios with its dark corners, scaffolding, and spaghetti jungle of electronic wiring. The Beatles are shown in various moods as they perform the music for album and film, occasionally surrounded by friends or relatives – Neil Aspinall, Yoko Ono, Mal Evans. Billy Preston is present (as a musician) contributing to the recording, and Yoko is seen keeping a watchful eye on John. One of the pictorial highlights is a tender shot of Paul playing with his stepdaughter Heather. Russell has presented a remarkable photo-essay, and a valuable addition to Beatlelore.

The text has been provided by Jonathan Cott and David Dalton, both contributors to the American magazine *Rolling Stone*. Cott, in fact, conducted the magazine's first interview with John. The 24 pages of text consist mainly of the edited conversation of film director Michael Lindsay-Hogg and the Beatles; this took place between sessions, and as such has a dreamlike, almost surreal quality – it ebbs and flows, touching on many subjects, meandering, drifting, sometimes drying up completely.

At times John's dialogue sounds as if it has come from the pages of *In His Own Write*: "Since then the group has become the hottest property in Japan due to being locked in a sauna bath by Her Royal Majesty Ho Chin Mind. Out tomorrow is our disc 'Come on in you will get pneumonia'..." Or: "Once upon a tarmac there lived a small baggade who suffered incredible distraction on his right leg. He took it out to the Doctors and they said that... One day... happy ever after." There are hints of George's growing discontent, shades of Ringo's sense of humour (we never do find the answer to Ringo's riddle: what goes under water, over water, and never gets wet?) and rambling recollections from Paul. ★★★★★

THE GIRL WHO SANG WITH THE BEATLES
Robert Hemenway. Alfred A.Knopf, 1970

The first example of published fiction about the Beatles, though the book is subtitled "And Other Stories" and the Beatles are not actually mentioned until page 203. There are nine stories in this first collection of the work of Michigan writer Hemenway, all originally published in the *New Yorker* magazine. "The Girl Who Sang With the Beatles" is the most prominent tale: it was awarded first prize in "Prize Stories 1970: The O.Henry Awards".

The story has a certain charm. Larry, aged 40, and Cynthia, aged 33, get married. After some months, Larry begins to harbour doubts about their mutual compatibility: he likes reading and listening to classical music, she watches old movies on TV until the early hours. Larry buys Cynthia ear-phones and she begins to listen to middle-of-the-road music for hours at a stretch. They are both saddened by the death of J.F. Kennedy and to console her he buys a Beatles' album.

Larry notices that she spends hours listening to the record, miming to it. She reveals to him that she has created a fantasy in which she has successfully auditioned to play with the Beatles. Describing an imaginary appearance at the London Palladium, she says: "The place is mobbed ... The Beatles are on stage .. I'm singing with them, and naturally everybody loves us. I work through the whole show. . . playing second guitar.

I back up George." Larry has become a Beatles' fan himself, believing that they have brought new hope to the United States after the tragedy of President Kennedy's assassination. "The Beatles are filled with the Holy Ghost. Do you know that? They came to bring us back to life! Out of the old nightmare. Dallas, Oswald, Ruby, all of it. . ."

Cynthia continues to inhabit her dream world and Larry to play his classical records, but the music of the Beatles seems to have brought them closer together.

The book was published in England by Macdonald. ★★★

WE LOVE YOU BEATLES
Margaret Sutton. Doubleday, 1971

This simplified picture-story of the Beatles' career is strictly for kids. A very slim, 48-page, hardbound children's book, written and illustrated by Sutton, it includes a number of colour drawings. ★★

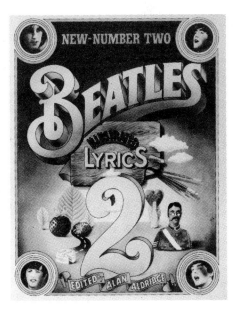

THE BEATLES ILLUSTRATED LYRICS: VOLUME TWO
Alan Aldridge. BCI Publishing Ltd, 1971

In his introduction, Ray Connolly refers to the Beatles as "the dream weavers of our generation"; and the book itself weaves a number of dream-like images in its illustrations to 88 song lyrics. These illustrations have been executed in a variety of styles by almost 80 artists, including such established names as Allen Jones, Adrian George, Ralph Steadman and Eduardo Paolozzi. Aldridge himself is a self-taught artist of exceptional skill with an individual style, rich in colour and detail. He has illustrated the songs 'Instant

Karma!', 'Across the Universe', 'Cold Turkey', 'I Don't Want to Spoil the Party', and 'I'm Happy Just to Dance With You' – all penned by John (providing us with a guide to Alan's individual tastes).

We are given an indication of how Aldridge asembled the book; Japanese artist Tadanori Yokoo includes the letter commissioning his work in his actual assignment. It reads, in part: ". . . I am preparing Volume II of *The Beatles Illustrated Lyrics* which will be a companion work to the first book published by B.P.C. in the Autumn of 1969.

"As with the first volume, I am trying to get all the people I admire involved, and I was hoping that you might like to participate.

"I am enclosing with this letter two sets of lyrics which I would very much like you to illustrate. Although I would prefer to have original work for the book it may be that you already have unpublished work that you think would portray the lyrics, and which you would allow us to reproduce. . ."

Pencil, ink, wash, guache, oils, photographs and papier mâché models are among the many methods used by the contributing artists to express their vision of Beatle masterpieces. Many of the lyrics are coupled with comments – assembled from quotes by John, Paul, George or Ringo – offering illumination on a particular composition. Discussing 'Woman' (a song he wrote for Peter and Gordon) Paul says: "It became very difficult for me to write with Yoko sitting there. I might want to say something like 'I love you girl' but with Yoko watching I always felt I had to come out with something clever and avant-garde. She would probably have loved the simple stuff, but I was scared." John comments on 'Give Peace a Chance': "The real word I used on the record was 'masturbation', but I'd just got in trouble for the 'Ballad of John and Yoko' and I didn't want any more fuss, so I put 'mastication' in the written lyrics. It was a cop-out, but the message about peace was more important to me than having a little laugh about a word."

The standard of the work is exceptionally high and – judging by the exotic, often erotic, drawings of Allen Jones, Michael English, Marcia Herscovitz, Dick Weaver and Adrian George – it is apparent that a number of artists find the Beatles' lyrics quite sensual. ★★★★

THE BEATLES
Aram Saroyan. Barn Dream Press, 1971

A curiosity item. A four-page book containing eight words, and selling for only five cents. Saroyan is known as a minimalist poet; the entire contents of the book, with two words per page, comprise the names: JOHN LENNON, PAUL McCARTNEY, GEORGE HARRISON, RINGO STARR.

LENNON REMEMBERS
Jann Wenner. Straight Arrow, 1971

The first gritty, no-holds-barred book about the life of a Beatle. *Rolling Stone* editor Jann Wenner conducted lengthy, in-depth interviews with Lennon following the release of the *John Lennon/Plastic Ono Band* album; they were presented as a two-part series entitled "Working Class Hero" in the innovative American rock magazine.

The interviews were collected and published by the magazine's own publishing arm, Straight Arrow Books, in 1971. They were issued in Britain in 1972 by Talmy, Franklin. Penguin Books brought out a paperback version in 1973 containing 60 photographs and a cover painting by Philip Castle. Penguin reprinted the book in 1980.

In this searing interview, John is abrasive, rude, angry and – at times – inarticulate. It proved to be very controversial, perhaps because he destroyed so many myths. He describes tours as being like "Fellini's *Satyricon*," tells of orgies, visits to brothels, aides securing drugs and groupies. Some enthusiasts were appalled that he had turned on long-time friends such as Neil Aspinall and Derek Taylor; but his criticisms were aimed at a number of people, most notably Paul McCartney. He dismisses the musical products of his former friends and associates, commenting on George's album *All Things Must Pass:* "I think it's all right. . . I wouldn't play that kind of music but I don't want to hurt George's feelings." And of Paul's *McCartney* LP: "I thought [it] was rubbish." Even his former idol Bob Dylan does not escape unscathed; John mentions Dylan's latest album *New Morning:* "It wasn't much. . . I haven't been a Dylan follower since he stopped rocking."

John discusses a wide range of topics: his attitude to cripples, primal therapy, George Martin, Phil Spector, the Beatles' break-up, the Maharishi, Apple, the MBEs, LSD and Yoko – covering all aspects of his career. He mentions that, among his own songs, his personal favourites are 'I Am the Walrus', 'Strawberry Fields Forever', 'Help', and 'In My Life". ★★★★★

APPLE TO THE CORE
Peter McCabe and Robert D. Schonfeld. Pocket Books, 1972

McCabe is a Liverpool-born, Cambridge graduate who moved to New York and became an editor for *Rolling Stone* magazine. Schonfeld is an American who received a BA in Political Science at Kenyon College before enrolling at the New York University Graduate School of Business Administration. They were both well qualified for dissecting and analysing the complex story of Apple, the business nightmares, the contractual muddles, the birth and death of a dream.

The first half of the book is familiar territory, charting the basic history of the Beatles' story. However, McCabe and Schonfeld are to be congratulated for carrying out their own inter-

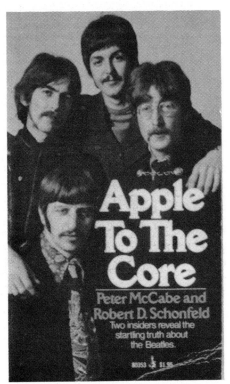

views with some of the lesser-known stars in the Beatles' firmament – Pat Delaney, the former Cavern doorman, Astrid Kemp, Wendy Moger, Tony Barrow and Nat Weiss. The book really gets into its stride when it documents the trials and tribulations of the fated company. The Apple boutique turned into a farce, with the Dutch designers – The Fool – spending vast sums of money. The only lasting image they created was the enormous psychedelic mural painted on the side of the Baker Street building.

Alexis Mardas was another person who thought that working for the Beatles was a licence to print money. He ran the electronics division of the company; yet although a small fortune was invested in this department, the only results were a succession of gimmicks (some of which fascinated John). Mardas then convinced them he could create astoundingly advanced electronic devices, as well as build a 72-track studio at Apple. But he never completed the studio and George Martin had to be called in.

Chapter six, "The Power Struggle Begins With Nems", details the group's abortive bid to purchase Epstein's management company. "Enter Pop Biz Demon Allen Klein" illustrates this man's ability to manipulate three of the Beatles – particularly John – with his act of being the underdog, an orphan like John, a person with knowledge about their records and career. He didn't fool Paul, though. "It's Only a Northern

Song" follows, showing that Klein was unable to secure Northern Songs, just as he was unable to obtain Nems Enterprises for the group. "The Long and Winding Road Through the English Courts" covers Paul's reluctant decision to wind up the partnership, and the unavoidable bitterness that resulted from this.

It is a sad tale, but an engrossing one. The reader is left feeling a sense of regret at what happened at Apple. . . and somewhat bewildered. Also published in a hardback edition in Britain. ★★★★

THE LENNON FACTOR
Paul Young. Stein and Day, 1972

Hardbound book with a simple cover of John in a white suit, with long hair and a beard, walking. There are no interior illustrations; the book concentrates on John, linking the story of the Beatles to the popular culture of the day. ★★

Richard DiLello
An insider's diary of the Beatles million pound 'Apple' empire and its wild rise and confusion.

THE LONGEST COCKTAIL PARTY
Richard DiLello. Charisma Books, 1972

Published in the United States by Playboy Books, and due to be reprinted by Pierian Press in 1984, this hilarious account of the Apple empire is in direct contrast to the sober *Apple to the Core*.

DiLello was given a job, by Derek Taylor, in the Press Office at Apple, where he became known as "The House Hippie". He brings a hip wit to his "insider's" story, written with genuine affection for the Beatles and their circle, and enhanced by over 50 photographs taken by DiLello himself. The pictures complement the text, covering not only the Beatles (Paul with Mary Hopkin, John and Yoko on various conceptual escapades), but the "Apple scruffs", interiors of Apple offices and the various members of staff – including Derek Taylor, Terry Doran, Frankie Hart, Peter Brown,

Mal Evans – as well as various Apple artists, Jackie Lomax, Mary Hopkin, Badfinger, White Trash.

The information is quite detailed, listing the structure and staff of the company, its initial formation, the signing of the first artist, the move to Savile Row and the involvement of each of the Beatles in the company – from their initial enthusiasm to their eventual disillusionment.

The influence of Derek Taylor is evident in the lively and unusual style of writing, broken up into 140 separate sections. They vary in length from items covering several pages, to small anecdotes such as: "I'll ball you if you introduce me to Paul McCartney." "All right." Two days later: "Hey, I thought you said you were going to introduce me to Paul McCartney." "That's what I tell all the girls."

The book is rich in amusing and atmospheric stories of the day-to-day running of the Press Office. The events mentioned are too numerous to list them all, but they include the *Two Virgins* album sleeve controversy; the arrival of Hell's Angels; the Christmas party with the world's largest turkey; the Fraser Gallery exhibition; the discovery of Mary Hopkin, Badfinger, White Trash and other Apple acts; the John/Yoko drugs bust; the Amsterdam Bed-in; the Allen Klein sackings; John's MBE; and the end of the cocktail party for DiLello when the Press Office was officially closed down on 1 August 1970.

"Silence in the Court Till the Judge Blows His Nose" is devoted to press reportage of the court case finalising the dissolution of the Beatles as a partnership. This section is followed by selected almanac dates covering the years between 1962 and 1967, and information on their major tours and a discography. ★★★★★

BODY COUNT
Francie Schwartz. Straight Arrow, 1972

This was the first of the kiss-and-tell books. Pennsylvanian-born Schwartz had spent some time in New York before arriving in London in 1968. She met Paul McCartney when she dropped into Apple's Wigmore Street Office to interest the organisation in a film script she had written. She began to work at Apple, started dating Paul and then moved into his St John's Wood house. This book is the story of that affair – and others – after Schwartz had already got full mileage out of her association with Paul in a *News of the World* and a *Rolling Stone* feature. ★★★

AS TIME GOES BY
Derek Taylor. Straight Arrow, 1973

Derek Taylor's famous Apple "memos" (none of which, unfortunately, are included here) were witty, sometimes utterly mad, always a thoroughly enjoyable read. Guests at Apple would often be asked to append their signature to a scrap of paper on which he had just written some cryptic

message; he would then send it on to the Beatles. There was often a near-surreal edge to the writings, as in his famous note: "A poached egg in the Underground on the Bakerloo Line between Trafalgar Square and Charing Cross? Yes, Paul. A sock full of elephant's dung on Otterspool Promenade? Give me two minutes Ringo. Two Turkish dwarfs dancing the Charleston on the sideboard? Male or female, John? Pubic hair from Sonny Liston? It's early closing, George (gulp), but give me until noon tomorrow." Hopefully, Taylor will include a selection of his memos in his *Fifty Years Adrift (in an Open-Necked Shirt)* book.

Derek has a rich, rather unusual sense of humour. His caption to the photograph of his wife and five daughters reads: "Don't take any white powders that don't have a name."

Derek describes the years between 1932 and 1972, from his birth in Hoylake to his home in Berkshire, covering his early years as a journalist, his stint at the *Daily Express* in Manchester (which eventually led to him joining the Beatles' bandwaggon), through the Apple years, his period as a PR on the West Coast of America and his return to Britain to take on an executive post at WEA Records.

"This book is my statement," he writes at one point; and in some ways it is a statement about a precious part of the sixties in London – the madcap days of Apple. He is careful to credit almost everyone who worked there, from the cleaning ladies and secretaries to the executives, such as Ron Kass, who were given the axe by Allen Klein. He claims responsibility for putting Klein in touch with the Beatles (as if confessing that his action led to the events that brought about the Beatles' demise). He admits to being frightened of Klein (which I don't believe for a moment), but also to liking him (but then Derek likes everybody). As in *The Longest Cocktail Party*, Apple is portrayed as an exciting and happy place to be until the reign of terror brought about by Allen Klein – was Klein trying to save the Beatles' money or put extra money into his own pocket?

Describing the black Friday when "the big and small men who had been fired left too," he mentions meeting Alistair Taylor in the lift: "He had been with the Beatles boy and man from the beginnings in Liverpool when Epstein had found them. Alistair Taylor's was the signature as witness on the contract they first signed. He had worked in the Nems record shop, he had been General Manager at Nems in London and he was mad about the boys." It must have been a bleak time at Apple when people who had worked so long for the Beatles, and found themselves sacked without explanation, and unable to contact the group to find some justification for their dismissal. In fact, although Apple had been losing money, it had also sold a lot of records; certainly the tree needed pruning, but it was fairly extreme of the

Beatles to find someone who then chopped it down completely.

It is obvious that Derek finds life fun. At one time, he was commissioned to turn Mae West into a rock and roll star. After a few conversations with the legendary lady, he was given a cheque and told to call it a day. The book is littered with the names of the celebrities Derek met in the course of his travels, but its strength lies in the depiction of that short, exciting "Camelot" in Savile Row when – like the sixties' era itself – the future looked so rosy.

As Time Goes By was published in Britain in 1973 in hardback by Davis Poyneter Ltd and in 1974 in paperback by Abacus. ★★★★

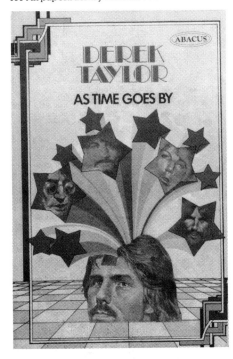

TWILIGHT OF THE GODS:
THE BEATLES IN RETROSPECT
Wilfred Mellors. Viking Press, 1973

The Beatles' music dissected and analysed by a leading British Professor of Music. For anyone who had been impressed by William Mann's talk of "major tonic sevenths and ninths built into their tunes...flat submediant key switches...
the Aeolian cadence..." in *The Sunday Times* and by the *Herald Tribune*'s "mixolydian mode", here was an entire book of the same. An unusual but worthwhile addition to any Beatles library.

One of the phrases used has come into common use and rates an entry in *To Coin a Phrase: A Dictionary of Origins* published by Papermac. Authors Edwin Radford and Alan Smith write:

"MUSIC OF NECESSITY. An academic term for 'pop' coined by Professor Wilfred Mellors of the University of York in his book *Twilight of the Gods: The Beatles in Retrospect*. Professor Mellors stresses the role of the pop musicians as fillers of the aching void in the mind of youth cultists, as dream weavers and occupiers of empty time. The phrase is an analogue of 'money of necessity', the bizarre coinages issued in besieged cities during the English Civil War..." ★★★

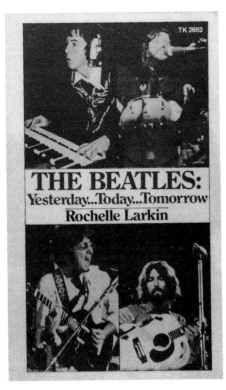

THE BEATLES:
YESTERDAY... TODAY... TOMORROW
Rochelle Larkin. Scholastic Book Services, 1974

A fan who was present among the thousands of youngsters waiting at John F.Kennedy Airport when the Beatles arrived in America in February 1964 has written her own book, ten years later. A commendable attempt, but not very well executed. The book is basically "Yesterday"; the "Today" section is only about 1,000 words long, and "Tomorrow" merely comprises a few hundred words.

In some ways it reads like a very lengthy school essay; although Larkin has a basic knowledge of the Beatles' story, she is thin on research and comes to some misplaced conclusions. She begins by claiming that Pete Best was "not of the same musical calibre as the three of them were

... he simply wasn't good enough to record." And claims that "in the rough and ready Liverpool clubs... the boys thought nothing of downing a couple of cokes and hamburgers between tunes." The hamburger invasion of Britain was years in the future; food at the Cavern usually consisted of limp cheese rolls. She also claims that the Beatles took their black leather look from Teddy Boys. Teddy Boys never wore black leather: they wore Edwardian-style jackets, hence their name.

It is a slim volume, but well illustrated with more than 85 photographs. ★★

THE BEATLES
Patricia Pirmangton. Creative Education, 1974

Another outline of the Beatles' story for young readers. ★★

THE PAUL McCARTNEY STORY
George Tremlett. Futura, 1975

The first 121 pages of this paperback document Paul's life up to 1974; and the following 71 pages comprise a detailed chronology containing such information as:

12/11/63: Paul McCartney taken ill with gastric flu, and their concert at Portsmouth Guildhall is postponed.

11/10/64: Jacksonville Gaitor Bowl, Florida – where they say they will not appear if the audience is racially segregated. "We all feel strongly about Civil Rights and the segregation issue" says Paul.

15/8/65: Jane Asher tells the *Sunday Mirror,* "No, I am not Paul's wife... but yes, we are going to get married."

26/3/66: Drake's Drum wins the Hylton Plate at Aintree at 20-1 and Paul McCartney leads his father's horse into the winner's enclosure.

The cover is a simple but effective portrait of Paul, against a background of blue sky with a Wings' symbol above his forehead; there are more than two dozen photographs inside.

Tremlett was one of the diligent journalists who went to Liverpool when the Mersey Beat scene first gained national prominence; he interviewed dozens of people who knew the Beatles and much of this information is utilised in the book. Among the people who have contributed their stories about Paul is his brother Mike McGear, who fills in background details about their father, and Ken Brown, a guitarist who played with John, Paul and George at the Casbah club.

Singer Johnny Gentle describes the Beatles' tour of Scotland as his backing band. "The promoter, Duncan McKinnon, thought they were no good and wanted to sack them at the end of the first week..." Tony Sheridan recalls their Hamburg period: "I shared a room with Paul and Pete, and John and George were in another with Stu, they just used to sleep there, because they were exhausted by the time they finished playing at the club, where they were often on stage eight hours a night."

The book covers the rising fortunes of the Liverpool lads, Paul's romance with Jane Asher, the "Paul is dead" hoax, the Francie Schwartz affair, Apple, Paul's court case against his fellow Beatles, his marriage to Linda and the formation of Wings. ★★★

THE BEATLES: THE FABULOUS STORY OF JOHN, PAUL, GEORGE & RINGO
Compiled by Robert Burt, edited by Jeremy Pascall. Octopus Books in association with Phoebus Publishing Company, 1975

The contents comprise 13 unrelated Beatle articles, originally published in the Phoebus partwork, *The Story of Pop.* (This weekly magazine, first issued to coincide with a BBC radio series of the same name, covered the history of pop music and could be bound into special folders and built up into an encyclopedia). The articles assembled in this collection are entitled: "The Mersey Sound"; "The Beatle Years 1956-1970"; "Beatlemania"; "The Beatles US Tour '64"; "The Music of the Beatles"; "The Beatle-Maker"; "Beatle Films"; "Beatle Headlines"; "The Beatles Break Up"; "John Lennon"; "Paul McCartney"; "George Harrison" and "Ringo Starr".

This large format hardback book succeeds mainly in its presentation: with 150 photographs, mainly in colour, and a bold and exciting layout. The text, however, offers nothing new and is quite thin on material. The section on Beatles' films, for instance, merely presents a couple of paragraphs of general information on each film: no synopsis, credit list or behind-the-scenes information, not even a critical comment or analysis of the films mentioned. ★★★

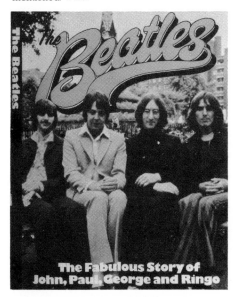

THE BEATLES LYRICS ILLUSTRATED
Dell, 1975

American paperback with an introduction written by novelist Richard Brautigan; the Alan Aldridge cover was previously used on *The Beatles Illustrated Lyrics*. This book differs from Aldridge's work since it utilises photographs to illustrate the Beatles' songs. A total of 100 separate photographs have been used. ★★★

THE BEATLES LYRICS COMPLETE
Futura Books, 1974

This paperback contains the lyrics to most of the Beatles' songs. Colin Campbell and Allan Murphy, in their *Things We Said Today* book, tell an anecdote about a schoolteacher called Allan Bacon who sued Futura under the Trade Descriptions Act because the book didn't contain the lyrics to 'Paperback Writer'. After all, there was the word "Complete" in the title. His complaint was upheld and the company were fined £25. The following year they reissued the paperback under the title *The Beatles Lyrics*. ★★★

THE BEATLES ILLUSTRATED RECORD
Roy Carr and Tony Tyler.
New English Library, 1975

This copiously illustrated, lavishly produced work (published in the United States by Harmony Books) followed John Lennon's books and Hunter Davies' biography into the best-seller lists.

The book is an unusual size: it has the dimensions of an album sleeve. There are over 220 illustrations, including album covers, membership cards, memorabilia, book and magazine covers, reproductions of clippings and photographs from childhood days through to the solo years. This 128-page book is not only visually stimulating; it contains knowledgeable and penetrating critiques of every Beatles' single and album to date, reviewed by Roy Carr and Tony Tyler. Roy, a journalist with the *New Musical Express* had previously contributed to *Mersey Beat;* Tony had also worked for the *NME*.

A concise history of the band precedes the year by year section. Beginning at 1962, the authors not only dissect each record but also contribute a year-by-year almanac of events in the life of the Fab Four; this is coloured by a choice selection of quotes from various sources. There was the religious reaction, of course. . .
Rev. Michael Brierly commented: "The Beatles are good, clean and enjoyable entertainment and the young people like them. There is nothing we can do about it. Unnecessary and superior criticism won't do any good, but merely strengthen the usual argument: 'You don't understand'." And examples of the Beatles' wit: Reporter: "Do you have a leading lady for your first film?" George: "We're trying to get the Queen. She sells."

The reviews are of varying and appropriate lengths, and the authors' comments on some of the records are very direct. On 'Please Please Me': "This is where the Beatle Legend really begins."
'She Loves You': "If a future archivist were to select one single tune to characterise the Beatles' appeal and the stylistic devices for which they became world famous, he would be forced to choose 'She Loves You'."
'I Feel Fine': "Just about the first constructive use of guitar feedback as we know and love her today."
'Paperback Writer': "The first Beatles' single to receive less than universal acclaim."
Revolver: "This almost flawless album can be seen as the peak of the Beatles' creative career."
Sgt. Pepper: "Surely the Beatles' greatest technical achievement."

The book proved so popular that there were several further editions containing updated material. ★★★★★

THE BEATLES COLLECTION
City of Liverpool Public Relations Department, 1975

This large, album-shaped package was designed by McCaffrey & Sharp and produced by Liverpool's own PR office as a tribute to their famous sons. Sixteen colour shots of Beatle albums are featured on both the front and the back covers. Inside, a large poster – mapped out chronologically – serves as an almanac of events in the

Beatles' lives; another contains details of their tour dates; yet another is a large fold-out souvenir drawing of the Fab Four; there is also a map of Liverpool indicating their homes, schools, clubs and so on. Also impressive is a circular card – simulating an actual album – that contains details of all their single and album releases. Additional items include a reproduction of Freda Kelly's last Beatles' fan club letter, dated March 1972; a Beatles' bookmark (listing Beatle books available at that time); and four postcard-size Peter Kaye photographs. An added bonus is a 30-page paperback book, *Nothing to Get Hung About: A Short History of the Beatles*, by Mike Evans. Mike, a former member of the Clayton Squares and author of *The City and the Slum Goddess*, contributes ten short chapters on the Beatles' career, beginning with "The Liverpool Background" and ending with "The Lonely Seventies". His summing up is contained in a few paragraphs entitled "Tomorrow Never Knows", in which he speculates whether the Beatles will ever reunite. He comments: "There's certainly been a revival of interest in the Beatles." In 1975, few were to realise just how extensive that interest was to grow in the years to come. ★★★★

THE BEATLES: DEZO HOFFMANN
Shinko Music Co., 1975

The Japanese books on the Beatles specialise in quality photographic reproduction; this collection of black-and-white photographs by Dezo Hoffmann contains his familiar shots, providing him with his second Beatles' gallery in book form. There is a brief text in Japanese relating to the Beatles. ★★★

THE BEATLES
Shinko Music Co., 1975

Another Shinko book, very similar to the Dezo Hoffmann photo collection, but this time reproducing photographs covering the Beatles' story from the group's early days until their break-up. ★★★

THE MAN WHO GAVE THE BEATLES AWAY
Allan Williams and William Marshall.
Elm Tree Books, 1975

The title has a touch of poetic licence: Allan Williams never had the Beatles to give away in the first place. When he states "I was the Beatles' first manager. I still have their contracts, ragged and burnt from being involved in a fire" he is referring to the contracts with Bruno Koschmeider. They were merely to book the Beatles into Hamburg. Allan Williams booked a handful of Mersey bands into Hamburg, he also booked the Beatles on a few Liverpool gigs, which in some ways would qualify him as a short-term, unofficial booking agent. But he never had any management contracts.

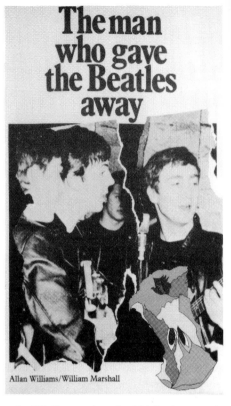

The man who gave the Beatles away

Allan Williams/William Marshall

Paul McCartney described this book as a work of fiction, while John gleefully sent Allan a letter ironically praising the book for its accuracy.

Coffee-bar owner Allan Williams became a close friend of Bill Marshall – a journalist with the *Daily Mirror* – when he was based in Liverpool during the Mersey Beat years. In the sixties, Allan commissioned Bob Azurdia, a local journalist, to ghost his biography – though the Beatles only featured in a minor role. During the seventies, Allan asked Bill Marshall to write the book for him; the obvious selling point was to bring the Beatles to centre stage. Bill then rather took the book over; it is written in his inimitable style and is full of invented dialogue. In the early chapters he has the Beatles mouth swear words in a way that makes them appear inarticulate. They never spoke that way. He writes: "The groups that patronised the Jac represented the really big time to the Beatles. They idolised them and didn't dare speak unless spoken to first." This is rubbish. He continues: "At that time I had the only Beat cellar going in Liverpool." Williams in fact ran a coffee bar in which a steel band played. When the steel band were away, he booked in a few groups because he could get them dirt cheap, but the Jac was never a Beat cellar club. He goes on: "I got them a few gigs playing at a coffee bar in a suburb of Liverpool, Heymans Green." That club was the Casbah (in existence long before the Jac), but the bookings there came about in other circumstances. Allan Williams was not associated with the group at the time.

It strikes me that not only the conversations have been made up. Allan has obviously forgotten a number of names and details, and substituted others in their place. After all, who is to challenge their accuracy? For instance, according to both the Beatles and *Mersey Beat*, (which printed a report at the time), the name of the stripper they backed was Janice, not Shirley.

Occasionally, the genuine Allan Williams emerges from Marshall's prose. Some of the letters Allan wrote have been reproduced, and for a flavour of the real man read his letter dated 20 April 1961. But as long as you read the book for its atmosphere, rather than as an accurate account, it should prove both humorous and enjoyable.

The Man Who Gave the Beatles Away was issued in America by Ballantine; there have been several paperback editions. ★★★

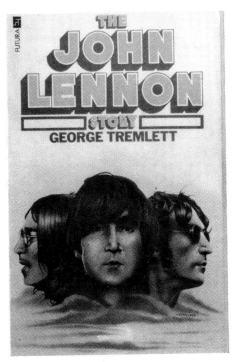

THE JOHN LENNON STORY
George Tremlett. Futura Books, 1975

Tremlett's series of paperbacks for Futura were always worth reading for their store of anecdotes, collected during interviews with friends, relatives or associates of the various stars he wrote about. He even interviewed the local tradesmen who provided the Lennons with their supplies when they lived in Weybridge!

The book begins with an account of the fifties' scene in Liverpool, following the Skiffle boom, details the interest in rock and roll and the cult of the teenager – manifesting itself in tribal style with groups such as the Teddy Boys – then describes the evolution of the Mersey scene itself with its myriad of bands. John's biography then unfolds with a portrayal of his father Freddie, the death of his mother Julia, his childhood escapades, time at Quarrybank School, the formation of the Quarrymen and his meeting with Paul. His life story is documented over the next 105 pages, when we reach 1974 – and Tremlett's summation of John's life and career. He comments: "In financial terms, Lennon is almost certainly one of the wealthiest artists the world has ever known with a fortune probably comparable to Picasso." Picasso was reputed to be worth a hundred million pounds. As John had complained only five years previously that he was down to his last thirty thousand, it might be supposed that the seventies had brought him more wealth than the whole of the sixties.

The 54-page chronology that follows is packed full of interesting background details and trivia:
15/2/65: John Lennon passes his driving test.
17/8/66: At a press conference Lennon says he is in favour of Americans going to Canada to avoid being conscripted for Vietnam. "If a man doesn't feel like fighting, he should have a right not to go into the army," he says.
25/1/67: Thieves try to steal Lennon's Mini Cooper from outside Epstein's home in Belgravia – and are foiled by an anti-theft device.
26/7/68: John Lennon spends the day at McCartney's house finishing 'Hey Jude'.

There are 16 pages of Beatle photographs, including the group's appearance at the *Mersey Beat* Awards; at the opening of the Apple boutique; with Pierre the Clown at Apple; and a shot of John and Yoko on stage at the Lyceum.

Tremlett's attempt to find a publisher for a Beatles' almanac had been unsuccessful and this book on John was not followed by ones on George and Ringo, as some fans had hoped. ★★★

THE COMPLETE BEATLES QUIZ BOOK
Edwin Goodgold and Dan Carlinsky.
Warner Books, 1975

The second quiz book devoted to the Beatles, and the first to be published in the United States. The authors have also included puzzles and a selection of black-and-white photographs. ★★

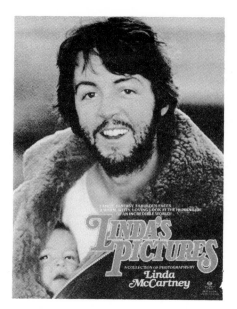

LINDA'S PICTURES
Linda McCartney. Alfred A.Knopf, 1976

A collection of 148 plates, both in colour and black and white, of Linda's favourite pictures. The flyleaf announces: "Reviewed by Paul McCartney", although the only contribution from that source is a single sentence: "The authoress, already a firm favourite of mine, scores with her first outing in print."

There is a lengthy introduction by Linda, adapted from an interview with Patrick Watson. It is a candid, informative view of Linda's love affair with the camera. An early comment: "I'm basically shy," provides us with some insight when she later says: "Taking pictures made me less shy."

Apparently, she never took her father's advice: "If you want to be a photographer, go to work for a professional. Get trained." She first began taking pictures when she was living in Arizona and her first camera was a Pentax. It was after she had moved to New York and taken photographs of the Rolling Stones at their reception on the Hudson River that she decided she would like to become a professional.

The photographer who says "if I like their music, I can get good pictures," reveals: "I was always a bit embarrassed to take pictures of the Beatles professionally because I felt I would be using Paul's friendship. So I used to take pictures and just sort of take them, not seriously."

The cover is the same colour photograph that adorns the sleeve of the *McCartney* album; it is of Paul with his recently-born daughter Mary peeking from inside his furry jacket. Like many of the family photographs inside the book, it was taken in Scotland. "The light in Scotland is the best light in the world for me," says Linda.

Linda's family pictures are particularly full of tenderness and joy, while her forays into the world of rock are intriguing. All the best ones of Jimi Hendrix disappeared: he used to take them from her, put them in a bag and she would never see them again. She only ever took one shot of Bowie, a polaroid that is reproduced here. As Linda mentions in the book, the shots of the Beatles are especially candid, benefiting from the informality.

It is with something of a shock that we see a series of happy faces – musicians making music – and realise that John Lennon, Brian Jones, Otis Redding, Keith Moon, Jim Morrison and Janis Joplin are all dead. Actor Steve McQueen (alas, also dead) is pictured with his wife Ali McGraw; other famous faces include Judy Collins, Grace Slick, Aretha Franklin, Bob Dylan and Simon and Garfunkel.

The first plate in the book features Mick Jagger, taken on that initial photographic jaunt on the Hudson. The photograph of the Beach Boys and the Maharishi is rather unfortunate: the way the paperback edition has been bound causes the guru to disappear from the picture completely if the book is held open in a certain way.

Ballantine produced a softback version of the book in the same year. ★★★

ALL TOGETHER NOW
Harry Castleman & Walter J.Podrazik. Pierian Press, 1976

The first Beatle project issued by Pierian Press, exquisitely bound and produced in a manner that was to become a hallmark of the company in their further Beatle book publications (available mainly by mail order). This book was also issued in paperback by Ballantine.

Only 1,000 copies of the book were printed in the first run. It was immediately reprinted with changes and additions made to the text. The scholarly, exhaustively researched discography is mapped out chronologically; "The Magical Mystery Tour" section details all the releases from 1961 to 1975. This is followed by an album and song title index; "Beatles for Others", an index to records by other artists performing Beatles' numbers; "By Lennon", listing all John's recordings; "Lennon for Others", listing all the recordings he participated in for other artists; there are similar indices for Paul, George and Ringo.

"The Beatles From Others" details the recordings the Beatles made of numbers written by other writers; "Bootlegs" is a lengthy listing of bootleg releases; "Pandemonium Shadow Show" is a section on Beatle-related records, including discographies of Mike McGear and George Martin.

"No You're Wrong" concerns records that have no connection with the Beatles even though people incorrectly assume that they do: thus, "The Girl I Love by the Beatles", issued in 1965 on Quest Records, was actually performed by a group called the Five Shits. "Apple Albums" lists all the LPs issued by the Beatles' company; this is followed by "Apple Singles", and releases from the "Dark Horse" and "Ring O' Records" labels.

"The Beatles on Film" is a brief filmography, as is "John and Yoko on Film". "Books for Boys and Girls of All Ages" is a selected bibliography; "Solid Gold – Rock 'n' Roll", a list of Beatle records certified as Gold. "Top of the Pops" is the complete listing of Beatle records from the *Melody Maker* charts; "American Top 40" the chart positions from *Billboard*; and "1975" a section on releases issued while this book was being compiled. ★★★★

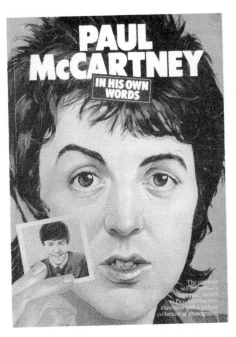

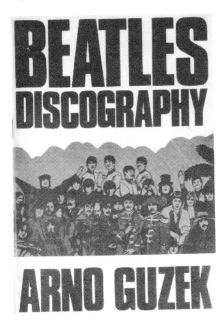

BEATLES DISCOGRAPHY
Arno Guzek. Privately printed, 1976

Danish fan Arno published his own 75-page paperback book because he wanted to make a really thorough discography available to fans. The book is divided into six parts. Part One covers the recordings the Beatles made both as a group and as solo artists; Part Two features the recordings they made guest appearances on as composer, producer or musician. Part Three is a supplement to the two previous sections; Part Four is a table of song titles. Part Five lists the releases from EMI, Apple and Capitol Records in America and Britain and the final part lists available books and fan clubs. ★★

PAUL McCARTNEY IN HIS OWN WORDS
Paul Gambaccini. Omnibus Press, 1976

This book became part of a series that included *The Beatles in Their Own Words* and *John Lennon in His Own Words*. But while the other books in the series were compilations of actual quotes, this particular one was written by Paul Gambaccini. It is adapted by articles he wrote for *Rolling Stone* magazine (compiled, in their turn, from tapes he made with Paul in 1973 and the summer of 1975). Gambaccini is an American disc jockey, domiciled in London, who has been a BBC Radio One regular for almost a decade.

The cover painting, by Roy Knipe, portrays a long-haired Paul holding up a snapshot of himself as he was in his early Beatle days. There are over 100 photographs tracing Paul's life from childhood days through his record career, and covering his successful era with Wings.

In the first chapter, "McCartney the Lad: Butlins to Hamburg", Paul destroys the myth that "Cunard Yanks" were responsible for introducing Mersey groups to American music. He talks about his early days, the first songs to impress him, the first songs he wrote, the initial influences of his formative years, the Liverpool gigs – at venues such as the Conservative Club – and the trek to Hamburg. In "Beatles: Liverpool to the World" he discusses his songwriting partnership with John, and the stories behind particular songs and records. This includes his dislike for Phil Spector's treatment of 'The Long and Winding Road': "I'm not struck by the violins and ladies' voices on it. . . But that's a bit of spilled milk. Nobody minded except me, so I shut up."

This chapter also deals with the "Paul Is Dead" rumours, *A Hard Day's Night,* and speculation about a Beatles' reunion. "The Rot of Apple: Sue Me, Sue You" discusses the lawsuit that John, George and Ringo took out against Allen Klein. "Of course, I loved that. My God, I hope they win that one." It is the story of Klein's involvement in the Beatles' affairs, and Paul's belief that Klein caused their break-up. Other subjects covered in the chapter include the group's various lawsuits, their fight to buy Northern Songs, the *Magical Mystery Tour* TV shows, and "James Paul McCartney". "Life With the Family: Mr and Mrs McCartney" is a brief chapter that includes the story of Paul's meeting with Linda, the recording sessions with his brother Mike, and Linda's pseudonym as Suzi & the Red Stripes.

Chapter Five, entitled "The Singer, the Songs and the Songwriter", is a discussion concerning a number of the songs Paul wrote – mainly his solo efforts and his hits with Wings. "Wings in Flight: Band on the Run" begins with a chat about the *Band on the Run* cover, the trip to Lagos and further discussion of tracks on the Wings' albums. Gambaccini ends the chapter with the question: "Do you think there is life after youth in Rock? Can someone Rock, in their thirties?"

The final chapter, "Venus and Mars Are Alright", is a lengthy discussion of the *Venus and Mars* album, Paul's willingness to remain in Britain and pay hefty taxes – to be "British to the core" with Linda being "honorary British."

The book ends with a short discography of Paul's singles and albums. ★★★

In Their Own Words Series

Bob Dylan In His Own Words
Compiled by Miles

The words dhe Kept most port Transcribed from audio and TV shows, press conferences and interviews

Beatles In Their Own Words
Compiled by Miles

A book for the record straight The truth about the music, myth and madness of the Beatles era from the four people who know the answers.

John Lennon In His Own Words
Compiled by Miles

For the first time in one volume the best of Lennon's wit and

wisdom, frank comment on what it was like to be one of the 'The Fab Four,' the fame, the lifestyle, his struggle in the Seventies to be more than just an 'ex-Beatle.'

The Who In Their Own Words
Compiled by Steve Clarke

Four distinct and very difficult personalities who have given rock some of its greatest

moments tell the story behind The Who.

Paul McCartney In His Own Words
Compiled by Paul Gambaccini

A searching look at McCartney from his Beatle days through to Wings, his work as a solo artist and glimpses of the family man behind the public persona.

BEATLES A-Z
John Neville Leppert, Privately published, 1976

A fan from the Crosby area of Liverpool has shown great enterprise in publishing his own book, a slim paperback basically listing all Beatle releases up to and including the single 'Yesterday. There are a couple of inaccuracies, including mention that 'It's All Too Much' was issued in 1964, instead of 1969, and the author has overlooked 'You Never Give Me Your Money'. ★★

GROWING UP WITH THE BEATLES
Ron Shaumburg. Pyramid Books, 1976

A novel and effective idea: a Beatles' fan from Kansas traces his life between the years 1964 and 1976, interweaving memories of his personal experiences with events in the life of the Beatles. Ron, aged eleven – skinny, big-eared, bespectacled, but no longer wearing braces on his teeth – hears a Beatles' record in a local drug-store and becomes obsessed with the group. We share his family secrets as he joins the Cub Scouts with his brother Robert, begins school at Shawnee Mission, sets off for Scout Camp, earns his Eagle and graduates from High School.

"The first year of the Beatles and Beatlemania in America will always be the best year of my youth" Ron recalls. Probably his most frustrating moment occurred when the Beatles actually appeared locally that year – on an unscheduled performance. Local baseball impresario Charles O'Finley offered the staggering fee of $150,000 for the Beatles to appear at Kansas City's Municipal Stadium. At $5,000 a minute, this was the largest fee that had ever been paid to an artist in America, and Brian Epstein agreed to the boys' appearance. Ron's sister Susie and her friend Nancy went to the gig, but Ron had to attend his piano lessons!

The book, subtitled "An Illustrated Tribute", is exceptionally well-illustrated with over 280 photographs and a large full-colour poster insert. Ron's pictures, chosen from a wide range of sources, provide a valuable pictorial record of the Beatles' career in the sixties. Of particular interest are shots of ecstatic fans and examples of Beatle merchandise; barber shops advertising Beatle cuts; local beauty queens awaiting the group's arrival at an airport; Paul learning to water ski; the headlines to the Kansas City concert; Paul and Jane in loving mood; the Beatles arriving in Japan; George with Ravi Shankar and friends; Paul at the piano with a parrot on his shoulder; the *Yellow Submarine* première; Paul's marriage to Linda; and the McCartneys at home in Scotland. More traditional shots show the Beatles with Ed Sullivan; making *A Hard Day's Night;* receiving their MBEs; on location for *Help!;* in the studio with George Martin; with the Maharishi; making *Magical Mystery Tour;* on the roof of the Apple building; and walking across the

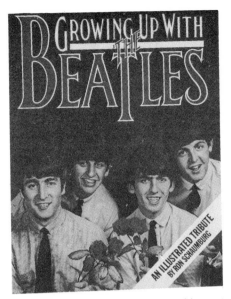

Abbey Road zebra crossing. Of special interest are the pictures of John and Yoko. There is also a shot of Yoko on stage during one of her conceptual "happenings", having her clothes snipped away by scissors. Below is a picture of her making the famous *Bottoms* film. All those people who harshly used to call Yoko ugly may well change their minds after seeing these photographs. ★ ★ ★ ★

JOHN LENNON: ONE DAY AT A TIME
Anthony Fawcett. Grove Press, 1976

Anthony Fawcett, an Oxford graduate who became an art critic, first met John at the Arts Laboratory. He became John and Yoko's personal assistant for two years, organising some of their artistic ventures. We can also thank him for suggesting and encouraging the famous "Bag One" erotic lithographs.

Fawcett explains in his introduction that "this book is about the growth of the artist John Lennon, a poet, a primitive musician, and certainly a practical dreamer." The creative world of the duo is explored with sympathetic insight: the National Sculpture Exhibition; Yoko's early conceptual "happenings" in London; "Exhibition No.2" at the Indica Gallery; the *Two Virgins* album; the John and Yoko films; the "Bed-Ins"; the Alchemical Wedding; the Peace campaign; the *In His Own Write* book and the erotic lithographs. In addition, the story takes in John and Yoko's personal and musical life from their first meeting until they had settled in New York. There is also a short chronology and a discography.

The book contains over two hundred photographs, taken by ten different photographers, including Bob Gruen, Annie Leibovitz, Chuck

Pulin and Elthan Russell. Various events are portrayed in a series of photographs, affording us a more intimate knowledge of specific experiences such as the acorn planting at Coventry Cathedral; the "You Are Here" exhibition; the Gibralta wedding; the Montreal bed-in; the Apple office and the One to One Concert. There are also reproductions of some of the less sensational erotic lithographs and a photograph of a wall painting John created in a friend's house in 1967.

The book was published in Britain the following year by New English Library. ★ ★ ★ ★

THE FACTS ABOUT A POP GROUP FEATURING WINGS
Dave Gelly. Andre Deutsch, 1977

The success of Wings brought about a renewed interest in Paul's career. This book, aimed at young readers, was part of the "A.G.Whizzard Fact Book Series" (others covered the making of a Hammer film, the background to a soccer club and, later, the making of an episode in the *Doctor Who* TV series). Gelly, the *Observer* music critic, was assisted by photographer Homer Sykes; there are over 50 photographs in the publication, many in colour.

The Facts About a Pop Group is written in a simple manner for youngsters, and describes the work that goes into putting a major group on the road. There are interviews with fans and wardrobe ladies, PRs and roadies; profiles of the members of Wings; and details of the equipment and sets used for the tour, illustrated with diagrams. The mechanics of a recording session are analysed, together with a description of a visit to a record pressing plant.

Paul McCartney has written the introduction, in his usual concise style. The book was issued in America by Harmony Books under the title *Facts About a Rock Group Featuring Wings.* ★ ★ ★ ★

PAUL McCARTNEY & WINGS
Tony Jasper. Octopus Books, 1977

Tony Jasper, one of Britain's most prolific rock writers, has penned nearly 50 books. This one follows the standard visual design of such publications and contains over 100 photographs, most of them in full colour. The chapters include: "The Formation of Wings", the events which led up to Paul's decision to form the group; "The Story of Wings", details of the group's development; "The Band (On the Run)", the various personnel changes; "The World Tour, 1975-1976", the story of their world tour; "Paul and Linda – The Family Way", the background to Paul's married life; and "Behind the Albums", details of the album releases. There is also a "Calendar of Events", a discography and a selection of quotes from Paul. ★ ★ ★

PAUL McCARTNEY & WINGS
Jeremy Pascall. Hamlyn, 1977

Pascall is another writer with a string of book titles to his credit, ranging from a history of sex movies to a history of rock music. Here he has written a sympathetic treatment of the Wings' story; the book is remarkably similar to Jasper's, and is lavishly illustrated with 70 photographs, many in colour. The chapter titles make clever use of song titles: "Yesterday", a recap of Paul's life and career with the Beatles; "Long & Winding Road", Paul's departure from the Fab Four; "Another Day", the formation of Wings: "Wings Take Off", the story of Wings' initial successes; "Band on the Run", the various personnel changes; and "Wings Across the World", detailing their tours and career up to 1976. ★★★

George Harrison Yesterday & Today
by Ross Michaels

GEORGE HARRISON YESTERDAY & TODAY
Ross Michaels. Flash Books, 1977

In the very first book devoted solely to George, Michaels has provided a clear, well-written description of George's life and a critical analysis of his work. He has drawn on a number of publications, from Hunter Davies' official biography to *Rolling Stone* magazine articles, and the result is a number of aptly chosen quotes with George chipping in with his comments at relevant points in the text.

There are five main sections to the book. The first, "Friends of Us All", sets the scene, covering George's greatest triumph, the Bangla Desh Concert. "From Liverpool to 'Let It Be'" spans George's early years and his career with the Beatles. "Commuting to the Material World"

recaps his solo career, "Gently Weeping" analyses his ability as a guitarist, whilst "In George's Words" turns attention to his talent as a songwriter.

There are 90 photographs, mainly of George's post-Beatles period, and a discography compiled by Wendy Schacter.

The most glaring error is the statement that Pete Best's mother owned the Cavern Club. She did, of course, run a much humbler cellar club called the Casbah.

The book was reprinted a few years later with a more striking cover. ★★★

PAUL McCARTNEY: A BIOGRAPHY IN WORDS AND PICTURES
John Mendelsohn.
Sire Books/Chappell Music Ltd, 1977

Well-illustrated, critical view of Paul, penned by American rock writer Mendelsohn as part of a series.

WINGS
Rock Fun, 1977

A Japanese photo-book in the "Rock Fun" series, crammed with photographs of Wings, mostly taken during their world tour. The book includes a discography and chronology. ★★★

A HARD DAY'S NIGHT
Edited by Philip DiFranco. Chelsea House, 1977

This is a marvellous souvenir of the Beatles debut movie, issued 13 years later, and containing the full screenplay, hundreds of stills from the film and a lengthy interview with director Dick Lester. Also published in Britain by Penguin. ★★★

YESTERDAY SEEMS SO FAR AWAY: THE BEATLES YESTERDAY AND TODAY
John Swenson. Zebra Books, 1977

Another straightforward biography, retracing the history of the group and illustrated with a selection of black-and-white photographs. The book was reissued the following year with a different cover and a briefer title, *The Beatles Yesterday and Today*. ★★

THE BEATLES AGAIN?
Harry Castleman and Walter Podrazik.
Pierian Press, 1977

This companion volume to the excellent *All Together Now* updates and amends material from the first book, while also presenting a mass of carefully researched discographical information not contained in the earlier volume.

The book is divided into four sections. "It's Like You Never Left" is a year by year survey of their musical career, both as a group and as solo artists, from 1961 until 1977. There are numerous small items – "The Case of the Belittled Beatles Tapes", for instance, investigates the making of the Hamburg tapes recorded at the Star Club. (The authors weren't to know, of course, that the tapes were originally made by Adrian Barber, who recorded all of the bands at the Star Club when he was stage manager there. Kingsize Taylor merely asked Adrian if he could have the tapes.)

"Pandemonium Aerial Ballet" contains further information on bootleg records, and the authors go on to answer a series of questions ranging from the "Paul Is Dead" stories to the collectability of "foreign" Beatles records.

Mike McGear is thoroughly covered in "Friends, Relatives and Strangers", and there is a discography of Mike's releases.

"Apple Records" provides details of all the artists who recorded for the label, and a discography. Further information concerns Dark Horse and Ringo O' Records, and the Beatles' stage appearances.

Scholarly, informative and well presented, with a cleverly assembled index. ★★★★

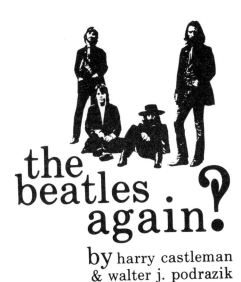

by harry castleman & walter j. podrazik

**1,000 BEATLES FACTS
(AND A LITTLE HEARSAY)**
Ed Nibbervoll and Evan Thorburn.
J. Albert 1977
A collection of Fab Four facts, with over 70 pages, issued in Australia. ★★

**MERSEY BEAT:
THE BEGINNINGS OF THE BEATLES**
Bill Harry. Omnibus Press, 1977

Until the British Press discovered the Beatles in 1963 the only source of information about the group was *Mersey Beat,* an alternative music paper virtually unknown to the general public.

From the very first issue, *Mersey Beat* promoted the Beatles more than any other band. This book is a collection of Beatles material from that period, reproduced as it was originally printed. And it's all here: John's "On the Dubious Origins of Beatles", his classified ads, his "Beatcomber" columns; the cover of page two proclaiming "Beatles Sign Recording Contract!"; Brian Epstein's record reviews; the reports by Paul McCartney of trips to Paris and Hamburg; Bob Wooler's predictive report "Well Now – Dig This!"; the famous Beatles Top Poll cover; the *Mersey Beat* Popularity Polls; the "Beatles Change Drummer" story... and much much more.

Also reproduced are ads for Beatles' appearances at dozens of venues ranging from the Cavern and the Majestic Ballroom to the Pavilion, Lodge Lane, and the Tower, New Brighton, as well as ads for Beatle cakes and Beatle books, Beatle guitars and Beatle amplifiers.

The book contains extracts from the first attempt to document the Beatles' lives in "The Beatles Story" series, drawing on interviews with Pete Best, Allan Williams, Howie Casey and others. There is also a selection of the famous "Mersey Beatle" pages, a special newspaper within a newspaper, dedicated entirely to the Beatles.

Most of the photographs reproduced were taken exclusively for *Mersey Beat* and have not been seen anywhere else: Ringo with Rory Storm & the Hurricanes; Mike McGear's pictures of Paul; the Beatles at local venues and with the Vernons Girls, Chris Sandford of *Coronation Street* and Mike and Bernie Winters.

The material ends at 1964 with John's visit to Stuart Sutcliffe's mother. There is a report on the American tour by Brian Epstein, who also describes the Beatles' first EMI recording session, and there are family album pictures of the four as babies.

This historic collection, relating to those early days in Liverpool when the Fab Four began their rise to fame, contains a 6,000 word introduction and is illustrated with photographs by Peter Kaye. ★★★★★

THE BEATLES: THE AUTHORIZED BIOGRAPHY
Hunter Davies. William Heinemann, 1978

This updated edition of the Davies book, issued ten years after the original, was also published in America by McGraw-Hill and as a British paperback by Granada in 1979.

In the introduction Davies reassesses the book: "I was a fly on the wall living with them for eighteen months. . . I was criticised by some at the time for not standing back far enough, not trying to analyse and evaluate. I'm glad I didn't . . . If I were writing it again now, I would try to improve the style. It seems too jumpy and staccato." He goes on: "Although no serious mistakes or lies crept in. . . I'd have to admit that quite a few important truths were omitted. Now it can be told. . ."

He mentions how critical John became after the book had been published and comments that, though all four Beatles were given the chance to suggest changes, apart from a few minor things, only George requested lengthy alterations ". . .in the last section where he thought I hadn't given enough space to his thoughts on religion." Davies allowed the Beatles' parents and close relatives to read the manuscript, receiving the most objections from John's aunt Mimi.

Davies reveals that it was "side-kicks at Apple (who) tried to clean up the book, cut out the bad language, stories about John thieving, reference to drugs and such like. Back in the sixties, one didn't write about such things as one does today." And he regrets he didn't mention that Brian Epstein was a homosexual.

Davies is still a big Beatles' fan. "Not long after this book first appeared I was asked by *The Times* newspaper of London to write their obituary. Every year the metal gets dragged out and the yellow galleys brought up to date as new marriages, new events are added."

The 1978 edition contains a postscript which brings the stories of the individual Beatles and their friends up to date. And another edition of the book was published following John's tragic death. ★★★★

THE BEATLES: AN ILLUSTRATED RECORD
Roy Carr & Tony Tyler.
New English Library, 1978

This revised and updated edition – also published in America by Harmony Books – has a more forceful cover design. The original photograph of the four in Sgt. Pepper uniforms has been replaced by a familiar Dezo Hoffmann shot placed on a blue background: notice Paul with a cigarette in his hand.

On page one, the notorious "butcher" cover of *The Beatles Yesterday and Today* American album sleeve has replaced the cartoon figure of John from *Yellow Submarine*. The contents page has been illustrated with some interesting memorabilia – a note from John stating that he never used the name Johnny Silver, the first ever mention of the group at an appearance at Neston Institute, a rejection letter to Mrs Best from Granada TV, some clippings of ads from the *Liverpool Echo* and *Mersey Beat*, a couple of early pictures and the ticket from their Davy Jones Show appearance at the Tower Ballroom, New Brighton. Additional pages illustrate 1974; there is a section on the group's American releases; details of bootleg recordings; an expanded "Odds & Ends" section; and photographs of the Beatles' "Fellow Travellers", The Fourmost, Cilla Black, Louise Caldwell, Peter & Gordon, Badfinger, Tommy Quickly, and P.J.Proby.

The back cover is based on the *Let It Be* sleeve; it is less interesting than the original design which featured a set of photographs of each of the Beatles from childhood to the mid seventies – an idea that has been used successfully since then in Philip Norman's *Shout!* ★★★★

BEHIND THE BEATLES SONGS
Philip Cowan. Polytantric Press, 1978

Philip Cowan, a dedicated Beatles' fan, began work on a Beatles' encyclopedia but then, after being beaten to the punch, decided to try his luck with a book containing the stories behind individual numbers recorded by the Beatles.

Robert Rankin, a friend of Cowan's and a fellow Beatles' fan, has illustrated the book with some charming and unusual black-and-white pen drawings. One wishes he had also been given a free hand to map out the cover, which displays some confusing typography and an indistinct black-and-white photograph. The picture is of a slightly balding middle-aged man, in a black tie and dinner jacket, playing an organ. A girl sprawls awkwardly in the background.

The book is divided into two sections. The first section, "Behind the Lyrics", is a very skimpy treatment and covers a limited number of songs. In many cases, a single sentence is all the information given about a particular song. The second section consists of various lists, handy for reference purposes and including: "Radio and TV Appearances in the UK"; "Unreleased Studio Songs"; "Contributions by the Beatles to Others"; and discography lists.

It is a slim and worthwhile volume, though *The Long and Winding Road,* published a few years later, covers the ground more thoroughly. ★ ★ ★

PAPERBACK WRITER
Mark Shipper. Grosset & Dunlap, 1978

You will either love or hate this book. The American critics thought it hilarious, and Greil Marcus wrote that it was "the finest novel ever written about rock and roll."

While appreciating that it is a lampoon of the Beatles' career, I can't help feeling that the writer hasn't really attempted to capture the real Beatles. The Liverpool background is quite untypical, the dialogue unrealistic – Shipper has Americanised the way the Beatles think and speak.

Personally, I find this spoof both unfunny and false. Having lived through the whole scene, it is strange to find it described in this way. Shipper's Liverpool, quite simply, never existed.

This book was published as a paperback in Britain by New English Library. ★ ★ ★

THE LIFE AND TIMES OF
THE BEATLES: THE SPURIOUS CHRONICLE
OF THEIR RISE TO STARDOM

THE BEATLES IN THEIR OWN WORDS
Miles. Omnibus Press, 1978

The previous book in the series, *Paul McCartney in His Own Words,* was adapted from interviews. In this one (Brian) Miles – once associated with the Indica Gallery where Yoko met John and at one time a leading light of the London "underground" scene and a contributor to the *International Times* – has collated scores of quotes made by the Beatles during their career. These quotes are assembled in several separate sections: "Beatles: The Story"; "Press Conferences"; "Songwriting"; "The Songs"; "The Films"; "Drugs and Politics".

The section on individual songs, like that in Philip Cowan's book, leaves something to be desired. The entry on 'Got to Get You into My

Life', for instance, is an uninformative, two-sentence quote from John: "We were influenced by our Tamla Motown bit on this. You see we're influenced by whatever's going." Many of the quotes seem to have been included merely for padding.

There are over 70 photographs, including some particularly interesting ones: Stuart and Astrid; Patti Boyd; the psychedelic Rolls; Paul and Mary Hopkin; the Beatles with Marlene Dietrich; Ringo with a Blue Meanie; and John and Paul with Richard Lester. Unfortunately, the reproduction of many of the pictures taken from newspapers and magazines is poor.

Although the book is an interesting read, the definitive collection of Beatles' quotes still remains to be assembled. ★★★

ends at midnight on 21 June in Los Angeles.

There are shots taken inside hotel rooms, in dressing rooms, concert halls and bars, on planes, on the road, on horseback, and at parties (there were no less than three to celebrate the birthdays of Paul, Jimmy McCulloch and artist Humphrey Ocean). In addition to the McCartneys and members of Wings, the gallery of faces includes security men, fans, cops, roadies, truck drivers, photographers, programme sellers, bodyguards, riggers, technicians, stage designers and lawyers, as well as visiting celebrities – Ringo Starr, Elton John, Cher, Peter Frampton and Roy Harper.

This handsome souvenir, the first in a number of publications which document Paul in his solo work, captures the atmosphere and the complexity of a tour.

Also published in America by Reed Books. ★★★

HANDS ACROSS THE WATER
WINGS TOUR USA
Hipgnosis. Paper Tiger, 1978

Paul's company, MPL Communications, produced this book – documenting Wings' tour of America between May and June 1976 – Hipgnosis were involved in the design, the editors were Storm Thorgerson and Peter Christopherson, George Hardie supplied graphics and illustrations, and Aubrey Powell took the photographs.

Paul contributes a miniature introduction; Storm explains the actual plan of the book: "This was to photograph on or very near to the hour: thus the order is relative only to the hour of the day rather than to the narrative or geographical sequence." The selection of 185 photographs begins at 11.45a.m. in New York on 25 May and

26 DAYS THAT ROCKED THE WORLD
O'Brien Publishing, 1978

This large format, 64-page paperback takes a nostalgic look at the Beatles' 1964 American tour, drawing largely on clippings collected from over 40 leading American newspapers published at that time. There are 150 shots and a number of interviews. ★★★

BEATLE MADNESS
Martin A.Grove. Manor Books, 1978

Yet another paperback telling the Beatles' story, complete with a selection of photographs. ★★

THE BEATLES TRIVIA QUIZ BOOK
Helen Rosenbaum. New American Library, 1978

The third quiz book devoted to the Beatles, and also fully illustrated. ★★★

PAUL McCARTNEY: BEATLE WITH WINGS
Martin A. Grove. Manor Books, 1978

Grove's second paperback for Manor Books
during the year (the first was *Beatles Madness*) is
a biography of Paul's solo career, including his
activities with Wings. ★★★

THE OFFICIAL SGT. PEPPER'S LONELY
HEARTS CLUB BAND SCRAPBOOK
Robert Stigwood and Dee Anthony.
Guild & Western, 1978

"The inside story behind the most mind-blowing
movie fantasy ever filmed!" reads the cover blurb
of this large format paperback. It's actually a
collection of 100 photographs, with 24 pages of
colour, and some text describing the making of
the film starring Peter Frampton and the Bee
Gees. ★★

SGT. PEPPER'S LONELY
HEARTS CLUB BAND
Henry Edwards. Pocket Books, 1978

Paperback novelisation of Robert Stigwood's
movie. A photo insert contains two dozen stills
from the film, which starred Peter Frampton as
Billy Shears and the Bee Gees as Sgt. Pepper's
Lonely Hearts Club Band.

It has none of the atmosphere surrounding the
original Beatles' album, merely incorporating the

characters originally introduced in the LP's lyrics
into an apple-pie story about happenings in
Heartland USA.

"Who were these musicians who could make
peace out of war? They were good American
boys – each and every one," we are told, as a
marching band appears on the battlefields dur-
in World War Two and drops dead when he is
trenches. The band has been led by Sgt. Pepper
and he is greeted as a war hero on his return to
Heartland. Sgt. Pepper cheers people up
throughout the Depression, entertains the troops
in the World War Two and drops dead when he is
about to be honoured once again by the citizens
of Heartland. The saccharine plot then goes on to
introduce characters such as Mr Kite, Mr Mustard, Father Sun, Strawberry Fields and Lucy &
the Diamonds.

The paperback includes lyrics to 'Sgt. Pepper's
Lonely Hearts Club Band'; 'With a Little Help
From My Friends'; 'Fixing a Hole'; 'It's Getting
Better'; 'The Long & Winding Road'; 'Here Comes
the Sun'; 'I Want You'; 'Good Morning, Good
Morning'; 'Polythene Pam'; 'She Came in Through
the Bathroom Window'; 'Nowhere Man'; 'Mean
Mr Mustard'; 'She's Leaving Home'; 'Lucy in the
Sky With Diamonds'; 'Oh Darling'; 'Maxwell's
Silver Hammer'; 'Because'; 'Strawberry Fields
Forever'; 'For the Benefit of Mr Kite'; 'Got to Get
You into My Life'; 'You Never Give Me Your
Money'; 'When I'm Sixty Four'; 'Come Together';
'Golden Slumbers'; 'Carry That Weight'; 'A Day in
the Life' and 'Get Back'.

The paperback was published in Britain the
following year by Star Books. ★★

A TWIST OF LENNON
Cynthia Lennon. Star Books, 1978

Cynthia's story of life with John makes pleasant, if
lightweight, reading. The style, at times, is rather
gushing: "I loved Maureen, she was down to
earth, honest. . ."; "Patti and I got on famously . . .
she was a friendly bubbly character...", "George
was a true gentleman and Judy a perfect lady. . ."
She even has generous things to say about Yoko:
"I understood their love. I knew I couldn't fight
the unity of mind and body that they had with
each other." One wishes she'd tell how she really
felt when John dropped her.

Her poems too are overly sentimental, while
her 12 black-ink drawings betray none of the
talent or flair of John's – they are merely the
competent illustrations of an expert student.
Cynthia also seems to know nothing about the
actual Mersey scene and what she does write
about is almost totally inaccurate. She even has
the date of her marriage wrong by a full year.

Despite this, the book is another valuable
"insider" contribution to the growing Beatlelore.
There is a selection of 14 photographs in an insert
and Cynthia presents numerous personal stories:
Paul's love affair with Dot; a trip to Paris in which

she and John had to share a bed with Astrid Kirchnerr and another girl; the flat that Brian Epstein lent to the newly married couple; their move to Kenwood; the sojourn at Rishikesh.

In the new temperature following the success of the "kiss-and-tell" books, Cynthia is writing another account of her marriage to John. This time, I expect, the claws will be out.

Although Cynthia used the name of her third husband John Twist in the title of the book, she has now reverted to the name of her first husband.

The book was published in the United States by Avon, and was reissued in 1980 after John's death. ★★★

THE BEATLES FOREVER
Nicholas Schaffner. McGraw-Hill, 1978

This book provides a detailed history of the group from 1964, when they first conquered America, to 1977.

The Beatles Forever contains more photographs than any of the previous Beatle books: 400 of them. They include memorabilia (bubble gum cards, badges, posters, dolls, wigs),; records (scores of album and single sleeve shots); Beatles with other celebrities (Muhammad Ali, James Taylor & Carly Simon, Alice Cooper, Gerry Ford, David Frost, Maharishi, Ed Sullivan) with sweethearts (Jane, Patti, Linda, Yoko); at premières (*How I Won the War, Yellow Submarine, Wonderwall*). There are photographs of Ringo's de-

signs for furniture, Paul's "Gotta Sing, Gotta Dance" routine for TV, John and Yoko in battle dress, George with Dylan at the Bangla Desh concert, with Brian Jones at the Rock and Roll Circus, singing 'Hey Jude' and hundreds of other shots, carefully selected to tie in with the text.

The detail is immensely readable as it contains interesting items of trivia missing from less substantial books. Each chapter ends with a discography of their American singles and albums and British singles with details of their chart positions on both sides of the Atlantic.

Schaffner's encyclopaedic knowledge is brought to bear as he fills in the background to each record release and major event in the group's career. Additional bonuses include: an International Beatle discography; Beatle Tributes and Novelty discs; lists of various awards they have received; a bibliography and an index.

Essential reading for Beatle enthusiasts. ★★★★★

POCKET BEATLES COMPLETE
Wise Publications, 1979

This small, hardbound book has been produced superbly: a transparent cover protects an exquisite full-colour painting of the Fabs by artist Allan Manham. Inside there are half-a-dozen, full-page photographs, arrangements with guitar chord symbols, lyrics to 184 Beatles' songs, and a discography of all their British recordings in order of release. ★★★

imately 400 records from 13 different countries. McGeary enlarged and reissued the book the following year: it was now 30 pages in length, and covered 600 listings from over 18 different countries.

Every Little Thing was inspired by the "Here, There & Everywhere" column by Jos Remmerswaal in *Beatles Unlimited* magazine and includes lists of information about Beatles recordings.

BEATLES MOVIE CATALOG
Toru Matahira, 1979

The photographs in this large-format paperback illustrate a number of the films and television shows in which the Beatles appeared. The stills of each film, often taking up several pages, are accompanied by a brief text in Japanese. ★★★

THE BEATLES CONCERT-ED EFFORTS
Jan Van de Bunt & Friends.
Beatles Unlimited, 1979

This enterprising book was published by the Dutch fan magazine *Beatles Unlimited.* The author spent three years gathering details of the Beatles' appearances at clubs, concerts and on television shows – from their early Liverpool gigs until after they split up and went solo. Although it is a basic listing with little background information on the individual dates, it makes a handy reference guide.

The illustrations, 60 in all – photographs, maps, posters and tickets relating to the various appearances – are enterprising. Of particular interest are the photographs of the Liverpool venues as they were at the time of the book's publication: the Jacaranda had become a steak bar, the Maxi San Suzie, and the Blue Angel had become the Galaxy Club. Photographs of the venues include the De Montfort Hall, Leicester; Candlestick Park, San Francisco; the Shea Stadium; Litherland Town Hall; and the Cavern. The maps provide an at-a-glance view of the Beatles' movements on each of the tours.

A yellow cover shows the Beatles in action in a television studio. ★★★

EVERY LITTLE THING:
THE BEATLES ON RECORD
Mitchell McGeary and William McCoy.
Privately printed, 1979

This discography was privately printed by two dealers in Beatles' memorabilia. McGeary had been involved in selling Beatles' merchandise during the seventies, and he originally issued *The Beatles Complete Discography* in 1975. This 18-page booklet had text printed on one side of the page only, and contained information on approx-

UP AGAINST IT:
A SCREENPLAY FOR THE BEATLES
Joe Orton. Eyre Methuen, 1979

The controversial playwright Joe Orton had enjoyed considerable success with his plays *Loot* and *Entertaining Mr Sloane* when Walter Shenson asked him to rewrite the script for a proposed Beatles film called "Shades of a Personality". Orton eventually persuaded Shenson to drop the original script in favour of a completely new screenplay that he had penned, called "Up Against It". The original four male characters have been reduced to a pair of boys called McTurk and Low who are banished from their town and become involved in the assassination of a female Prime Minister. Unfortunately neither Brian Epstein nor Paul McCartney liked the screenplay.

Orton then rewrote it for Oscar Lewenstein of Woodfall Productions. The director intended to film it, but Orton was murdered by his lover Kenneth Helliwell and the movie was never made.

The script presented here is the second version. The book contains a 12-page introduction by John Lahr describing the story behind the screenplay and Orton's meetings with the Beatles. There are also excerpts from Orton's private diaries. Titbits of information include mention that Shenson wanted the Beatles to make *The Three Musketeers* (with Brigitte Bardot cast as Lady DeWinter), that Orton thought the group were fed up with Dick Lester as a director and didn't want experienced actors like Leo McKern in their films because they stole scenes from them.

The book was published in America by Grove Press. ★★★

ALL YOU NEED IS EARS
George Martin. Macmillan, 1979

As the Beatles' recording manager, Martin was one of the most important of the "insiders", and his book was eagerly awaited by enthusiasts. But although the Beatles played a very important part in Martin's life, they are not allowed to dominate the book: Martin existed as a recording man both before and after his time as their producer.

Chapter Seven, "Hard Days and Nights", takes the story from April 1962 (when Martin received a call from Syd Coleman regarding the Beatles tape and the setting up of a meeting with Brian Epstein) through the next several years of his involvement with the Fab Four. We learn of the famous incident that originally broke the ice between himself and the band from Liverpool: after listening to a playback, he asked them if there was anything they didn't like and George Harrison replied: "Well, for a start, I don't like your tie." There was the compromise over 'Love Me Do'; with session drummer Andy White playing drums on one version and Ringo on the other; Martin's insistence that they record 'How Do You Do It?'; Martin's contributions to the actual arrangements of various Lennon and McCartney numbers; his success with other Epstein artists; his use of mobile equipment at the Apple studio because Magic Alex hadn't fulfilled his promise of a 72-track studio. The book bristles with anecdotes and with Martin's feelings of injustice at being so poorly paid by EMI when his productions were raking in millions for the company.

The book covers Martin's early life in detail, his initial work at EMI in 1950, his advancement to record label chief, and his recording sessions with a range of stars, including Sir Adrian Boult, Shirley Bassey, Tommy Steele, the Temperance Seven, the Goons, Stan Getz, Bernard Cribbins and Ella Fitzgerald. There is also the story of his attempts to go independent and of the setting up of AIR Studios.

There are, of course, inaccuracies, inevitable in a book of this sort. Billy J.Kramer, for instance, feels sorely and unfairly treated by Martin's comments: "Billy J.Kramer. . . had to be double tracked nearly all the time" and by the implication that the sessions conducted with him were particularly hard work. George also says, "Brian [Epstein] brought me a singer named Priscilla White. All her friends called her Cilla and Brian, for some reason best known to himself, didn't like the idea of Cilla White, so he'd gone to the other end of the spectrum and called her Cilla Black." One has only to look at issue No.1 of *Mersey Beat*, dated July 1961, before Epstein or Martin had ever heard of her to see her name printed as Cilla Black.

Since this is a biography, readers may be surprised to find an incredible amount of detailed technical information presented as Martin analyses record production and arranging.

There are 25 photographs, half-a-dozen picturing Martin with members of the Beatles. The book was co-written with professional journalist Jeremy Hornsby and was published in the United States by St Martin's Press. ★★★★

THINGS WE SAID TODAY
Colin Campbell and Allan Murphy.
Pierian Press, 1980

Webster's Third New International Dictionary defines "concordance" as "an alphabetical verbal index showing the places in the text of a book or in the works of an author where each printed word may be found often with its immediate context." In the past there have been concordances on Shakespeare and the major works of poets, but never on the lyrics of popular songs.

Things We Said Today is just that, "A Concordance of the Beatles Songs, 1962-1970". It is a formidable work of scholarship carried out by the authors with some university assistance and access to a computer terminal. The result has been luxuriously produced in a large-format, hardbound limited edition.

In addition to the concordance itself, which runs to hundreds of pages in length, there is a preface by the authors explaining the process by which their brain child was born, and there are several pages of notes explaining the ways in which the book can be used. "From Romance to Romanticism" analyses the lyrics. There is a list of the songs included in the concordance, 189 in all, and a list of the songs not included (these are songs written but not recorded by the Beatles and songs recorded but not written by them). This is followed by "Song Title Abbreviations", which also furnishes information on release dates, composer credits and lead vocalist designations; a chronological list of songs; the complete lyrics and lyrics to all the songs contained in the book.

An "Alphabetical Word-Frequency List" follows the concordance; this numbers the times any word has been used in the Beatles' total output of songs. Thus we learn that the most frequent word is "the", mentioned 1,027 times, while "me" comes second with 825 appearances. "California" is mentioned twice, "Liverpool" is not mentioned at all.

The illustrations in the book are reproductions of the actual handwritten notes of various songs, including 'I'm Only Sleeping', 'Paperback Writer', 'Good Day Sunshine', 'Blue Jay Way', 'Help', 'And Your Bird Can Sing', 'Yesterday', 'For No-one', 'I Want to Hold Your Hand', 'The Word', 'Lucy in the Sky With Diamonds', 'Eleanor Rigby', 'Michelle' and 'Yellow Submarine'. ★★★★

THE BEATLES:
A DAY IN THE LIFE
Compiled by Tom Schultheiss.
Pierian Press, 1980

Tom Schultheiss begins his introduction: "Hundreds of books and thousands of periodical issues devoted to the Beatles have been published over the years; not a single one of them can be totally trusted, including the one you hold in your hands." He then goes on to mention some of the many inaccuracies in Beatle books, the variety of ways certain names are spelt (Astrid Kirschner, Kircherr, Kichener, Kirchner, Kirchherr, Kitchener), the different dates given for specific events (John met Paul on either June 15, 1955, June 15, 1956, or June 15, 1957).

The book lists day-by-day events in the lives of the Beatles between the years 1960 and 1970, though there is a section dealing with some relevant dates prior to that time. It is an extremely engrossing volume and a valuable reference work, but it does have several drawbacks. A little judicious pruning would have improved the book. There is too much trivia concerning relatives, particularly those of George: "Nov 16 1967: Ian Harrison is born, son of George Harrison's brother Peter and sister-in-law Pauline. Nov 16 1968: Ian Harrison, George's nephew, is one year old. Nov 16 1969: Ian Harrison, George's nephew, is two years old."

But the main criticism of the book is that the author mixes in spoof items from Mark Shipper's *Paperback Writer,* the National Lampoon's Beatle parody, and the Rutles' comic history among the dates without separating them sufficiently from the genuine entries.

The book was published as a paperback in Britain later the same year by Omnibus Press. ★★★★

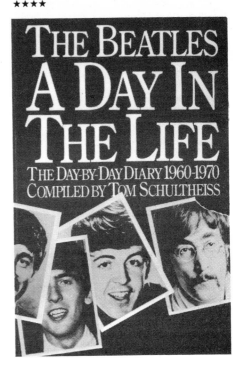

STRAWBERRY FIELDS FOREVER: JOHN LENNON REMEMBERED
Vic Garbarini, Brian Cullman,
Barbara Graustark. Delilah/Bantam, 1980

One of the first paperbacks issued as a tribute to John, sporting photographs by Jack Mitchell on its front and back cover and a photo insert with over two-dozen photographs. The book was cobbled together in a very short time yet it manages to achieve a standard of readability not maintained by the many similar books that followed.

It is, in some ways, three short books in one. Dave Marsh contributes the introduction; this is followed by six chapters. The first, "The Dream Is Over", reports the news of John's murder. "Seven Days in December" details the events leading to the assassination. "Sometime in NYC" is the story of John and Yoko's love affair with New York. "All the Lonely People: The Early Years" describes John's life in Liverpool and his career as a Beatle. "Strawberry Fields" covers part of the Beatles' story and their music, and includes a great many quotes from John. "The Plastic Ono Band" concerns John's solo career.

The next section of the book, "Two Virgins", contains the text of the *Newsweek* interview conducted by Barbara Graustark. The third and final section of the book, "Liverpool to New York: 1940-1980", is a chronological biography. ★★★

ACROSS THE UNIVERSE
Arno Guzek. Privately published, 1980

Another information-crammed discography from Arno, once again privately printed. He presents details of Beatle records issued in all parts of the world, from Argentina to the USSR, and packs quite an amount of text into the book's 27 pages. ★★★

THE BOYS FROM LIVERPOOL: JOHN, PAUL, GEORGE, RINGO
Nicholas Schaffner. Methuen, 1980

When Methuen were looking for an authority to write a book about the Beatles, they turned to Nicholas Schaffner, who had already penned *The Beatles Forever*. The book is knowledgeable and well written, though skimpy in places. The Beatles' entire career prior to their "conquest of America" has been condensed into a mere 19 pages. After the chapter "Apple Corpse" (ouch!), there is a "Solo in the Seventies" section dealing with the individual careers of the four following their break-up.

Described by the publishers as "juvenile literature," the book nonetheless compares favourably with other previously written biographies. It has been handsomely produced in hardback, with a colour wraparound cover (the familiar Camera Press shot of the Beatles sitting on a red staircase) and 49 interior photographs. ★★★

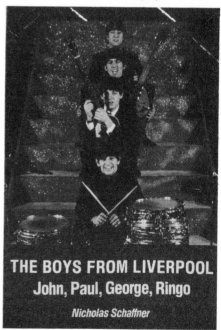

THE BOYS FROM LIVERPOOL
John, Paul, George, Ringo
Nicholas Schaffner

THE BEATLES ILLUSTRATED LYRICS
Volumes One and Two. Edited by Alan Aldridge. Macdonald Futura, 1980

A reissue of both books, sold as a two-volume set. It retailed in Britain at £9.95, and was published in the United States by Delacorte Press. ★★★★

JOHN LENNON 1940-80: ONE DAY AT A TIME
Anthony Fawcett. New English Library, 1980

Republished after John's death with the subtitle "John Lennon 1940-1980" and a publisher's comment: "For this reprint it was decided to leave the text in the present tense, but to update the chronological sections and the discography." There is a quote on the flypage from Yoko: "John loved and prayed for the human race. Please do the same for him." And Fawcett has added a two-page item "Epilogue: The Last Four Years", filling in details of John's activities in the years not covered in the original edition. ★★★★

JOHN LENNON: DEATH OF A DREAM
George Carpozi Jr. Manor Books, 1980

This publication was put together literally overnight to cash in on John's death. It contains some poorly reproduced photographs that look as if they have been clipped from magazines and newspapers. "This is the first, biggest, and fastest selling book on the life and death of John Lennon . . . a monumental publishing effort to produce the story of the Gentle Beatle's phenomenal career, report every detail about his murder, and make a penetrating study of the life of his crazed assassin" reads the blurb.

It has been penned by a *New York Post* journalist who specialises in crime stories and has written over 70 books, most of them about true-life murders.

Carpozi has concentrated on the sensational elements of the killing, in true crime-reporter style, while most of the information about the Beatles is already contained in a previously published Manor paperback by Martin Grove, *Beatle Madness.*

Book One, "A Heinous Crime", concerns itself solely with the murder. Book Two, "His Legacy", is the basic Beatles' history with details of films and record releases; and it ends with a chapter entitled "The Fifth Beatle", an interview with Murray the K. Book Three, "Last Words", covers the aftermath of the tragedy and the various tributes. ★★

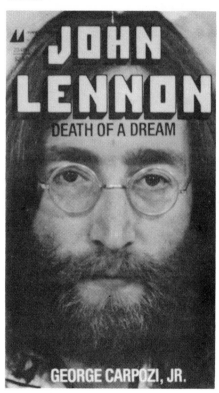

I.ME.MINE
George Harrison. Genesis Publications, 1980

This was a milestone in Beatles' publishing history: the most expensive and unique book issued so far. *I.Me.Mine*, in a limited edition of 2,000 copies, cost £184. Despite the furore created at the time by fans who considered the price too high, the original edition has become a valuable collectors' item, already increasing in value.

In his foreword, George relates how two drunks cornered him in a hotel room and suggested that he should have his lyrics bound in a book. They showed him a copy of *Log of H.M.S.Bounty,* published by Genesis at £158. George was intrigued; he had been collecting his song lyrics, written on envelopes, letterheads and scraps of paper, for some years. And he liked the idea of a book produced with the care and attention Genesis had lavished on Bligh's Bounty Log, originally intending his book to be called "The Big Leather Job".

I.Me.Mine was hand-bound in leather, printed on fine, antique-laid paper, and issued in a slipcase. Each copy was hand-numbered by the publisher and personally signed by George.

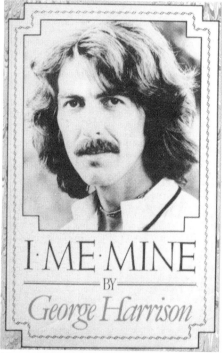

Derek Taylor aided George in the preparation of the manuscript; he penned an introduction and interviewed George about his life and career, from his early memories of Liverpool until his solo years. The story of George's life is illustrated by a series of masterly engravings by Roy Williams. A photo gallery containing 48 full-page photographs follows, and then the main section of the book – facsimiles of George's song lyrics reproduced from the original scraps of paper he had written them on. There are lyrics to 82 songs, complete with printed lyrics, and accompanied by George's own comments on each of the songs.

The book which he describes as a "little ego detour," is very much George's personal view of the world, including his feelings of his years as a Beatle: "There was more good than evil in being a Beatle." John was enraged with the book and attacked it in his *Playboy* interview: ". . . my influence on his life (in the book) is absolutely

zilch and nil. . . he mentions every two-bit sax player or guitarist he met in subsequent years. I'm not in the book." John is, in fact, mentioned more than any other person in the book, a total of eleven times.

Those people who were under the impression that only 2,000 copies of the book would be printed, will be disappointed. The book was issued in both hardcover and paperback editions, in less lavish style and at a much reduced price, by Simon & Schuster in the United States and W.H. Allen in Britain. ★ ★ ★ ★ ★

THE BEATLES A TO Z
Goldie Friede, Robin Titone, Sue Weiner.
Eyre Methuen, 1980

This first Beatles encyclopedia is a large format book with more than 3,000 separate entries and over 100 photographs. The photographs, many presented here for the first time, were taken by freelance photographers Friede and Titone; they have been divided into six sections – the Beatles, George Harrison, John Lennon, Paul McCartney, Ringo Starr and the album covers. Sue Weiner, editor of an American women's magazine, has tackled much of the actual writing, albeit with a little help from her two friends. "Together, they have collected, over the past sixteen years, every scrap of information, photographs, records, clippings, and books about the Beatles," says the blurb.

It is a formidable piece of research work, although there are inevitably many omissions. The entries on the records themselves tend to be skimpy, though much of this information can be found in discographies. The real strength of the *A to Z* lies in the range of subjects covered – books, movies, people, performances and recording sessions, as well as many other aspects of the Beatles' lives not previously available in such an easily accessible form.

Many of the one-line entries are tantalisingly short. Thus: "Bob Bain, performer on the bill with the Beatles during their 1964 British Fall tour." Who was he? Why was he selected to appear? What did he do before and after his brief association with the Beatles?

Also included is a list of tour dates, a list of the Beatles' special performances, and a selection of television appearances. ★ ★ ★ ★

IN HIS OWN WRITE/
A SPANIARD IN THE WORKS
John Lennon. New American Library, 1980

The 1967 paperback edition, reissued following John's death. ★ ★ ★ ★ ★

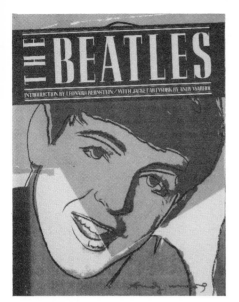

THE BEATLES
Geoffrey Stokes. Rolling Stone/W.H.Allen/
Omnibus Press, 1980

This is *the* coffee table book and so lavish that
three publishers have co-operated in its production. Full credit should go to art director Bea
Feitter for a visually stunning book. There are 320
photographs, printed on quality paper, many of
them spread boldly across two pages.

A full colour section features dozens of items of
memorabilia. There is also a set of full page, full
colour reproductions of Richard Avedon's famous
psychedelic posters. The cover is by Andy
Warhol; in addition, a wraparound cover – the
design, without the lettering – comes with the
book, and is suitable for framing.

The strength of the book lies in its visual
impact, but the text – though neither very long nor
particularly novel – is a good read and the large
type is easy on the eyes. Leonard Bernstein has
contributed the introduction. ★ ★ ★ ★ ★

THE WRITINGS OF JOHN LENNON
John Lennon. Simon & Schuster, 1980

This major publishing house reissued their two
John Lennon books, *In His Own Write* and *A
Spaniard in the Works.*
★ ★ ★ ★ ★

LENNON: WHAT HAPPENED!
Edited by Timothy Green Beckley.
Sunshine Publications, 1980

This is not a sensational exposé of John's life,
along the lines of the similarly titled *Elvis: What
Happened!*, but an investigation into the assassination and its aftermath. Mainly concerned with
the killing – analysed in such chapters as "Why
John Lennon of All the Beatles?" – the book barely
touches on the history of the Beatles. There is,
however, a mild probing into John's relationship
with Yoko; "John & Yoko: Witchcraft or True
Love?" is one chapter heading.

Beckley edited the text, written by reporters
B.R.Ampolsk, B.Schofield and Chris Rowley.
There are more than 40 photographs, supplied by
Wide World, Globe Photos, UPI, AP and
Gamma/Liaison. ★ ★

LENNON: UP CLOSE & PERSONAL
Edited by Timothy Green Beckley.
Sunshine Publications, 1980

The companion volume to *Lennon: What Happened!* and published simultaneously, this is the
history of John's life from 1940-1980.

The book contains a year-by-year chronology
and over 50 photographs, many of which were
also featured in *Lennon: What Happened!*. Unfortunately, the rather cheap paper leads to poor
picture reproduction.

The book was edited by Beckley, with contributions from Arthur Crockett, Barbara Leeds, Carol Rodridque, Diane Quest, Bob Morse and David Stoller. ★★

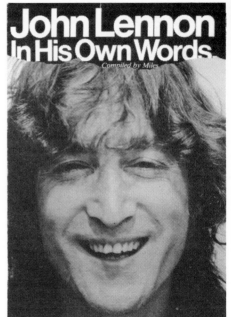

JOHN LENNON IN HIS OWN WORDS
Compiled by Miles. Omnibus Press, 1981

In the huge wave of books published immediately after John's death, this was one of the more popular offerings. It ties in with the Omnibus "In His Own Words" series, although the format is slightly different. Miles has placed the quotes and background history in chronological order; they cover the years 1945, 1952, 1955, 1957, 1958, 1960-1976, 1979 and 1980. The quotes have been assembled from a variety of sources and cover dozens of topics: politics, Hamburg, Brian Epstein, Beatlemania, tours, books, drums, the MBE, films, the Maharishi, Yoko, Apple, primal therapy and New York City.

Almost three quarters of the book is taken up by photographs, laid out in a bold style by designer Pearce Marchbank. There are 120 pictures in all, covering John's life from his childhood to his final days at the Dakota apartments. ★★★

IN THE FOOTSTEPS OF THE BEATLES
Mike Evans & Ron Jones.
Merseyside County Council, 1981

The book begins with a Beatle Trail around the centre of Liverpool, and describes places associated with the Beatles – schools, homes, pubs, places of work, shops. There are several maps and approximately 80 entries, ranging from Prescot Grammar School (where Stuart Sutcliffe studied before going on to Liverpool College of Art) to St Luke's Hall, Crosby, affectionately known as "The Jive Hive".

The book contains over 50 photographs, mainly ones used in early issues of *Mersey Beat*. There are many pictures of the original Mersey venues, with entries on many others: Knotty Ash Village Hall, Hambleton Hall, Aintree Institute, Litherland Town Hall, the Plaza, St Helens and the David Lewis Theatre. The David Lewis was flattened in 1981 and went the way of the Cavern, the Mardi Gras and other popular venues of the Mersey Beat years.

The entries, though brief, are informative. Mike Evans had been around in those days as a member of the Clayton Squares, and he wrote from experience. Ron, working for the Merseyside Tourist Office, was partly responsible for the handsome *Beatles Collection* package, issued some years earlier, but a complete sell-out. This book, in fact, was printed in an original edition of 5,000 copies, but sold out so rapidly that a further 10,000 had to be printed.

The book is dedicated to John and there are many photographs of him, most never seen before except in *Mersey Beat*. There is a picture of the "Lennon" production with Mark McGann portraying John, and a school photograph taken at the Liverpool Institute in 1956. Among the scores of clean-scrubbed faces can be detected Paul and Mike McCartney, Neil Aspinall, Len Garry (who joined the Quarrymen), Don Andrew and Colin Manley (who joined the Remo Four), Ivan Vaughan (who first introduced Paul to John), George Harrison, and Les Chadwick (who joined Gerry and the Pacemakers).

Other interesting shots include Paul and George chatting with Alderman Bill Sefton at their civic reception, mourning Merseysiders at St George's Plateau paying tribute to John, and Japanese fans posing outside Ringo's former home in Dingle. Penny Lane, Strawberry Fields, all the famous places are here, and a fan visiting Liverpool couldn't ask for a better guidebook. ★★★★

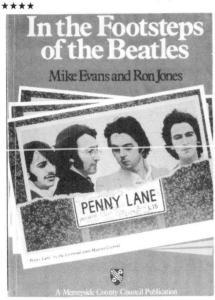

ROCK 'N' ROLL TIMES
Jurgen Vollmer. Google Plex Books, 1981

I was the first person to publish Jurgen Vollmer's pictures of the Beatles; Paul McCartney had given me a stack of photographs of their early trips to Hamburg to use in *Mersey Beat*. Jurgen was an art student friend of Klaus Voorman who, with Astrid Kirchnerr, had become close friends of the Beatles on their first trip to Hamburg. Jurgen and Astrid took some striking photographs of the Beatles in 1960. As John himself comments in the book: "Jurgen Vollmer was the first photographer to capture the beauty and spirit of the Beatles. . . "

Part One of the book illustrates the Beatles' Hamburg trip. There are exactly 25 photographs, including the shot – later used on the cover of John's *Rock 'n' Roll* album – of John in a doorway with some eerie, blurred figures passing by.

Part Two, the main section of the book, is taken up with photographs of Rockers. Shot in the early sixties after Jurgen moved to Paris, the photos produce some haunting images and are captioned with the titles of popular rock songs of the time. There are also pictures of his friends making love in sad-looking flats.

But while the book proved very welcome, I was disappointed to find so few shots of the Beatles. Was this all that Jurgen took during that 1960 visit? There are no photographs of the interior of clubs, such as the Kaiser Keller, or the St Pauli district itself, and no pictures of the Beatles' tatty room behind the Bambi cinema screen. It is some consolation perhaps, that his photographs are among the best ever taken of the Beatles. Jurgen contributes a chatty scenario describing the clubs and filling in the atmosphere. ★★★★

THE COMPLEAT BEATLES
Delilah/ATV/Bantam, 1981

This huge, ambitious work is well worth its price of over £20. It comprises such a large amount of material that it has been divided into two separate volumes, gathered in a slipcase. The books are 1,024 pages in length, and contain over 100 photographs, and the complete sheet music and lyrics to 211 songs with special arrangements by Milton Okun.

Volume One contains "Dedication: John Lennon" by Vic Garbarini and an introduction by John Rockwell. Then comes David Fricke's "Musical History: Vol. 1 (1962-1966)", followed by David Sheff's *Playboy* interview with John. "Don't Pass This Boy By: Ringo & the Beatles" is a Martin Torgott offering, while "Reminiscence of Merseyside" is an interview I gave to David M. Klein. Milo Reice's "The Private Pleasures of a

Beatles Collector" is followed by "Power and Intimacy" by Dave Marsh. Lenny Kaye contributes an article on "The Beatles' Instrumentality"; "Rubber Soul: Wood and Smoke" is by Ron Schaumburg, author of *Growing Up With the Beatles.* "Say the Word I'm Thinking Of" is a series of letters showing the difficulty the publishers had in gaining permission to gather so much copyright music together in a single work. "The Long and Winding Road" is followed by "Lennon & McCartney: Who Wrote What", which originally appeared in *Hit Parader* magazine. Jeannie Sakol's piece, "Richard Lester Remembers", is followed by a filmography and a discography. The discography contains details not only of record releases (chart placings, release dates, whether they qualified for a gold disc and so on, but also of artists who made cover versions of a particular song. Samuel S. Trust writes "A Music Publisher's Perspective"; "The Arrangements", a lengthy feature by Milton Okun, documents the songs featured in Volume One. The next 392 pages contain arrangements to 106 songs.

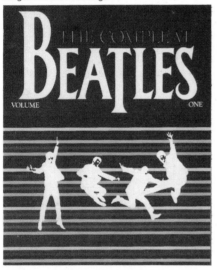

Volume Two covers the years 1966-1970 and begins with "Musical History: Volume Two (1966-1970)" by David Fricke. There is Vic Garbarini's interview of Paul McCartney and Jeannie Sakol's "George Martin Remembers"; this is followed by "Musical Innovations", an article by Lester Bangs. Nicholas Schaffner has written "Transformations" which is followed by "Who's Who in Sgt Pepper's Band", a list of names of the figures on the album sleeve. "Because: John Lennon" is a series of poems by Joel, Lem and Nat Oppenheimer. The discography contains details of the songs contained in the book and Milton Okun's "Arrangements" also analyses the individual numbers in this volume. The next 422 pages feature arrangements for the 105 songs.

To promote the book, the publishers commissioned a video of the Beatles' career. The film turned out to be a far more successful enterprise than anyone had envisaged, and it became one of the best-selling videotapes on both sides of the Atlantic. ★★★★

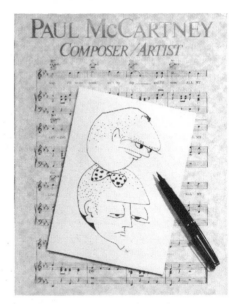

PAUL McCARTNEY COMPOSER/ARTIST
Paul McCartney. Pavilion Books, 1981

This book was publicised as being "an extra-special glimpse into McCartney's creative mind . . .revealed through songs and never-before-published drawings," encouraging readers to believe that it was Paul's equivalent of George Harrison's *I. Me. Mine.* However, it offers little more than a collection of sheet music for 48 songs, illustrated by the author's doodles.

Aside from a brief introduction by Paul of just over 100 words, his drawings and three photographs by Linda, the book contains no new material: the words and music to the songs included therein are available in excellent songbooks such as *The Beatles Complete.*

The drawings are of uneven quality; some, such as those for 'Eleanor Rigby' and 'Here, There and Everywhere', show a degree of latent artistic talent. They tend to detract from the lyrics, few of them succeeding in capturing the mood or mystery, the excitement or exoticism of some quite outstanding songs. ★★★

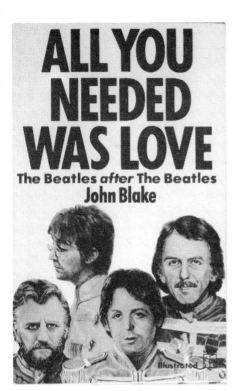

SHOUT! THE TRUE STORY OF THE BEATLES
Philip Norman. Elm Tree Books, 1981

A massive feat of research by *Sunday Times* journalist Philip Norman, this is the best biography of the Beatles currently in print. Norman is also a novelist and in 1982 was one of a select band of authors promoted in Britain as "the young writers of the year."

The book took three years to complete and was begun during a long-running strike at *The Sunday Times* in the late seventies. Norman initially ran into difficulties because he was unable to secure interviews with any of the former Beatles, so I suggested that he contact many of the people who had known the Beatles and provided him with a number of contacts. Although he took great pains with his research, his lack of personal experience of the Beatles' story led to him being purely dependent for information on what others told him; he was also forced to use his imagination in order to dramatise certain events that he had not witnessed himself. As a result, the book contains a number of inaccuracies and several dubious conclusions, rendering the subtitle somewhat inappropriate; this was altered for the American edition (published by Simon and Schuster/Firestone) to read "The Beatles in Their Generation". The subtitle was deleted from the British Corgi paperback edition published the following year.

ALL YOU NEEDED WAS LOVE: THE BEATLES AFTER THE BEATLES
John Blake. Hamlyn, 1981

Rock journalist John Blake's detailed appraisal of the Beatles' private lives from 1969 until the death of John in 1980 is written with the style and verve – and at times the invention – normally associated with novels.

This paperback is a gripping read from its first sentence: "An icy wind blasted down Savile Row; it seems sometimes there is nowhere more wretched on earth than London on a bleak winter's day." The author has also allowed himself a measure of artistic licence when attempting to describe his subjects' inner feelings and preoccupations at various points in the narrative.

The (uncredited) cover painting features the four – head and shoulders only – wearing Sgt. Pepper uniforms. Paul, George and Ringo are white-haired and ageing, though John remains youthful. The book contains 15 photographs and 24 chapters, most of them ingeniously utilising the titles of Beatles' hits. ★★★★

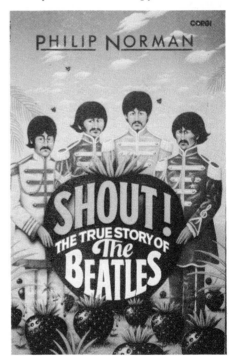

This book was the first to give substantial background to Brian Epstein's homosexuality, details of which were mainly culled from interviews with Joe Flannery. This almost certainly led to the inclusion of similar material in subsequent works and probably inspired the rush of "kiss and tell" books that followed publication. The book definitely became a valuable source for several authors who simply condensed its contents to provide material for their own works. Unfortunately, in so doing they also perpetuated a number of the book's inaccuracies.

Shout! became a best-seller, its sales fuelled by Norman's implications that Epstein had been killed by the Mafia. While this theory obviously helped to sell books, there is no truth in it. Norman also inferred that Epstein fell in love with John the moment he saw him on the Cavern stage, and that this was the reason he signed the Beatles. As someone who witnessed the actual event, and who observed the development of the Epstein/Beatles relationship, I can state that he signed them because he believed he had found his vocation as the manager of what he regarded as a potentially world-famous group.

There are over 100 photographs, well researched by Helen Stinson. The book's jacket features a design by Ken Reilly based on the Robert Freeman photograph (used as a cover for the *With the Beatles* album). ★★★★★

LENNON AND McCARTNEY
Malcolm Doney. Midas Books, 1981

The book is a straightforward retelling of the Beatles' story and the solo careers of John and Paul after the group's break-up. It offers nothing new, although there is a clear indication that the author has read Philip Norman's *Shout!* Some of the theories in *Shout!* are repeated here, almost parrot-fashion. The author makes an attempt to analyse Lennon and McCartney as a songwriting team, but his efforts are somewhat half-hearted. There is a discography and a selection of 13 familiar photographs.

Published in America by Hippodrome Books, and as a paperback by Omnibus Press the following year. ★★★

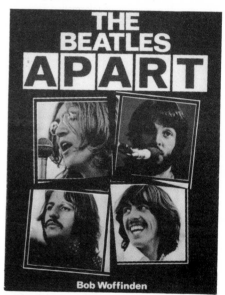

THE BEATLES APART
Bob Woffinden. Proteus Books, 1981

Bob Woffinden, a *New Musical Express* contributor and co-author of *The Illustrated New Musical Express Encyclopedia of Rock* follows the Beatles' careers from 1967 through their solo years until John's murder. This large-sized book is illustrated with 60 black-and-white and 17 colour shots and has a cover adapted from the *Let It Be* LP sleeve.

While this period of their lives was of great importance it was not as colourful as their early years. The disintegration of the partnership, the break-ups of marriages, the mixed fortunes of their solo recordings, and their various drug busts, followed by the tragic demise of John make for a somewhat depressing read.

We are reminded of other rock tragedies by pictures of Ringo with Keith Moon and Marc Bolan, while chapter headings such as "End of a Dream" do little to relieve the gloom. ★★★

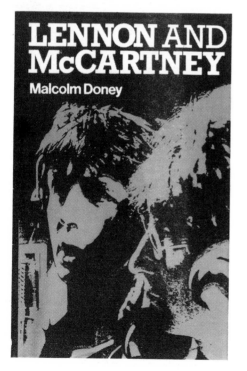

JOHN LENNON & THE BEATLES FOREVER
Ed Naha. Tower Books, 1981

Naha, who has compiled a number of interesting books in the sci-fi media field, edited this collection of pieces about John; he uses material from Starlog's *Beatles Forever* magazine and includes the details surrounding John's murder and the world-wide reaction to it.

The book was one of a number of US paperbacks speedily rushed on to the market and it draws upon familiar photographs and basic historical and discographical data. ★★

YOU CAN'T DO THAT: BEATLES BOOTLEGS & NOVELTY DISCS
Charles Reinhart. Pierian Press, 1981

This is another immensely informative reference work from Pierian Press, with a formidable compilation of 1,394 entries, covering over 1,000 song titles from 178 different labels and illustrated with 80 pictures featuring the sleeves of various bootleg albums and single releases. Wally Podrazik, co-author of *All Together Now* and *The Beatles Again,* contributes a foreword and publisher Tom Schultheiss provides the introduction. There is a wealth of information about bootleg recordings in general and Beatle bootlegs in particular in an appendix by Schultheiss, entitled "Everything You Always Wanted to Know About Bootlegs, But Were Too Busy Collecting Them to Ask".

Reinhart, who has become a specialist in the compilation of information about novelty discs – he has gathered together lists of Lennon tributes following John's death, which may be included in new editions of this work – divides his contents into three main categories: bootlegs, counterfeits and novelties. Expertly assembled indices on each of the sections are extremely useful. The book lists no less than 390 novelty discs with some amazing titles and artists: American Beatles, Beatle Buddies, Beatles Costello, Beatles Revival Band, Beatlettes and Beetles, with singles such as 'I Want a Beatle for Christmas', 'Beatle Bug Jump', 'Bring Back My Beatle to Me' and 'The Beatle Bit My Dog'.

The book's one major failing is a general lack of background information on the bands that recorded these and the other songs listed in the book. ★★★★

JOHN LENNON 4 EVER
Conrad Snell. Crown Summit Books, 1981

This book was one of a plethora of American paperbacks published just after John's death. Without illustrations to brighten it up, it relies on a text that is full of inaccuracies.

THE JOHN LENNON STORY
John Swenson. Leisure Books, 1981

This US paperback was penned by rock journalist Swenson, author of *Yesterday Seems So Far Away*. Similar to most of the other Lennon biography "quickies" and based on newspaper clippings and previously published books, it begins with the murder outside the Dakota building and then moves back in time to cover John's life, music and career with the Beatles. The book is littered with glaring errors.

THE BEATLES
Alan Clark. Alan Clark Productions, 1981

The author has published his own work, a 60-page "special limited collector's edition" featuring the American ads for the Beatles' records, together with some articles and photographs. ★★

LENNON '69: SEARCH FOR LIBERATION.
Edited by Jeff Long.
The Bhaktivedanta Book Trust, 1981

Steeped in the Hare Krishna religion, this publication contains excerpts from conversations the Swami Bhaktivedanta had with John, Yoko and George at Tittenhurst Park in 1969. There are various references to John in a book containing material on the Krishna movement, with information about the various branches of the Krishna Consciousness Society.

The Swami, a believer in reincarnation, recounts a dream he had concerning John and his belief that John had formerly been a wealthy Indian musician in a previous life.

A TRIBUTE TO JOHN LENNON 1940-1980

A TRIBUTE TO JOHN LENNON 1940-1980
Edited: by Lyn Belanger, Michael Brecher,
Jo Kearns, Nicolas Locke and Mike Shatzkin.
Proteus Books, 1981

The royalties from this hardbound book of Lennon tributes were divided equally between the Spirit Foundation and Handgun Control Inc. J.P. Tibbles contributes a fine cover drawing of John, printed on quality tinted paper. The tributes have been selected from newspapers – most of them American, a few of them British – and include: "This Is All About the John Lennon I Lost", by Denny Boyd; "'Yesterday' Mourning Before Sunrise" by Richard Roberts; "How John Was Overwhelmed by Life and Death", by Phil Sutcliffe; "They Loved Him, Yeah, Yeah, Yeah", by Leon Taylor; "Lennon Remembered for More Than Music", by Russ Christian; "Within His Music", by Richard Dyer; "The Lighter Side of John", by Don Short; "Lennon: Always Up Front", by Tony Kornheiser and Tom Zito; "Intellectual Lennon: Social Revolutionary", by Clive Barnes; "Everyone Should Speak Lennon's Language", by Rabbi Marcus Kramer; "John Lennon: No Secret Interior, Just Integrity", by Robert Hilburn; "A Lot of People Were Crying", by Al Carter; "The Surreal Genius of Rock", by Ray Connolly; "John Lennon's Music Will Never Die", by John Murray; and "The Promise Is Gone", by Ellen Goodman.

The book is illustrated with 16 full-page photographs. ★ ★ ★

A CELLARFUL OF NOISE
Brian Epstein. New English Library, 1981

This slim, paperback reprint of the 1964 book has no interior illustrations. A black-and-white photo of Brian above a colour shot of the Beatles in collarless jackets adorns the cover, which bears the slogan "The one essential Beatles book."

In the light of Epstein's tragic death, the book's final words are especially poignant: "I think the sun will shine tomorrow." Those words sum up how a lot of people in the sixties felt about the future. It was the last decade of optimism. ★ ★ ★

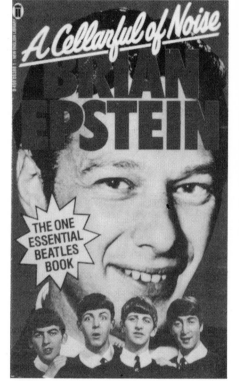

THE BEATLES FOR THE RECORD
Stafford Pemberton Publishing, 1981

No author is credited, but the text takes second place to the magnificently reproduced photographs in this large format book; like The Beatles Illustrated Record, it is the same size as a record album. Part of a series that includes volumes on Abba, Elvis Presley and Barry Manilow, it contains almost 140 photographs, most of them in colour. This lavish production was printed in Italy on art paper.

The text is informative, owing something to the research carried out in other books, such as Philip Norman's Shout! It contains the usual errors, such as the statement that Kingsize Taylor recorded the Beatles at the Star Club, which he didn't. Apart from documenting the Fab Four's career from their Quarrymen days, it also fills in details of their solo careers. The book was published in North America in 1982 by Totem Books. ★★★

JOHN LENNON
AND YOKO ONO
IN CONVERSATION
WITH ANDY PEEBLES
6 DECEMBER 1980

THE LENNON TAPES
Andy Peebles. BBC Publications, 1981

A team from Radio One travelled to New York to interview John and Yoko while they were recording *Double Fantasy* at the Hit Factory. The team comprised executive producer Doreen Davies, producer Paul Williams and DJ Andy Peebles. On Saturday, 6 December 1980, they began what they believed would be a half-hour interview about the making of the LP; to their delight this became a three-hour chat in which John talked about his entire life and career. The team arrived back in Britain on 9 December to learn that he had been murdered. Some short excerpts from the interview were broadcast that day and the entire tapes were broadcast in five parts beginning on 18 January 1981.

This slim volume is the transcript of those broadcasts; its publishing royalties were donated to charity. There is a colour photograph of John and Yoko at the Hit Factory on the back cover; and the contents comprise a foreword by Paul Williams, an introduction by Andy Peebles and the 88-page interview. The topics and personalities John discusses include memories of early BBC recordings; his meeting with Yoko at the Indica Gallery; the making of *How I Won the War*; *Two Virgins*; the film *Rape*; Bagism; 'The Ballad of John & Yoko'; *Live Peace in Toronto*; the Lyceum concert; *Double Fantasy*; feminism; Liverpool art school; Elton John; David Bowie; and Phil Spector and *The Rock 'n' Roll* album. ★★★★

JOHN LENNON: 1940-1980
Compiled by Ernest E.Schworck.
ESE, 1981

This large-size, 90-page paperback reproduces the front pages of newspapers with headline stories relating to John's murder. The majority of them are American, but there are a number of foreign-language newspapers represented. ★★★

JOHN LENNON:
A PERSONAL PICTORIAL DIARY
Sportomatic Ltd, 1981

This small booklet was published by a New York firm in January 1981. It was designed with the newsagent in mind rather than the bookseller, and is little more than a pictorial essay. ★★

JOHN LENNON: 1940-1980
Ray Connolly, 1981

Of all the biographies issued within 12 months of John's death, this was the best. Ray had been a journalist in Liverpool before he moved to London to join the *Evening Standard* in 1967. He interviewed the Beatles on numerous occasions and also wrote several separate features about John and Yoko. Ray was privy to the information that John was leaving the Beatles but as a favour to John he sat on the story. Four months later Paul announced he was leaving. It would have been Ray's biggest scoop – and John also came to regret losing the opportunity of making his statement first.

In the winter of 1980, Ray was due to fly to New York to interview John, and Yoko called him on the afternoon of 8 December to confirm it. At 5.30 the following morning he received a telephone call giving him the tragic news of John's murder. He then wrote the obituary for the *Standard*. (John had said to him in December 1970: "Have you written my obituary yet? I'd love to read it when you do.")

The book is well-written and informative and contains many anecdotes. It displays none of the haste evident in many of the books that were rushed out to satisfy public demand for information about John following his death.

The book is divided into three sections: Liverpool, the World, and New York. Ray never attempts to sensationalise, but he brings a degree of insight into John's story that is lacking in many other books.

There are 60 photographs, including some rare and unusual ones: John dressed as a Rocker at the *Magical Mystery Tour* party; eating an apple at the Apple boutique opening; handing Michael X a bag of hair for him to auction; compaigning for a posthumous pardon for James Hanratty; with Elton John at Madison Square Gardens and being leapt upon by a fan on stage in Rome. One of the most intriguing photographs shows John and Yoko standing among some of their possessions at Tittenhurst Park. The illustrations also include a lithograph for John's "I Ching" project, an *Evening Standard* poster "Police Raid Lennon Art Show", and a framed photograph of *three* virgins – yes, three naked people in full frontal pose. Most people assumed that the shot of John and Yoko naked, used on the *Two Virgins* sleeve, was taken using a delayed action device; apparently there was a third "virgin" around to take the picture. ★★★★

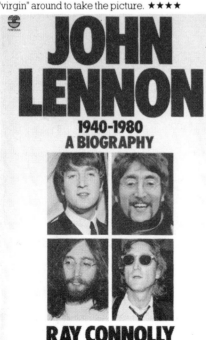

THANK U VERY MUCH
Mike McCartney. Arthur Baker, 1981

The best book to document the life of a single member of the Beatles (Paul) containing reproductions of the most extensive collection of personal memorabilia so far published.

Mike is, of course, Paul's brother, and for many years lived under the pseudonym Mike McGear while he pursued his own career as a member of the Scaffold and author of children's books.

Mike and Paul are shown on the front cover, standing shoulder to shoulder, holding wine glasses. The subtitle reads: "Mike McCartney's Family Album". This is an apt description of the book; Mike documents the life of the McCartney family from the turn of the century with photographs, a "Maclineage" and drawings. There are almost 200 illustrations in the book including ticket stubs to Beatle concerts, business cards, invitations, sleeve designs, letters, newspaper clippings, call sheets, postcards, telegrams and posters.

Many of the photographs from the late fifties and early sixties were taken by Mike himself, who is clearly no mean photographer. Among the many pictures printed here for the first time are shots of Paul with his former girlfriend Dot in the back garden of his home in Forthlin Road; playing the drums with Pete Best at the Cavern; with Stu Sutcliffe at the Casbah Club; with Rory Storm; and at the Cavern with Gene Vincent.

The story of the McCartney family through the years, and of the two brothers in particular, is written with a great deal of wit, Scouse humour and loving sentiment.

The book ranks alongside *The Longest Cock-*

tail Party as one of the funniest Beatle books available; it also brings Paul's early years to life in a highly readable style.

It was published in America by Delilah Books under the title *The Macs.* ★★★★★

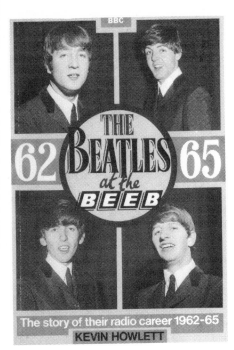

THE BEATLES AT THE BEEB
Kevin Howlett. BBC Publications, 1982

Radio One producer Kevin Howlett has written an excellent book detailing one special aspect of their career – their BBC radio appearances. Kevin was also co-producer of *The Beatles at the Beeb*, the two-hour show that celebrated the twentieth anniversary of the group's first BBC studio performance. The book was issued a few months after the programme was broadcast with a foreword by Jeff Griffin.

The first section of the book presents the story of the group's appearances on over 50 shows between March 1962 and June 1965. The following section, "The Songs", combines alphabetical listing with background information on the 88 different songs they performed on the air. "The Date Chart 1962-1965" details various highlights in their career during this period, with specific information relating to the Radio One appearances. "The Programmes" provides information on the many radio shows the Beatles appeared on during those years and there is also a brief bibliography and discography.

There are almost 50 photographs in the book, the majority taken during BBC appearances and a number of them previously unpublished. ★★★★

LIVERPOOL 8
John Cornelius. John Murray, 1982

This book hardly mentions the Beatles but it does convey an idea of the character of the particular area of Liverpool associated with the group.

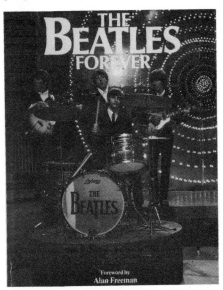

THE BEATLES FOREVER
Helen Spence. Colour Library Books, 1982

Not to be confused with Nicholas Shaffner's work. This is another beautiful picture book similar to *The Beatles for the Record*. There are 210 colour shots, presented in bold and exciting layouts and 18 black-and-white photographs. Unfortunately Helen Spence's text, which follows a foreword by Alan Freeman, is little more than a recycled version of Philip Norman's *Shout!* In fact, the text could have been ditched to make room for more photographs.

Most of the photographs have been provided by Keystone Press who clearly delved into their extensive Beatles' files to present several rarely-seen pictures. The publisher, Colour Library International, specialises in quality photographic reproduction and they have produced a book that is a handsome document of certain moments in the Beatles' career.

It was published in America by Crescent Books under the title *The Beatles.* ★★★

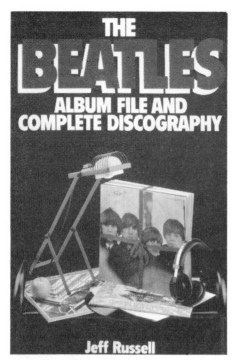

THE BEATLES ALBUM FILE
& COMPLETE DISCOGRAPHY
Jeff Russell. Blandford Press, 1982

A much maligned book: reviews were virtually unanimous in condemning it for a fairly large number of inaccuracies. Merseyside Beatles' fan Russell has obviously worked hard compiling the book, but he probably needed a "reader" thoroughly conversant with Beatles' records to double-check his copy. It was issued at a time when two other books covering the same subject were published, both of which proved more accurate.

The book has a striking cover, and the reproduction of the album sleeves is clean and legible. Russell begins by taking the British albums one at a time, and presenting the background to each record in a track by track analysis. Their first British LP *Please Please Me* is the fifth to be reviewed as Hamburg and Decca recordings have been placed before it. The next section deals with American albums and is followed by several appendices. There is a chapter on "Recording Oddities", another on the unreleased Beatles' tracks, and a complete discography.

It was published in the US by Scribner's under the title *The Beatles on Record.* ★★★

THE BEATLES ON RECORD
Mark Wallgren. Simon & Schuster, 1982

Another book concentrating on the group's recordings and also written by a Beatle fan – though it is more thoroughly researched than Russell's book and was warmly received by reviewers. It features 250 records and, as the cover blurb explains, the book comprises: "The story behind every single and LP released by the Beatles, John and Yoko, Paul McCartney/Wings, George Harrison and Ringo Starr, including title, artist, label, release date, highest chart positions and photos of each record jacket." The book is a pleasant read and there are several appendices, including a section of reissues and special items of interest, quick reference guides to chart positions in America and a similar chart on world-wide releases. ★★★★

THE LONG & WINDING ROAD
Neville Stannard. Virgin Books, 1982

The third book concerning Beatles' records to be issued within months of each other. Subtitled "A History of the Beatles on Record", it contains details of every Beatles' release: singles, albums, EPs, boxed sets and bootlegs, with catalogue details, chart positions, titbits about the actual recordings and anecdotes about the composition of the songs – all meticulously researched, with photographs of the record covers and a welcome selection of the promotional material originally used to advertise the records.

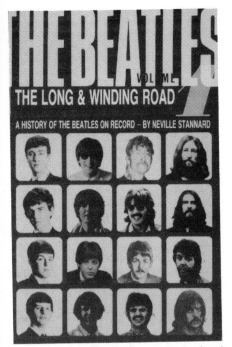

The facts are presented in an organised and readable manner; the Beatles' recordings are placed in the context of the time in which they were released, with added details to give a broader picture. In the case of 'Money', for example, we learn of the song's writers, Janie Bradford and Berry Gordy, its history, and which other artists went on to cover it.

At the end of each year we are given details of all the awards the Beatles' records have received, their chart positions throughout the world and the volume of their sales. The main section of the book comprises information on their British and American releases. There then follows 13 appendices: "With a Little Help From My Friends" – the stories of 21 Lennon and McCartney songs recorded by other acts between 1963 and 1969; "British Chart Statistics"; "British Chart Sales"; "Weekly British Chart Positions"; "Paul Is Dead" (a somewhat sketchy account); "Unreleased Studio Recordings"; "The Beatles' Million Sellers"; "The Hamburg Recordings"; "The Beatles' Rare Tracks"; "The Beatles' Bootlegs"; "The Beatles in the BMRB Chart 1962/1970"; "Song Recording Dates"; and "The Beatles' Christmas Records".

The first edition did not have an index, but the second – published later in the same year – corrected this omission. ★★★★

LOTS OF LIVERPOOL
A Beatles Unlimited Special, 1982

Another modest but enterprising publication from the editorial team of Dutch fans who produce the quarterly *Beatles Unlimited*. This is a guide book for Beatle fans visiting Merseyside detailing seven different areas of the region and including photographs, maps, information and routes for anyone wishing to tour the area in search of Beatle memories. The first section deals with Liverpool city centre and is the largest of the tours, containing many places associated with the Beatles, including theatres, clubs, schools and hospitals. The second trip covers the north-east side of Liverpool and the areas of Kirkdale, Walton and Fazakerley. There is a photograph of Brian Epstein's gravestone and one of Walton Hospital, where Paul was born. Trip three covers Toxteth and Dingle, where Ringo lived, including his schools, homes, even his former local pub the Empress, (which was featured on the cover of his *Sentimental Journey* album). Trip four covers Wavertree, Woolton and Hunt's Cross, taking in Penny Lane, Strawberry Fields and Quarrybank School. The Kensington, Knotty Ash and Huyton areas are covered in trip five, which includes the area where there are now streets named after the Beatles: John Lennon Drive, Ringo Starr Drive, Paul McCartney Way and George Harrison Close. Trip six crosses the Mersey to look at Wallasey and New Brighton, and the final trip takes us to Birkenhead, then goes off at a tangent by including Arnold Grove, and the former Casbah Club in West Derby.

There are almost 50 photographs and over 20 maps. ★★★

THE BEATLES' ENGLAND
David Bacon and Norman Maslov.
Columbus Books, 1982

The third book within 12 months to follow in the footsteps of the Beatles. Of the three, this is the most lavish, with superbly reproduced photographs on coated paper. Maslov is from San Francisco; Bacon was born in Japan and moved to San Francisco as a boy. The authors set out to track down all the places in England of interest to Beatles' fans, and have done so in such a dedicated manner that they are able to offer us information as detailed as the fact that Nems record store was exactly 98 steps from the Cavern. During their travels they took literally thousands of photographs and the book is basically a photo record of their journey, the actual text being quite sparse. There are over 150 black-and-white shots and a further 80 in colour.

The book is divided into three main sections, the first covering London, taking in Abbey Road, its famous zebra crossing and studios, Apple buildings, Carnaby Street, Decca Studios, EMI House, the locations for *A Hard Day's Night*, galleries, theatres, hospitals, flats and other venues with Beatle associations. Part two takes us to Liverpool, featuring the birthplaces, homes and original clubs that witnessed the birth of the Beatles. The third section, entitled "Daytripping", takes in various other places in England of interest to the Beatle fan, plus a trip to the St Pauli district of Hamburg.

The Beatles' England is not only one of the most handsome Beatle books ever published, but also provides some fascinating titbits of trivia. For example, it states that the Beatles posed at the Abbey Road zebra crossing at 10a.m. on 8 August 1969; that the field the Beatles horse around in during *A Hard Day's Night* is St Margaret's Field, near Heathrow Airport; and that the garbage from MPL Communications is placed in large plastic bags in doorways next to

their offices in Soho Square each Friday night – inviting the attentions of scavenging Beatle fans.

There are a few entries that have only the most tenuous links with the Beatles: Battersea Power Station is mentioned simply because it is seen in *Help!*; a Wall's Ice Cream sign because the company issued a promotional disc, featuring four Apple acts, that was given away at their West End shops; and Virgin Megastore in Oxford Street, presumably because it sells Beatles' records.

Generally, though, the sites are well chosen, well photographed and of immense interest to fans. ★★★★

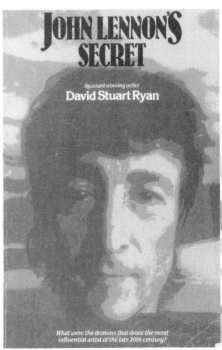

JOHN LENNON'S SECRET
David Stuart Ryan. Kosmik Press, 1982

In company with Ray Connolly's *John Lennon: 1940-1980,* this is a sincere attempt to produce a biography of John that delves a little deeper into the man than the rash of superficial paperbacks that appeared within weeks of his death. David spent some time in Liverpool and New York researching his material and obtaining first-hand information from friends and associates of John, including Bob Wooler and Clive Epstein. He also had access to the manuscripts of an unpublished book by the late Freddy Lennon, John's father.

This independently published book is well produced and contains a colour poster portraying John on the last day of his life and 32 full-page photographs. There is also a list of John's compositions, a bibliography and a section discussing 22 of John's songs in detail.

The 24 chapters cover John's life more closely than previous publications, although there are few surprises. The depiction of John's childhood is highly readable, the author covering the ground in much the same way as Philip Norman did in *Shout!* The influence of Norman's book is also evident in the scene where Brian Epstein first sees the Beatles at the Cavern: "From the moment the furtive figure of Brian Epstein saw the black leather clad shape of the sardonic, joking, superior Lennon, he was fixated." Norman's wild contention in *Shout!* that Brian fell in love with John at that moment, and as a result signed the Beatles, has been reiterated by several authors and is thus a particularly tiresome inaccuracy. ★★★★

THE LEGACY OF JOHN LENNON
David A.Noebel.
Thomas Nelson Publishers, 1982

Published simultaneously in both hardcover and paperback editions in the US, this is another of Noebel's anti-Beatle books. *Communism, Hypnotism & the Beatles* and *The Beatles: A Study in Sex, Drugs & Revolution* also revealed his obsession with John's comments in 1966 that: "Christianity will go. It will vanish and shrink. . . we're more popular than Jesus now."

The book is subtitled "Charming or Harming a Generation" and the blurb on the publisher's advertisement reads :"David Noebel's extensive research reveals direct and deliberate encouragement in rock music for young people to abandon biblical morality and embrace sexual perversion and promiscuity, drug abuse, Satan worship, rebellion against society, and violence. Noebel offers page after page of quotes from religious writers, secular commentators, and rock entertainers themselves to support his contention that rock music is a blatant attempt to brainwash its followers with anti-Christian propaganda."

AS I WRITE THIS LETTER
Marc A.Catone. Greenfield Books, 1982

Greenfield Books is a division of Pierian Press, and this is another quality hardback production from their presses. The foreword is by Tom Schultheiss and the introduction by self-confessed Beatlemaniac Catone, who first switched on to the Fab Four in 1964 at the age of 13. Marc began placing ads in magazines and newspapers in May 1979, inviting people from all walks of life to write to him and relate how the Beatles had affected their lives. He received approximately 200 letters for his planned work, which was to be "a book written *by* Beatle fans *for* Beatle fans about how Beatle fans view the Beatles".

Marc has organised the letters into eleven chapters, each one preceded by a personal commentary. The letters are all from American fans, which explains the book's subtitle: "An American Generation Remembers the Beatles". Schultheiss points out elsewhere: "More than any other people, Americans as a nation have enjoyed a special relationship with the Beatles."

The book is illustrated with 70 remarkable drawings by Beatle fans, gathered with the help of Bill King, editor of the fanzine *Beatlefan*. Eleven separate artists supplied the material and the work of John Covert, April Geiger and Jaime Sustaita is particularly commendable. ★★★★

An illustration from As I Write This Letter.

THE BEATLES: A COLLECTION
Robcin Associates.
Robert and Cindy DelBuno, 1982

Beatle fans, inspired by their heroes, have taken up their pens and produced a number of books. The authors of *The Beatles: A Collection* were unable to find a publisher for their book, so they decided to go ahead and publish it themselves. The work is subtitled: "A Comprehensive Guide to Beatles Collectibles and Their Values" and comprises five sections. The first deals with "Memorabilia", the second "Publications", the third "American Pressings", the fourth "Foreign Pressings" and the fifth "Bootlegs". Prices are included for each of the several hundred different items mentioned and, realising that price lists are liable to date quite rapidly, the authors have included an "Additions, Corrections and Suggestions" sheet so that readers can provide them with specific information for subsequent editions.

THE BEATLES: A COLLECTION

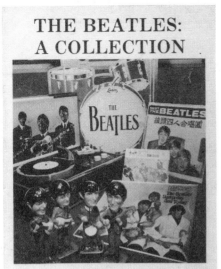

Robert and Cindy DelBuono

The price of an English Beatle dress is set at 300 dollars; a complete set of 55 *A Hard Day's Night* bubble-gum cards is priced at 50 dollars; a set of inflatable Beatles' dolls are priced at 50 dollars and a Beatles' diary, *circa* 1964, at 50 dollars. All these items would fetch considerably higher prices now.

The book is illustrated with hundreds of colour and black-and-white photographs, featuring a large number of books, magazines, dolls, records, wigs and other memorabilia. ★ ★ ★

COLLECTING THE BEATLES
Barb Fenick. Pierian Press, 1982

The essential guide to memorabilia, published in a large hardback edition with a bright yellow cover. Barb is editor of *The Write Thing*, a Beatles' fanzine of inestimable value to collectors. Her book imparts the knowledge she has gained during her years spent as a dealer in Beatle souvenirs. Aware that the prices she quotes in her book are subject to change, she presents a sample of the inflation rates of Beatle items, contrasting the prices of 1978, 1980 and 1982. For instance, a Corgi yellow-submarine toy which could be bought for 35 dollars in 1978 was worth 75 dollars in 1980 and between 100 and 125 dollars in 1982.

Barb abhors the counterfeiting that has become a feature of the now lucrative market in Beatles' memorabilia. With prices quadrupling within a few years, some skyrocketing within the space of months, unscrupulous dealers have been eager to grab a piece of the action. She comments: "The worst offence [of this] I've ever seen was at a recent Beatles' convention where a counterfeit cover of the 'original' art work for *Somewhere in England* was made into an LP

jacket, sans record, and passed off as a genuine rarity selling for 35 dollars!... this counterfeit slick could legitimately be sold for three to four dollars merely as a widely distributed novelty piece, but to deliberately make it appear to be the real thing and charge such an outlandish price is pure banditry. . . "

The first section of the price guide contains several chapters of detailed information on all aspects of the subject, beginning with the author's initial inspiration for the book. There is a chapter on the history of collecting, in which she describes a Woolworth's store in 1964 as an "Ali Baba's cave". This is followed by a description of the new era of collecting that took root in the early seventies, when the tenth anniversary of Beatlemania was celebrated and conventions began to become popular. "The Counterfeit Controversy" examines the subject of counterfeiting in detail and there is also a chapter on bootleg material. This is followed by an examination of potential sources of memorabilia and a section on the professional dealers in Beatles' artefacts.

The main section of the book is the price guide, which lists prices of over 850 separate items under the following headings: Beatles Albums; Beatles Singles; EPs and Compact Records; Promo Records; Bootleg Records; Beatles Related and Novelty Records; Books; Magazines, Pamphlets and Programmes; Memorabilia and Other Special and Promotional Items. There follows a list of the original, exclusive, licensed manufacturers and a section on the Sotheby's auction, reproducing the original catalogue.

There are also 138 pages of photographs.
★ ★ ★ ★ ★

THE COMPLETE BEATLES LYRICS
Omnibus Press, 1982

This large paperback is well designed and was issued to celebrate the twentieth anniversary of 'Love Me Do'. The cover is Robert Freeman's "onion head" pic from the *Beatles for Sale* sessions, although it is uncredited. The remaining 19 photographs in the book each take up a full page, are black and white and come from the files of Camera Press, Rex Features and Leslie Bryce. The cover announces: "For the first time ever together in print. . . " referring to the lyrics of over 180 Beatle numbers, each one given its own page. The book also presents a discography of all their British records listed in order of release. ★ ★ ★ ★

THE 1975 JOHN LENNON INTERVIEW
Privately printed. Lavinia Van Driver, 1982

The author has set out to print a series of booklets transcribing legendary Beatle interviews. She has edited and transcribed *The Old Grey Whistle Test* interview with John, conducted by Bob Harris. This particular booklet is 16 pages in length. ★★★

THE PLAYBOY INTERVIEWS WITH JOHN LENNON & YOKO ONO
David Sheff. Playboy Press, 1982

Playboy magazine was granted the first interview with John for almost five years following his period as a recluse and house-husband. However, *Newsweek* magazine pipped them to the post with Barbara Graustark's interview (later printed in *Strawberry Fields Forever: John Lennon Remembers*). David Sheff took three weeks to tape the interviews in September 1980 and eventually wrote a 20,000 word piece, which was too long for the magazine. An edited version appeared in the issue for January 1981, although it was on the news-stands in early December, before John was killed. The complete interviews are presented in this book.

John discusses many subjects ranging from his "lost weekend" period on the West Coast and his well-publicised drunkenness at the Troubadour Club to his guilt feelings over his and Yoko's attempts to take Kyoko away from her father. His relationship with Yoko is probed, as is his memory regarding the songs he personally

wrote under the Lennon/McCartney banner. He discusses feminism, early influences, being a father and the merits of the individual members of the Beatles. Yoko, of course, also has her say.

The book is illustrated with an eight-page photo insert and was published in Britain by New English Library. ★★★★

THE BALLAD OF JOHN & YOKO
The editors of Rolling Stone.
Rolling Stone Press, 1982

A collection of material, most of which was previously published in *Rolling Stone* magazine, that explores the life of John and his relationship with Yoko with great thoroughness in a series of well-written, sometimes probing, sometimes critical, but always thought-provoking articles Yoko's childhood in Japan and John's early life in Liverpool are examined and there is a lengthy chronology. The first *Rolling Stone* interview, which Jonathan Cott conducted in 1968, is reprinted, with various articles written between the years 1968 and 1976 by top rock journalists such as Ritchie York, Chet Flippo and Jann Wenner. Chet also provides "The Private Years", covering the period between 1976 and 1980, while Annie Leibovitz has contributed a portfolio of intimate pictures of John and Yoko at the Dakota in December 1980. Mick Jagger and Harry Nilsson have recorded their memories of John in short articles in a section that also contains brief tributes from a range of people, including Gerry Marsden, Frank Sinatra, Ray Charles and Chuck Berry. The book includes critical analyses of John and Yoko's films and of Yoko's songs and conceptual happenings.

The eighty photographs, six of them in colour, are well selected and include many that are quite rare. Of particular interest are the childhood photographs of Yoko and a range of pictures of her conceptual creations. The book was published in England by Michael Joseph. ★★★★

PHOTOGRAPHS
Linda McCartney. MPL Communications, 1982

This large-sized book comprises a collection of Linda's photographs taken between the years 1966 and 1981. Although panned by the photographer David Bailey, when it was published in Britain, Linda's talent is plain for all to see.

Rather than cram the book with pictures of Paul and the other Beatles – which some buyers would have doubtless preferred – she has selected her own favourite photographs, thereby widening the book's scope.

During the sixties, Linda met and photographed a number of stars, including Jim Morrison, Mick Jagger and Jimi Hendrix; these are just some of the rock personalities featured in the collection. ★★★★

Abbey Road – perhaps the most famous recording studio in the world. Abbey Road received its greatest boost when the Beatles named their biggest-selling album after it. The studios have since been opened to the public for "Beatles at Abbey Road" presentations, which drew audiences from all over the world during the summer of 1983.

Since the early fifties, the studio has been used by many successful artists, and the author has included a list of the 76 British No.1 records produced there between 1954 and 1982: the Beatles were responsible for 15 of them and Liverpudlian acts for a further 10.

Paul McCartney has supplied the foreword and George Martin the introduction to this fascinating biography of a recording studio. There are over 200 photographs, many of them showing the Beatles relaxing and performing at Abbey Road, and a series of photographs of other Mersey acts such as Billy J. Kramer and Cilla Black.

The Beatles' connection with the studio is covered in chapter six, "I Don't Like Your Tie"; and chapter seven, "Yesterday – McCartney Remembers", relates the association between Paul's group Wings and Abbey Road. ★★★★

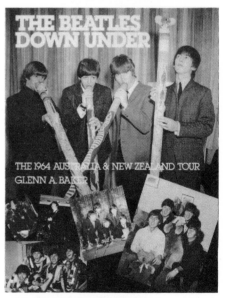

ABBEY ROAD
Brian Southall. Patrick Stephens Ltd, 1982

Brian Southall, an EMI publicity executive who was a popular guest at several Beatles' conventions, has exhaustively researched the history of

THE BEATLES DOWN UNDER
Glenn A.Baker. Wild & Woolley Press, 1982

This is one of those rare books that takes a small aspect of the Beatles' career and places it under a microscope. In this case it is their 1964 tour of Australia and New Zealand.

This is the best document of a Beatles' tour available and Baker ("a radio announcer, journalist, scriptwriter, record company owner and terminal music addict") has thoroughly researched his subject, interviewing more than 50 people.

Until reading this book, few would have realised just how fervent Beatlemania was during that particular tour; but the hysteria that greeted the Fab Four when they arrived in Australasia was truly staggering. As Baker comments: "No street crowds in New York, London or Liverpool ever eclipsed the Antipodean hordes which, at times, comprised more than half the entire population of a city."

The first chapter deals with the early negotiations to promote the tour, the details of the arrangements, the behind-the-scenes organisation and the mixed reaction of the Australian media to the news that the Beatles were actually Australia-bound. In chapter two we arrive in Sydney, learning that the first fans to arrive at the airport, Kay Strickland and Vicki Griffin, were patiently waiting the day prior to the landing and that the two had already queued 18 hours to secure tickets to a Beatle concert. The book is filled with such stories, recording the excitement of fans of all ages. In the following chapters we accompany the Beatles on the tour, with Baker providing an almost moment-by-moment commentary.

The book is crammed with over 300 photographs, the majority of them previously unpublished. There are also scores of newspaper clippings, and an Australian discography. ★★★★★

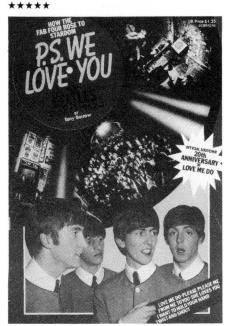

P.S. WE LOVE YOU
Tony Barrow. Mirror Books, 1982

Written by Tony Barrow, a public relations officer for Nems Enterprises who handled the Beatles' press on a number of occasions, this book features 100 carefully selected photographs, a number of them in colour, illustrating the Beatles' career between 1962 and 1963. The book was published to tie in with the twentieth anniversary of 'Love Me Do'.

There are 16 brief chapters that cover the hectic days of the birth of Beatlemania in Britain, the group's rise in status from Liverpool's No.1 band to Britain's biggest musical export. Tony has interviewed a number of early associates such as Freda Kelly, the secretary of the Beatles' fan club, in addition to including his own recollections of the time. ★★★★

THE BEATLES WHO'S WHO
Bill Harry. Aurum Press, 1982

There are over 300 different biographies in this book, and over 100 photographs. My aim was to view the Beatles' lives through the eyes of their friends, associates, relatives and immediate families and also to include information on some of the lesser-known people who featured in the Beatles' story. The selection was presented in a chronological form, rather than in A to Z fashion, which seems to have confused some reviewers. Their main criticism concerned the brevity of the entries on people who were associated with the band once they had achieved success. This is a valid point as I preferred to concentrate on the "Liverpool end" of their career, in order to present intimate portraits of the many people on the scene I knew personally. ★★★★

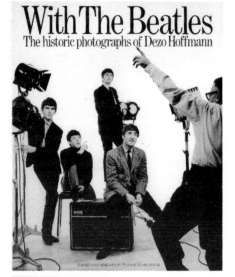

With The Beatles
The historic photographs of Dezo Hoffmann

WITH THE BEATLES
Dezo Hoffmann. Omnibus Press, 1982

Dezo Hoffmann is a Czech-born photographer who worked for a number of publications in the early sixties, including the musical weekly *Record Mirror*. He travelled to Liverpool in 1962 to take photographs of the Beatles and regularly photographed the group over the next three years.

His photographs have been collated in book form before, yet this is by far the best and most complete collection of Dezo's pictures of the Beatles.

There are over 300 photographs: shots include Dezo supervising a Beatles' photo session; the Beatles auditioning at Abbey Road in June 1962; at their homes in Liverpool; romping around in Sefton Park; at the Cavern; Paul with Frankie Howerd; having their hair cut; performing at Stowe School; broadcasting from the Albert Hall; with Marlene Dietrich; arriving in America; with Ed Sullivan at Carnegie Hall; at Washington Coliseum; filming *A Hard Day's Night;* with Sir Laurence Olivier; at their Christmas Show at Hammersmith Odeon; and filming *Help!*

There are a few captions and some text taken from an interview with Dezo in July 1982. But the pictures speak for themselves. ★★★★

THE OCEAN VIEW
Humphrey Ocean.
MPL Communications/Plexus Books, 1983

Paul McCartney, regarded as the most "media-conscious" Beatle, has been careful to provide posterity with adequate information about his career. In the case of the Wings' tour of America, a film team accompanied the group; the tour was

documented by a series of photographs published as *Hands Across the Water: Wings Tour USA;* and Paul also commissioned an artist, Humphrey Ocean, to make a visual record of it.

Paul has contributed his usual brief introduction, and there is a tour itinerary and several pages of diary notes by Ocean. The rest of the book comprises paintings and drawings of a quality excellent enough to be described as "art". There are more than 50 paintings and drawings contained in the volume, all executed between April and June 1976. ★★★★

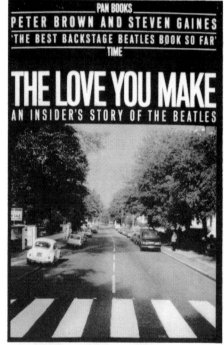

THE LOVE YOU MAKE
Peter Brown and Steven Gaines.
McGraw Hill, 1983

There isn't much fun in this book. The stupendously exciting, stimulating story of the twentieth-century's greatest musical phenomenon has been reduced to a tale of squalor, perversion, drugs, sex and betrayal. The most depressing aspects of the Beatles' career have been stressed, the complicated and frustrating financial details of Apple brought to the fore and the private life of Brian Epstein exposed in the most unsavoury fashion.

Beatle fans were so appalled that Mark Lapidos, organiser of various Beatle conventions in America, withdrew the book from his Beatle-fests. In addition, many of the people interviewed by Brown and Gaines were upset by the book's revelations – the Epstein family and Yoko Ono in particular.

The Love You Make was the first of the "kiss and tell" books; it sold in huge numbers and made a fortune for its authors. I read the British edition, published by Macmillan, and have been informed that it differs from the American one in that a number of cuts had to be made. The ads claimed that the work was "illustrated with never-before-seen photos from Peter Brown's private file," though most of its 37 photographs have been published before.

Brown knew little about the actual Mersey scene: he worked on the record counter in Lewis's department store and became one of Brian Epstein's small circle of friends. Brian brought him into the family business, making him manager of a branch of Nems and later, when he had established himself in the music industry, invited Brown to join him. Brown's view of the Mersey scene is sketchy at best, but terribly inaccurate in the main. He has looked to other sources for his information of this period – and has picked out all the inaccuracies and false impressions given in other books.

Many of the stories of a sexual nature that Brown recounts cannot be substantiated – who can actually prove that Brian and John went to bed together in Spain? Brown himself admits that his story of Ringo's wife and George Harrison sleeping together has never been proved. The book is a terribly depressing read for a Beatles' fan, but its salacious gossip makes it ideal for the general reader who enjoys a good squirm. ★ ★ ★ ★

LOVING JOHN
May Pang and Henry Edwards.
Warner Books, 1983

Like *The Love You Make*, this book made an incredible amount of money for its authors in publisher's advances. May Pang was the Chinese-American secretary who worked for the Lennons; Pang suggests that she was forced into a relationship with John by Yoko herself. This assertion made great copy for the Sunday papers and brought in more bucks from serialisation rights. May's close encounters of the sexual kind are described in suitably titillating detail.

The book's promotional material says it all: "Never-before-published intimate account of her life with John and Yoko. . . the drugs, the chaos, the bouts of violence, the intimate details . . . the Lennons' whims were May Pang's commands, and no matter how strange, May followed them. . . sizzling."

The book is illustrated with over 40 of May Pang's own photographs. ★ ★ ★

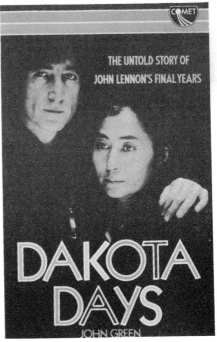

DAKOTA DAYS.
John Green. St Martin's Press, 1983

Another "kiss-and-tell" book by a former employee of the Lennons, this time their ex-tarot-card reader (sic) who comes up with various revelations concerning the intimate relationship of John and Yoko between the years 1975 and 1980. Yoko has since vehemently denied the truth of Green's various assertions.

During the time Green worked for the Lennons, he was very well paid and, presumably, for him to be present at so many private and personal moments, he must have been trusted by the couple. A trust, it seems, that wasn't warranted!

Green relates some startling accounts of the sexual relationship between the couple – and of John's violent temper. He even claims that John kicked Sean when he was a toddler. ★★

JOHN LENNON: SUMMER OF 1980
Perigee Books, 1983

A collection of photographs of John and Yoko taken in 1980 by eight different photographers. There is an introduction by Yoko and the photographers relate their memories of the sessions. A slim volume with photographs by Annie Leibovitz, Bob Gruen, Allan Tannenbaum, Jack Mitchell and others. ★★★★

THE BEATLES: 24 POSTERS
Colour Library Books, 1983

The publisher of *The Beatles Forever* has collected a selection of photographs, most of them already featured in the previous book, and presented them in this rather slim paperback. ★★★★

JOHN LENNON: A FAMILY ALBUM
Photographs by Nishi F.Saimaru, 1983

A superb Japanese book with outstanding reproductions of over 100 colour prints of John, Yoko and Sean, taken between 1977 and 1979. The majority of the photographs were taken in Japan (there are some shots of Sean's birthday party in New York) and none of them have previously been published. Saimaru's book was issued in a limited edition in Japan and is relatively rare. ★★★★

THE COMPLETE BEATLES
U.S. RECORD PRICE GUIDE
Perry Cox and Joe Lindsay.
O'Sullivan Woodside & Co., 1983

A book for record collectors, crammed with details of the Beatles' releases in America and illustrated with many photographs of picture sleeves and album covers. This paperback presents details of every Beatles' record issued in America and also presents lists of their current values. Its subtitle, "First Edition", indicates that future editions will monitor any variations in these prices. A limited edition of the book at almost twice the price of the ordinary copy was also published; this contained a red flexi-disc with the tracks 'Till There Was You' and 'Three Cool Cats'. ★★★

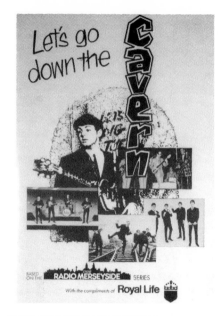

LET'S GO DOWN THE CAVERN
Spencer Leigh. Royal Life Insurance, 1983

Spencer Leigh is a young journalist/broadcaster from Liverpool who spent several months tracing a formidable number of original Mersey Beatsters for a 12-programme series on BBC Radio Merseyside called *Let's Go Down the Cavern*. His notes appeared on the sleeves of the Edsell Records series of albums of Liverpool bands and capture some of the down-to-earth humour of the 200 Scouse musicians he interviewed.

This publication will be followed by a full-scale book sporting the same title, to be issued in Britain in September 1984 by Vermillion Books.

Leigh's experiences of the early sixties' Liverpool scene have all been obtained at second-hand – a major obstacle to the success of what is a very worthwhile venture. Perhaps the only satisfactory accounts of the Mersey Beat days can be written by people who experienced them (although this may not be strictly true as *Follow the Merseybeat Road* proved). However the insight and perspective of someone who was actually a part of the scene is clearly missing. For instance the author states: "Merseybeat was a male-dominated sound. . . there were very few female singers on Merseyside." It was just the opposite in fact; Liverpool was bustling with female talent, over a generation before "women in rock" came into vogue. Every band who toured American bases in France had to take a female singer with them (Rory Storm and the Hurricanes, Faron's Flamingos, the Remo Four *et* al); there were also several bands led by girls, such as Joan and the Demons, Irene and the Sante Fe's and Jenny and the Tallboys, in addition to all-girl groups like the Liverbirds and singers such as Barbara Harrison, Irene Carroll, Beryl Marsden and Cilla Black. Spencer also seems to believe that the black music scene was almost non-existent, apart from the Chants and Derry Wilkie. There were, in fact, a number of black vocal groups based in the Liverpool 8 district, including the Sobells, the Challengers and the Poppies, and solo singers such as Steve Aldo.

This 30-page book was published in conjunction with Royal Life Insurance, the company behind the Cavern Walks, and contains 36 photographs. ★★★★

WORKING CLASS HEROES
Neville Stannard. Virgin Books, 1983

This is the second volume in the *Beatles Library* series from Virgin. It was initially issued in a slipcase with *The Long & Winding Road* in time for Christmas 1983. Neville is aided by rock journalist John Tobler in this illustrated discography, subtitled "The History of the Beatles' Solo Recordings". It contains details of all the solo releases by the individual members of the Fab Four, fleshed out with facts, chart details and anecdotal stories, as in the style of the first book. The entries on records are well illustrated with picture sleeves, and promotional material surrounding the releases. Once again, there is a

series of appendices. The first is a chronological list of the band's British releases; the second is a chronological list of their American releases; the third contains details of songs and sessions involving other artists; "The Beatles in the BMRB Chart" follows, and appendix four lists Yoko Ono's solo releases. A bibliography and index complete the book. ★★★★

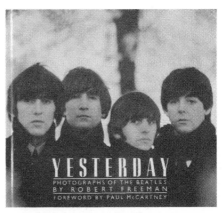

YESTERDAY: PHOTOGRAPHS OF THE BEATLES
Robert Freeman. Weidenfeld & Nicholson, 1983

Freeman's second photographic collection of Beatle pictures, was published 19 years after his first book. Paul McCartney contributes a foreword in which he says: "I have a feeling that his photos were amongst the best ever taken of the Beatles." The cover photograph is the colour shot from the *Beatles for Sale* sleeve and the back cover the colour shot of the *Rubber Soul* LP. There are over 100 black-and-white photographs and they are among the best ever taken of the Fab Four, capturing mood and atmosphere, displaying an eye for composition and including moments of wit and humour.

Freeman was, for a while, a favourite in Beatle circles and travelled with them to Sweden, France, America, Austria and the Bahamas. He handled the design and photographs for five of their albums and for John's two books; *Yesterday* also contains a nine-page piece by Freeman, relating his experiences with the Beatles between 1963 and 1965. ★★★★

PAUL McCARTNEY
Alan Hamilton. Hamish Hamilton, 1983

This book is one of many biographies of twentieth-century celebrities in the "Profiles" series, issued by Hamish Hamilton's children's book section. The author, who also wrote a volume about Queen Elizabeth II in the series, is a journalist with *The Times* newspaper. Although the book is only a few thousand words in length, Hamilton manages to get quite a number of details wrong. This is not so much because of his lack of research (for basic information on the Beatles the author obviously owes a debt to Philip Norman's *Shout!*), but his inability to place certain facts in context.

Referring to *The Beatles* and *Yellow Submarine* albums, Hamilton says: "The fans thought they were very poor... and there were new heroes for young people to listen to, performers like Bob Dylan... and the Rolling Stones." *The Beatles* and *Yellow Submarine* were issued in 1968 and 1969 respectively, whereas Dylan had been having chart hits in Britain since 1965 and the Stones since 1963.

Apart from misleading items such as this, the book serves its purpose, while the pen-and-ink illustrations by Karen Heywood are pleasing to look at. ★★

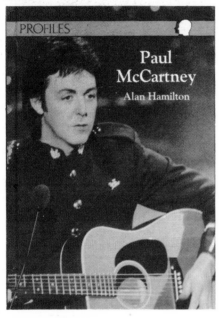

PROFILES

Paul McCartney
Alan Hamilton

THE LITERARY LENNON
Dr James Sauceda. Pierian Press, 1983

The most scholarly and detailed study of a much neglected aspect of Lennon's genius: his ability with words. Subtitled: "The First Study of All the Major and Minor Writings of John Lennon", the book is true to its title in unearthing items ranging from John's review of *The Goon Show Scripts* to his sketch for the musical revue *Oh Calcutta!*

In his introduction the author talks of how his life was changed one day in Pickwick's bookstore in Hollywood when he picked up a copy of James Joyce's *Finnegan's Wake.* This eventually led to him writing a doctorial dissertation on the book at USC in 1977. Three years later, in the

same bookstore, he came across a passage of work which he mistook for Joyce, but discovered to be a piece by John. Sauceda continues: "Like millions of others, I knew he was simply 'the best', meaning the best musical poet, the best rock artist, the best personality; I was stone-cold ignorant of the *literary* Lennon." He then set out to track down further examples of John's work, a task of research that proved difficult but exciting. The result is this seven chapter book, which is divided into three parts. Part one covers Lennon's major works; part two his minor works; and part three his future ones. The first chapter deals with the critics' reaction to *In His Own Write*, followed by a chapter analysing the book. The third chapter deals with the reviews to *A Spaniard in the Works*, followed by an analysis of it. Chapter five covers John's early work, from childhood to his *Mersey Beat* contributions and chapter six reviews his works between 1965 and 1979. The final chapter discusses *The Lennon Play: In His Own Write* and suggests directions for future research.

Dr Sauceda not only attempts a thorough analysis of John's writings, but seeks to understand how John's mind worked when he wrote his stories and poems, revealing many little-known facts about John's life and career. ★★★★★

THE BEATLES: AN ILLUSTRATED DIARY
Har van Fulpen. Plexus Books, 1983

Previously published in Holland as *Beatles Dagboek* and in France as *Souvenirs des Beatles*, this work is scheduled to be published in America by Simon & Schuster. Fulpen was arguably Holland's major Beatles' fan and he launched a fanzine there as early as 1964. The events in the life of the Beatles are covered year-by-year in much the same way as Tom Schultheiss' *A Day in the Life*, but in less depth. The main difference is in the quality of the illustrations; although numbering almost 1,000, many are only thumbnail size. The early ones draw on my own *Mersey Beat: The Beginnings of the Beatles* and later sources include the photographs of Dezo Hoffmann. Among the book's best features are the numerous short articles placed in between the dates, covering the Beatles' Decca audition, the *Mersey Beat* poll, Pete Best, Brian Epstein, the *Please Please Me* recording sessions, the Beatles' homes and the "Paul Is Dead" episode. ★★★

FOLLOW THE MERSEYBEAT ROAD
Sam Leach. Eden Publications, 1983

Another magazine-style book covering the Beatles' Liverpool trail, following the ground already explored by *In the Footsteps of the Beatles, The Beatles England* and *Lots of Liverpool*. Sam was one of several promoters who actively supported the Mersey groups during the heyday of the local scene in the late fifties and early sixties.

Although it is a good idea to cover a "tour" by introducing personal memories, Sam unfortunately tends to colour some of his recollections with a touch of fantasy. He mentions the Jacaranda Club, "where one Saturday night Bill Harry and I planned *Merseybeat*". This is untrue. Admittedly, Sam did once offer me financial assistance to produce a jazz magazine called "Storyville/52nd Street", but he never came up with the cash, so I dropped the idea.

However, I can understand Sam's attempts to justify his position as a commentator on the Beatles' life and times since he, like so many other people, have been given scant credit for their part in the growth of the Liverpool scene. This was perhaps due to Brian Epstein's book *A Cellarful of Noise*, which suggested that Brian created the scene almost singe-handedly, when in fact he was something of a latecomer.

A number of Sam's anecdotes concerning his adventures with the Beatles appear in print for the first time. He has published the book himself and it is well illustrated, with almost 100 photographs. ★★★

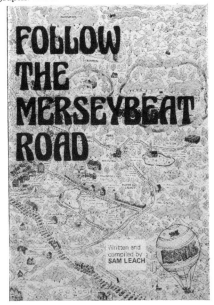

JOHN LENNON: IN MY LIFE
Pete Shotton & Nicholas Schaffner.
Stein & Day, 1983

Pete Shotton was one of John Lennon's closest friends and, in the wake of so many books about John, he naturally felt that there would be some interest in his personal recollections. He approached several American publishers and it was suggested that he team up with American Beatle expert Nicholas Schaffner, author of *The Beatles Forever* and *The Lads From Liverpool*.

Naturally, since Pete's relationship with John began in their early schooldays, his story is rich in anecdotes of the sixties when Pete was able to observe the personal life of the Beatles following their initial success.

The book is illustrated with a number of Pete's own photographs and provides another insight into the life of John Lennon. It was serialised in the *Daily Star* in Britain in December 1983. ★★★★

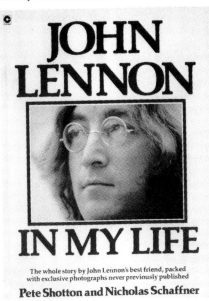

THE BEATLES RECORDS IN AUSTRALIA
Bruce Hamlin. Privately published, 1983

Hamlin first compiled a discography of Beatle records in Australia in 1979, but has since gathered so much further information that he has collated it in book form and published it himself. This is an amateur publication with stencilled pages, illustrated with pictures of record sleeves. Hamlin has had the co-operation of EMI Australia in compiling his lists and has stuck to the releases of the Beatles as a group, disregarding their solo releases. ★★★

THE BEATLES
Robert Burt, Jeremy Pascall.
Treasure Press, 1983

This is a reprint of the 1975 book, previously entitled *The Beatles: The Fabulous Story of John, Paul, George & Ringo*. The contents are the same, only the cover is different – this time it reproduces four Bob Freeman Beatle album covers. ★★★

THE BEATLES
Colour Library Books, 1983

A reprint of the 1982 publication *The Beatles Forever*. It contains the same excellent selection of pictures, although it sports a different cover. ★★★

LIVERPOOL – THE 60's
Brunnings, 1983

Subtitled "A Photographic Celebration", this handsome portfolio of photographs presents the magic of Merseyside in the sixties. A glossy, softback book, it features 127 photographs in its 100 pages.

The collection is ideal for the growing army of "Beatlemaniacs" thirsting for more information on Liverpool as it was when the Beatles lived there. ★★★★★

THE MERSEY SOUND
Adrian Henri, Roger McGough, Brian Patten.
Penguin, 1983

A revised edition of the book by the Liverpool poets that sold over a quarter of a million copies in the late sixties. These poets were contemporaries of the Beatles and mention the Fab Four in their work, which is full of Scouse wit. ★★★★

NEW VOLUME
Adrian Henri, Roger McGough, Brian Patten.
Penguin, 1983

There were 15 different editions of *The Mersey Sound* anthology, a unique collection of poetry with a Merseyside flavour. The three poets continue to amuse and entertain. ★★★★

STARDUST MEMORIES
Ray Connolly. Pavillion Books, 1983

Connolly was a Merseyside journalist who first came to prominence as a columnist for London's *Evening Standard* during the sixties. It was while researching material for his column that he met and interviewed members of the Beatles. Fifty-two of his interviews have been collected in this volume, including two pieces on Paul and one each on John Lennon, Yoko Ono and Ringo Starr.

Connolly's first interview with Paul took place at the star's Cavendish Avenue house. Their conversation touched on a number of topics, ranging from the *Magical Mystery Tour* film to the group's forthcoming trip to India. Connolly adds a postscript to the article, bringing Paul's life and career up to date. His interview with Ringo Starr was conducted in March 1968. Connolly paints a happy picture of Ringo's home in Weybridge and of his life with his wife, Maureen, and son Zak. A postscript brings Ringo's life up to date. Connolly's Yoko Ono interview took place in October 1968 and begins with a chat about her and John's *Two Virgins* album and their *Bottoms* film. The rest of the

interview covers her childhood and the years prior to her meeting John. Connolly's second McCartney interview took place in a Soho restaurant in April 1970 and was a detailed discussion of the Beatles' break-up. Later that year, Ray interviewed John at his home in Ascot; Yoko also joined in the conversation, which concentrated on John's solo career. ★★★★

THE BEATLES:
IT WAS TWENTY YEARS AGO
Michael Press, 1984

A limited-edition book that comprises a collection of newspaper clippings of Beatles' stories between 1964 and 1966. ★★★

THE MUSIC OF THE BEATLES
Martin E. Horn. Big Eye Publications, 1984

This American work contains a collection of searching reviews of every Beatles' album and single release. ★★★

THE BEATLES READER
Charles P. Meises. Pierian Press, 1984

Meises has collected 20 major articles about the Beatles from sixties magazines and newspapers. The articles span the entire career of the group. The book is No. 6 in the "Rock 'n' Roll Remembrance Series". ★★★★

A CELLARFUL OF NOISE
Brian Epstein. Pierian Press, 1984

This is a revised, hardback edition of Epstein's autobiography with photographs, a new index and a specially written foreword by Brian's younger brother Clive Epstein. ★ ★ ★ ★

THE LONGEST COCKTAIL PARTY
Richard DiLello. Pierian Press, 1984

This is a revised, hardbound edition of a book originally published in 1972; it is subtitled "An Insider's Diary of the Beatles, Their Million-Dollar Apple Empire and Its Wild Rise and Fall". Another title in the "Rock 'n' Roll Remembrance Series". ★ ★ ★ ★

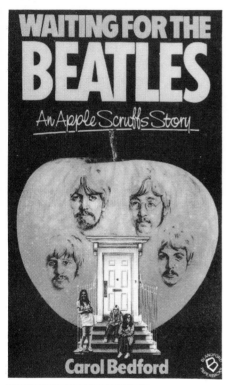

WAITING FOR THE BEATLES
Carol Bedford. Blandford Press, 1984

The story of the Apple Scruffs, that dedicated band of girls (plus one gay guy) who haunted the steps of the Apple offices. The author became an Apple Scruff herself, winging her way from Texas to be near the Fab Four. Her book vividly describes the bizarre, monomaniacal mentality of these dedicated pop fans, who were willing to go to almost any lengths for a fleeting glimpse of their idols. ★ ★ ★ ★

AS TIME GOES BY
Derek Taylor. Pierian Press, 1984

Pierian's "Rock 'n' Roll Remembrance Series" intends to reprint many of the out-of-print books about the Beatles. Derek's book, a vivid portrait of life in the sixties, contain a new index. ★ ★ ★ ★

THE BEATLES AT THE BEEB
Kevin Howlett. Pierian Press, 1984

This is a hardback edition of the 1982 BBC book, with an expanded index. ★ ★ ★ ★

THE BOOK OF LENNON
Bill Harry. Aurum Press, 1984

Published in May, this John Lennon encyclo-pedia has over 600 separate entries. I was originally asked to write a book about John following his death, but I refused. However, so many people asked me questions about John that – rather than write yet another biography – I decided to provide an informative book about his films, records, writings, personal life and career.

THE DAY THE MUSIC DIED
Various Authors. Plexus Books, 1984

The famous Bob Gruen photograph of John Lennon on the roof of the Dakota building is featured on the cover of this collection of essays about various rock legends. Philip Norman has written a piece about John, and I have contri-buted an article about Brian Epstein.

THE BEATLES
Bill Harry. Beatle City, 1984

The catalogue for Beatle City, which opened in April 1984. I won't give this a star rating as it is available exclusively from Beatle City in Liver-pool. Local designer Peter Mathews has pro-duced a bold, exciting, visual souvenir with large photographs, many of them in colour and excel-lently reproduced. My brief was to condense the Beatles' story into ten chapters of approximately 350 words each. I was thus forced to limit myself to recording the bare essentials of their fasci-nating career.

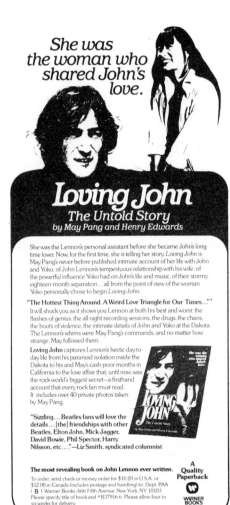

FOR BEATLE BOOKWORMS

FOR BEATLE BOOKWORMS

The amount of Beatle books in circulation is considerable, but the voracious appetites of Beatle bookworms cry out for more. There is a tremendous wealth of Beatle information to be found in books for various reasons ineligible for inclusion in our bibliography section; but since they may of be interest to Beatle fans, here is a short selection.

ROCK DREAMS

A book of visually stimulating rock fantasy, featuring the paintings of Dutch artist Guy Peellaert, that was first published in Britain in 1974 by Pan Books. The Beatles' section comprises six paintings: the first is a portrait of Stuart Sutcliffe seated between French windows overlooking a garden. Peellaert has captured the mystique of the group's original bass guitarist whose creative talents and sensitivity had a marked effect on the Beatles during their formative years. A Hamburg street scene follows, with Ringo Starr in Teddy-Boy guise entering the picture from the left and an isolated Pete Best standing on the extreme right. In between, John, Paul and George are shown standing on the steps of the Star Club. In the next painting, a frenetic Fab Four are being pursued by policemen – a scene reminiscent of the "Keystone Cops" chase sequence in *A Hard Day's Night*. The fourth painting is a sedate scene inside Buckingham Palace showing the boys taking tea with the Queen. Brian Epstein is featured as a guru in place of the Maharishi in the following painting which shows the group, accompanied by their wives and girlfriends, looking suitably

Eastern in colourful Indian garb. A touch of show-business glamour surrounds the final picture, which shows the four dressed in snow-white evening dress. Another interesting painting in the book captures the Ad Lib club in London with its exclusive membership of the top rock stars of the mid sixties, including George and Patti, Ringo and Maureen and John and Paul.

OXTOBY'S ROCKERS

This is the first published collection of the works of Yorkshire painter David Oxtoby, who specialises in the rock field; it was published by Phaidon Press in 1978 (and simultaneously in the US by E.P.Dulton, New York). There are 80 works in the book, with text by David Sandison. Page 59 features the full-colour reproduction of an aquatec on canvas of John Lennon. Oxtoby comments: "This painting is no longer as depicted. I decided to rework certain sections a little and the result is now in America, the property of Bernie Taupin." The final reproduction in the book is a black-and-white aquatec and pencil work of Paul McCartney, entitled "Yesterdays with a Blue Guitar." Oxtoby comments: ". . .the background contains drawings based on the works of many of my friends while badges scattered across Paul's chest have names of other friends. The drawing was born out of a conversation with David Hockney who told me he was working on a series of etchings based on a poem inspired by a Picasso painting. I figured one thing missing from that sequence was a drawing!"

TOP TWENTY

This paperback by Phil Buckle, was published in 1963 by Four Square Books. It contains a photograph and two-page biographical feature on the Beatles. A section called "Vital Statistics" informs the reader that John's favourite actress is Brigitte Bardot and that his ambition is "Money and everything." Paul's hates are listed as "False and soft people, shaving," while his ambition is "to make money and do well". George's favourite food is "egg and chips" and his ambition is "to retire rich!"; Ringo's favourite clothes are sleek suits and ties" and his ambition is "to get to the top".

ALL NIGHT STAND

A novel by Thom Keyes, published by W.H.Allen in 1966. Keyes, an American who was living in Liverpool during the Mersey Beat years, wrote this story of four Liverpool musicians and their experiences on Merseyside and in Hamburg and their eventual rise to fame as one of the most popular groups in the world. Reviewers at the time naturally assumed it was a fictionalised version of the Beatles' story, but it was actually based on Thom's travels with other Mersey bands such as Faron's Flamingoes and the Searchers.

POP FROM THE BEGINNING

Nik Cohn's highly personalised view of pop music, published by Weidenfeld and Nicholson in 1969, featured a chapter on the Beatles. Cohn is an able writer, but one whose views often seem unduly biased. He clearly doesn't like the Beatles and his work attacks them with a blunderbuss rather than a rapier, coming to such conclusions as: "I don't enjoy them much and I'm not at all convinced that they've been good for pop" and "the Beatles have brought pop to its knees." Still, I liked his reference to John's ". . .doddled drawings."

THE ROLLING STONE
ROCK 'N' ROLL READER

Hefty paperback published by Bantam Books in 1974, edited by Ben Fong-Torres. Almost 80 pages at the beginning of the book are devoted to the Beatles in a selection of 15 articles about the group which were previously published in *Rolling Stone* magazine. Article titles include: "The Beatles Open a Boutique: Apple"; "New Things for Beatles: Magical Mystery Tour"; "The Maharishi Meets the Press"; "Mystery Tour Shot Down"; "Apple Closed: Beatles Give It All Away"; "John, Yoko and Eric Clapton Kick Up Their Blue Suede Shoes"; "Beatles Splitting? Maybe, Says John"; "McCartney, Solo, Clearing Up a Few Things"; "Let It Be" and "The Beatles: on the Occasion of Their Authorised Biography."

CELLULOID ROCK

A lavishly illustrated book of cinema rock by Philip Jenkinson and Alan Warner, first published by Lorrimer Books in 1974. In addition to details of Beatle films in the text, there are numerous photographs, including six stills and the poster from *A Hard Day's Night*, six stills and the poster from *Help!*, two shots of John from *How I Won the War*, four shots from *Yellow Submarine*, three from *Let It Be*, a *Record Mirror* cover featuring *Magical Mystery Tour* and three photographs from *The Concert for Bangla Desh*. As Ringo was the one who found his footing in films, it's no surprise to find that he is featured more than any of the others with a full-page picture from *Help!*, with Marc Bolan from *Born to Boogie*, in a scene from *That'll Be the Day* and as Frank Zappa in *200 Motels*.

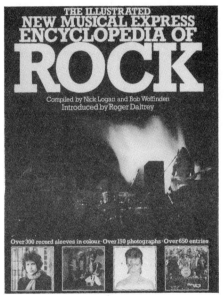

THE ILLUSTRATED NEW MUSICAL EXPRESS ENCYCLOPEDIA OF ROCK

This was first published in a large format, hardbound edition by Salamander Books in 1976. It has since been available in different paperback editions, some without illustrations. The original edition features a three-page article on the Beatles, illustrated by a large colour shot, two black-and-white photographs and four album sleeves. The entry on George features a black-and-white picture of George and Pattie and the *All Things Must Pass* cover. John's entry sports a full-colour portrait and the covers of *Imagine* and *Sometime in New York City*. Paul's article includes a colour photo and the covers of *Band on the Run* and *Red Rose Speedway*. Ringo's entry has a thumbnail reproduction of the *Goodnight Vienna* cover. The book also contains articles on George Martin, Yoko Ono and Derek Taylor.

THE ILLUSTRATED HISTORY OF ROCK MUSIC

A large-format book by Jeremy Pascall, first published by Hamlyn in 1978. A straightforward chronological history of rock music, it features over 20 photographs of interest to Beatle fans. The black-and-white shots include four group poses; a scene from a television show; the group with George Martin; a shot from the Shea Stadium concert and portraits of George and John. There are colour shots of Paul; Yoko; George; Ringo and John; of John with his psychedelic Rolls; a selection of album covers; the Apple mural; Brian Epstein with Tommy Quickly; Cilla Black and Billy J.Kramer; a scene from *Yellow Submarine* and shots taken during the band's performances.

THE ENCYCLOPEDIA OF ROCK

A three-volume paperback lexicon of musical reference published by Panther in 1976. Volume 2, entitled *From Liverpool to San Francisco*, is of particular interest to Beatle fans as it contains a six-page history of the group and entries on Brian Epstein, Liverpool and various Mersey bands of the sixties.

THE GREAT BRITISH

In 1978 *The Sunday Times* in association with the National Portrait Gallery commissioned Arnold Newman, the American photographer, to come to London and photograph some of the most prominent people in Britain for an exhibition at the National Portrait Gallery. These portraits are now part of the Gallery's permanent collection, and a book, co-published by *The Sunday Times*/National Portrait Gallery/Weidenfeld and Nicholson, was issued in 1979, entitled *The Great British*. Among the celebrities, such as Lord Olivier and Cecil Beaton, is George Harrison, one of only eight "great Britons" to be portrayed in colour. The photograph of George, which is also reproduced on the cover, shows him by a recording console at his Victorian mansion in Henley.

THE SONGWRITERS

This paperback book by Tony Staveacre, published by BBC Publications in 1980, is based on an eight-part BBC TV series of the same name which was first screened in the spring of 1978. Tony Staveacre, who wrote the original series, has a chapter on the Lennon and McCartney songwriting partnership called "A Hard Day's Night". This is 26 pages long and illustrated with 11 photographs.

THE POPULAR VOICE (A MUSICAL RECORD OF THE SIXTIES AND SEVENTIES)

A collection of articles by music journalist Derek Jewell, who has contributed a regular column to *The Sunday Times* newspaper for over 20 years. This hardback, published in 1980 by André Deutsch, features several articles on the Beatles and the dates when they were first published. They include: "Beatles Breaking Out" (15/9/63); "Beatles Breaking Down" (22/1/67); "Sergeant Pepper: The Freedom to Change" (4/6/67); "A Sort of Pop Forsyte Saga" (24/11/68); "Last Will & Testament" (10/5/70); "George and John minus Paul and Ringo" (20/12/70); and "McCartney Takes Wings" (27/5/73). I particularly liked one early, confident quote from Paul: "Of course, it could well fold, but it doesn't worry us. We could all start modest little businesses now."

ENCYCLOPEDIA OF BRITISH BEAT GROUPS AND SOLO ARTISTS OF THE SIXTIES

Published in 1980 by Omnibus Press, this work was compiled by Colin Cross with Paul Kendall and Mick Farren. There is a full-page feature on the Beatles and small articles on Brian Epstein; the Pete Best Four; Badfinger; the Cavern; Cliff Bennett and the Rebel Rousers; Tommy Quickly; the Scaffold; Gerry and the Pacemakers; Billy J.Kramer and the Dakotas; and Cilla Black. For those wishing for a taste of the Mersey scene there are items on the Big Three; Lee Curtis and the All Stars; the Del Renas; the Dennisons; Faron's Flamingos; the Fourmost; David Garrick; Ian and the Zodiacs; Beryl Marsden; the Merseybeats; the Mojos; Mark Peters and the Silhouettes; Earl Preston and the T.T's; the Remo

Four; Earl Royce and the Olympics; the Searchers; Denny Seyton and the Sabres; Freddy Starr and the Midnighters; Rory Storm and the Hurricanes; the Swinging Bluejeans; Kingsize Taylor and the Dominoes; Cy Tucker; the Undertakers; and Derry Wilkie and the Seniors.

THE GUINNESS BOOK OF RECORDS

The world's best-selling book, detailing the Beatles', considerable achievements. Paul McCartney was the most successful songwriter in the world between 1962 and 1978 and participated in 43 songs that each sold over a million copies; the Beatles were the most successful group and their sales until 1978 included 100 million singles and 100 million albums; 'Yesterday' has been recorded over 1,000 times; the top-selling British record of all time is 'I Want to Hold Your Hand' with world sales of over 13 million; the first single to sell over two million copies in Britain was 'Mull of Kintyre'; the fastest-selling British record was *The Beatles* double album which sold almost two million in its first week; the biggest advance sale for a record was the £2,100,000 for 'Can't Buy Me Love'; and the largest advance order for an album in Britain was the £750,000 for *Beatles for Sale*.

ART & THE CITY

John Willett's book, published by Methuen & Co.Ltd. in 1967, is an intriguing exploration of the Merseyside renaissance in music and art that began in the fifties. The Liverpool artists represented at the John Moore's Exhibitions at the Walker Art Gallery, for instance, included Stuart Sutcliffe (1959); Arthur Ballard (1959, 1961); Adrian Henry (1961, 1965); Nicholas Horsefield (1959, 1961); G.W.Jardine (1957) and Sam Walsh (1963).

There is quite a large section on Stuart Sutcliffe and his work and various references are made to the Beatles' contribution to the Liverpool arts scene. Willett points out some of the exciting events of the early and mid sixties: Liverpool FC winning the FA Cup in 1965; Everton FC winning the cup in 1966; Ken Dodd voted British Entertainer of 1965; the Liverpool Roman Catholic Cathedral opening; the success of the Liverpool poets, and so on. The book has vitality and covers art in Liverpool from the distant past to the present day, pointing out some of the choicest examples, such as the mosaic pavement inside St George's Hall. At the end of the book he suggests that a travelling exhibition could be launched to convey the essence of Liverpool to other countries. Adrian Henry, Arthur Ballard and Peter MacKarell acted as consultants in the preparation of the lists. In the section on pop music, he lists: a Cavern-type space, also to be used for actual performance; documents and other souvenirs of the Beatles;

documents and other souvenirs of other groups; photographs from *Mersey Beat;* facilities for listening to records; record sleeves; Lennon's drawings and any others relevant to the theme.

Considering Willett outlined his idea in 1967, it took until 1984 to see something similar actually come to fruition with the opening of Beatle City and the Walker Art Gallery's "Art of the Beatles" exhibition.

ALL YOU NEED IS LOVE

Written by Tony Palmer, and first published by Weidenfeld & Nicholson and Chappell & Company in 1976 to tie in with the 17-part London Weekend TV series of the same name. A paperback version from Futura Books was published the following year. Palmer who had become a controversial figure in Britain because of his tough approach to rock music in his *Observer* column and in various TV documentaries was also involved in the making of the television series.

Subtitled "The Story of Popular Music," the book is just that, expertly covering its history from the birth of jazz to modern rock. Although the Beatles' section is quite condensed, it contains some interesting anecdotes, as when Paul McCartney relates to Palmer: "My Dad used to work the lights in the local music halls. He actually burnt bits of lime for the limelights. He also used to bring home the programmes from the first house so that my Aunt Millie could iron them out in time for him to resell at the second house."

CHASE THE FADE

The autobiography of Britain's leading female DJ, Anne Nightingale, was published by Blandford Press in 1981. Of special interest is the 11-page chapter "Let It Be," mainly concerning the Beatles' break-up, illustrated with eleven pictures. Her account doesn't reveal anything new, except when she recalls how she inadvertently caused Richard DiLello to be sacked as Apple press officer and describes a party at Ringo's house on New Year's Eve, 1969.

THE ROAD GOES ON FOREVER

When Philip Norman's *Shout!* became a best-seller, Elm Tree Books swiftly published this collection of the author's rock interviews from *The Times* and *Sunday Times* in 1982. It features four related interviews: "I Was Never Lovable: I Was Just Lennon," a short biography of John that reads like a draft of the research for *Shout!*; "Yoko: Life Without John"; and "Ringo: A Starr Is Bored," a report of a visit to Ringo at the George V Hotel in Paris when the ex-Beatle was promoting his album *Photogravure.*

THE RECORD PRODUCERS

BBC Radio One presented a series *The Record Producers* in 1982 and this handsome book, written by John Tobler and Stuart Grundy, was published by BBC Publications to tie in with it. The production, photographs and text are commendable and Beatle enthusiasts will be interested in no less than four separate sections of the book. The first is the chapter on George Martin, which deals with his entire career but concentrates on his recording days with the Beatles and other Mersey acts such as Gerry and the Pacemakers and Billy J.Kramer. In another chapter, Phil Spector's work is discussed, including his involvement with the Beatles at Apple, his recordings with George Harrison and his failure to complete John Lennon's *Rock 'n' Roll* album. Less well-known is Glyn Johns' association with the band, but he initially worked as an engineer on Jack Good's *Around the Beatles* show and several years later was asked by Paul McCartney to work on *Let It Be*. Finally, the chapter on Tony Visconti relates the story of John Lennon's recording sessions with David Bowie in New York.

THE ESSENTIAL GUIDE TO ROCK RECORDS

A discography of British releases by hundreds of artists, compiled by Fred Dellar and Barry Lazell and published by Omnibus Press in 1983. There is a complete list of the Beatles' British singles and album releases. Other discographies of interest to Beatles' fans include: George Harrison, John Lennon, Paul McCartney and Wings, Ringo Starr, Badfinger, Eric Clapton, Gerry and the Pacemakers, Harry Nilsson and Yoko Ono.

THE GUINNESS BOOK OF FIVE HUNDRED NUMBER ONE HITS

A compilation by Jo and Tim Rice, Paul Gambaccini and Mike Read of stories and facts concerning the first 500 records to reach the top of the British charts. There are detailed entries from 'From Me to You'; 'She Loves You'; 'I Want to Hold Your Hand'; 'Can't Buy Me Love'; 'A Hard Day's Night'; 'I Feel Fine'; 'Ticket to Ride'; 'Help!';

'Day Tripper'/'We Can Work It Out'; 'Paperback Writer'; 'Yellow Submarine'/'Eleanor Rigby'; 'All You need is Love'; 'Hello Goodbye' 'Lady Madonna'; 'Hey Jude'; 'Get Back'; 'The Ballad of John & Yoko'; 'My Sweet Lord'; 'Mull of Kintyre'; '(Just Like) Starting Over'; 'Imagine'; 'Woman'; 'Ebony and Ivory'; and also 'Bad to Me'; 'A World Without Love'; 'Michelle'; 'With a Little Help From My Friends' and 'Ob-La-Di, Ob-La-Da'.

The various factual tables informs us that the Beatles share the record with Elvis for having the most No.1 hits, 17 in all, but that they came second to Elvis in the category "Most Weeks at No.1" with 65 weeks compared to the King's 73. They top the chart of "Most Consecutive No.1s" with eleven in a row, stretching from 'From Me to You' to 'Yellow Submarine/Eleanor Rigby'. They are placed third in "Most Weeks at No.1 in Calendar Year" with 16 weeks in 1963. John Lennon is top of the "Most Successful Writers" list with 26 No.1s, followed by Paul with 24. "The Most Versatile Writers" – who have written No.1s for at least five different acts – are John and Paul with eight each.

THE CUSTARD STOPS AT HATFIELD: AN ILLUSTRATED AUTOBIOGRAPHY

Published by Collins Willow in 1982, this autobiography by leading British TV star and former DJ Kenny Everett, contains numerous anecdotes about the Beatles. Kenny was born in Liverpool and in the sixties decided to become a DJ. He joined Radio London and was commissioned to cover the Beatles' tour of the US in 1966. Everett was so nervous, he couldn't bring himself to fulfil his assignment: an interview with the Beatles. Paul noticed him wandering along a motel hallway with a hang-dog expression on his face and took him into a nearby bathroom and told him: "Why don't you just ask me one question and I'll rabbit on for ages. Then you'll have enough material for ages."

The book contains several other Beatle stories, many of them hilarious.

NO ONE WAVED GOODBYE

Subtitled "A Casualty Report on Rock and Roll," this paperback – published in Britain in 1973 by Charisma Books – contains a number of essays by American writers on rock stars who have died, including Brian Jones, Jimi Hendrix and Janis Joplin. There is a double-page photograph of Brian Epstein and several anecdotes concerning him by Lou Reed and Jeff Nesin. Robert Somma edited the book.

ALVIN STARDUST

One of the many paperback biographies written by George Tremlett (others in the series include *Paul McCartney* and *John Lennon*) and published by Futura in the mid-seventies.

Born Bernard Jewry, in London, Alvin Stardust changed his name to Shane Fenton and led a group called the Fentones, who achieved some modest success. His first marriage, in 1963 was to Irish Caldwell, sister of Liverpool group leader Rory Storm and a former girlfriend of George Harrison and Paul McCartney. The book contains many anecdotes about the Beatles, including a tale about their appearance at the Granada, Mansfield, when Alvin Stardust climbed over rooftops to bring them some food. He also appeared at the Royal Albert Hall concert in 1963 and during the same year turned down an offer of management from Brian Epstein.

Stardust recollects the time he invited John, Paul and George to a party at the flat which his girlfriend Maureen shared with some other girls. When the boys arrived McCartney said to the girls: "Are we sleeping with you tonight?" A deathly hush fell over the room. "The girls couldn't believe it," recalls Alvin. "They just looked at [the Beatles] with expressions of total astonishment. They had all been used to smoothies. . .and the girls just blew us all out. They weren't used to this sort of bluntness, and they weren't having it."

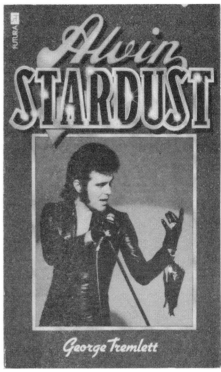

CHANT AND BE HAPPY

Another book from the Bhaktivedanta Book Trust, the publishing arm of the Hare Krishna sect. This particular paperback dwells on the Hare Krishna mantra. There is a lengthy interview with George Harrison that took place in September 1982, in which he discusses his relationship with the Krishna Consciousness sect.

PHANTASIA

This collection of the best of Alan Aldridge's artwork, published by Jonathan Cape in 1981, includes a selection of pictures from his *Beatles Illustrated Lyrics*, six pages on the Beatles, and his account of how he designed the cover for the *The Penguin John Lennon.*

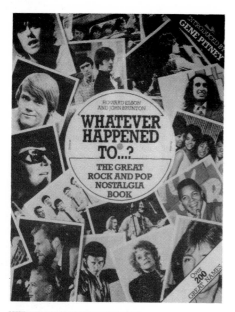

34 illustrations and a discography of their British and American releases. More Beatle information is to be found in the ten-page introduction; other bands of interest in the 316-page book include Badfinger, the Bonzo Dog Doo Dah Band, Eric Clapton, Gerry and the Pacemakers, Billy J. Kramer, Peter and Gordon, and the Searchers. There are a number of mistakes however, such as the entry on Billy J.Kramer, which ends: "In the meantime, his sister, Elkie Brooks, established herself as a leading British singer."

WHATEVER HAPPENED TO. . .

Subtitled "The Great Rock and Pop Nostalgia Book", this collection of biographies of former music stars, mainly from the sixties, was published by Proteus Books in 1981. Sadly, what is lacking is information on what eventually happend to the stars when their careers ceased being successful. Authors Howard Elson and John Brunton have collected information on 200 artists and those of interest to Beatle fans are the entries on Peter Asher, Badfinger, the Bonzo Dog Doo Dah Band, the Dave Clark Five, Joe Cocker, Delaney and Bonnie, Gerry and the Pacemakers, George Harrison, Mary Hopkin, Billy J.Kramer, the Merseybeats, Harry Nilsson, the Searchers, Helen Shapiro, Hurricane Smith, Phil Spector, Ringo Starr and the Swinging Blue Jeans.

GRAPEFRUIT

Yoko Ono's book of conceptual verse which she once promoted by sending out copies to the Press wrapped in a pair of panties. She sent the book to John, who kept it by his bedside table, often referring to it, sometimes with exasperation, sometimes with delight. It was originally issued in America in 1964 by Wanternaum Press. John added a two-line introduction to the book when Simon & Schuster reissued it in 1970.

THE BRITISH INVASION

This giant book by Nicholas Schaffner, published in America by McGraw-Hill in 1983, is subtitled "From the First Wave to the New Wave", and documents the success of British bands in the US. There is a 41-page section on the Beatles – almost a book in itself – containing

MAKING MUSIC

This, book subtitled "The Guide to Writing, Performing & Recording", was first published in Britain by Pan Books in 1983. George Martin, the editor, has collected several articles and interviews by such prominent British music industry people as Jeff Beck, Eric Clapton and Cleo Laine. George pens an introduction and contributes an article on record producing. There are two articles by Paul McCartney, one on songwriting, the other on playing bass guitar.

THE BRITISH MUSIC BOOKS

A HARD DAY'S NIGHT

Words and Music by
JOHN LENNON and
PAUL McCARTNEY

THE BRITISH MUSIC BOOKS

Music Sales Limited is one of the major music publishing companies in Britain and is the Beatles' exclusive printed-music publishers. Their other book divisions, such as Omnibus Press, also publish a range of Beatle titles, including *The Beatles in Their Own Words, With the Beatles, Mersey Beat: the Beginning of the Beatles* and *A Day in the Life*.

The company has produced literally scores of music book titles relating to the Fab Four and news and information on their current catalogue can be obtained by writing to: Information Department, Music Sales Limited, 78 Newman Street, London, W1P 3LA.

Among the various published music books are *The Beatles Ballads,* one of a series of five books published by Music Sales in 1977. The book includes the words and music to 20 Beatles' ballads, with cover art by Mick Browfield. The other titles, which also sport a Browfield cover and music to 20 songs, are: *The Beatles Rock 'n' Roll, The Beatles Fantasy, The Beatles Pop* and *The Beatles Humour.*

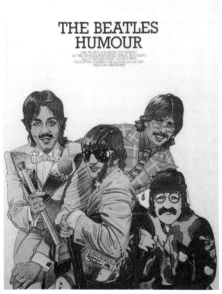

Wise Publications, one of the Music Sales imprints has published a series of songbooks featuring the music and lyrics of the individual albums. These include *Beatles for Sale, Rubber Soul, A Hard Day's Night, Abbey Road, The Beatles (White Album), Let It Be, Help!, Sgt. Pepper's Lonely Hearts Club Band, With the Beatles, Revolver, The Beatles at the Hollywood Bowl* and *Love Songs.*

In 1974 Wise Publications issued a series of eight songbooks covering the Beatles' career. They were *Beatles '63,* which featured music and lyrics to 33 Beatles' songs, including all the titles from the *Please Please Me* and *With the Beatles* albums and a cover collage of photographs of the period; *Beatles '64* featured music and lyrics to 38 Beatles' songs, including all the titles from the *Hard Day's Night* and *Beatles for Sale* albums; *Beatles '65* featured music and lyrics to 33 Beatles' songs, including all the titles from the *Help!* and *Rubber Soul* albums; *Beatles '66* featured music and lyrics to 13 Beatles' songs, including all the titles from the *Revolver* album; *Beatles '67* featured music and lyrics to 23 Beatles' songs, including all the titles from the *Sgt. Pepper's Lonely Hearts Club Band* and *Magical Mystery Tour* albums; *Beatles '68* featured music and lyrics to 33 Beatles' songs, including all the titles from *The Beatles (White Album)* and *Yellow Submarine* albums; *Beatles '69* featured music and lyrics to 17 Beatles' songs, including all the titles from the *Abbey Road* album; last of the series was *Beatles '70* with music and lyrics to 26 songs penned by John and Paul and a cover collage of newspaper clippings relating to the break-up of the Beatles. All the other covers featured a photographic collage of shots taken of the Beatles during that particular year.

The John Lennon material includes songbooks of his albums, such as *Shaved Fish; Walls and Bridges* (which is illustrated with 27 photographs of John by David Gahr and Bob Gruen), and *Imagine,* (which also contains 36 photographs of John and Yoko by Tom Hanley, with captions by Mike Hennessey). *Songs of John Lennon* contains 20 photographs by Ethan Russell, Richard DiLello and Annie Leibovitz and a 33-page John Lennon interview, which originally appear-ed in *Rolling Stone* magazine in 1970, and *The John Lennon Songbook* published in 1981 following John's death. Compiled by Brian Miles, this is a collection of songs arranged for piano/vocal with complete lyrics and chord symbols to all the songs included. The 80-page book has several illustrations.

Magical Mystery Tour contains the words and music to all eleven of the songs featured in the television film and *Wings: Wild Life,* is one of the series of titles featuring the music and lyrics to the songs on Wings' albums. This title is illustrated by a series of black-and-white prints of wild animals.

The Beatles Singles Collection 1962-1970 is a songbook originally published in 1976 which contains arrangements for piano/vocal with guitar chord boxes of all 26 of the Beatles' singles. A two-page spread of information relating to the British and American chart positions and background to the songs, compiled by Brian Miles, is supplemented by eleven pages of photographs.

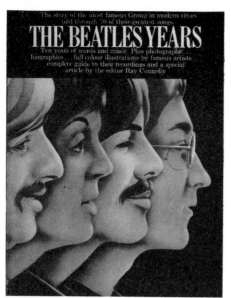

The Beatles Years is a substantial songbook encompassing ten years of the Beatles' career with 70 of their most famous songs. A cover painting by Philip Castle highlights a special 36-page editorial section on art paper which includes an introduction by Ray Connolly entitled "The Beatles Years", a reproduction of the famous Mersey Beat poll cover, several illustrations from Alan Aldridge's Beatles Illustrated Lyrics, discographies and biographies of each of the Fab Four.

The Beatles Complete (Guitar Edition) is a weighty volume featuring the music and lyrics of over 180 songs arranged for the guitar. The

first 24-pages printed on art paper is mainly material from The Beatles Illustrated Lyrics, with an introduction by Ray Connolly. The Beatles Complete (Piano/Vocal/Easy Organ) is in the same format as the guitar edition.

Lennon & McCartney: 50 Great Songs is a series of four book containing the music and lyrics to 50 Lennon and McCartney compositions. The cover sports a photograph of a bespectacled John and a bearded Paul. One book is for "Easy big note guitar", another for "Easy big note piano", a third for "C & G chord organs" and the fourth is an "All organs" book.

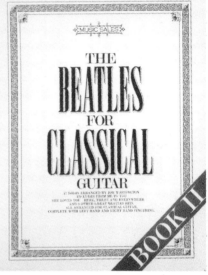

The Beatles for Classical Guitar is the title of two books published by Wise Publications. The blurb comments: "Solos arranged by Joe Washington, a noted Classical guitar teacher and arranger. Every one of these arrangements has been fully fingered for left and right hands and there are notes on how to play each solo. In addition, John Washington has included valuable hints on Classical guitar technique which will enable you to perform these famous solos to perfection." The first book contains 20 solo arrangements, the second has eleven.

Beatles to Bacharach is a series of four books containing the music and lyrics to 25 songs by Burt Bacharach and Hal David and John Lennon and Paul McCartney. There is a piano/vocal edition, an easy guitar edition, a chord-organ edition and an all-organ edition.

The First Book of Fifty Hit Songs by John Lennon and Paul McCartney is the first of a series of four songbooks containing the words and music to 50 songs by Lennon and McCartney, ending with The Fourth Book of Fifty Hit Songs by John Lennon and Paul McCartney. Each book sports a superb black-and-white pen drawing by Oliver Williams.

The second book of fifty hit songs by John Lennon and Paul McCartney.

A Collection of Beatles Oldies has a colour cover by Robert Whittaker and contains the words and music to 15 of the most famous Lennon and McCartney songs.

Beatle Songs for the Recorder features 20 Lennon and McCartney songs arranged for the recorder by Clive A.Sansom. The book also includes a six-page introduction containing instructions for playing the instrument, with lyrics and guitar chord diagrams.

Beatles: Themes and Variations: Clarinet. is one of a series of three books published in 1977, the other two concerning *Flute* and *Trumpet*.

Seven numbers – 'Eleanor Rigby', 'Here, There and Everywhere', 'Hey Jude', 'Yesterday', 'Michelle', 'The Long and Winding Road' and 'Penny Lane' – have been specially arranged by Donald Rauscher. The blurb explains: "Rauscher has taken some of the best known Beatles tunes and arranged them in the form of theme and variations. Each theme has three variations. The first is in a lively Classic style; the second is in the style of improvised jazz; while in the third the clarinet player is given the chance of exploring other rhythms." A special pull-out insert of piano accompaniments included for duets or ensemble playing is contained in each of the books.

It's Easy to Play Beatles contains 20 Beatles' numbers arranged by Cyril Walters in simplified arrangements, easy to read for piano/vocal, as well as guitar-chord symbols. The cover drawing depicts an aspiring mop-topped, one-man band, happily playing guitar, drums and trumpet.

The Beatles Bumper Songbook is another hefty compilation, containing the music and lyrics to 100 Beatle favourites.

Beatles Big Note contains 38 Lennon and McCartney numbers arranged for easy piano, with chord symbols and complete words to all the songs.

Finger Picking Beatles includes 16 of the most popular Beatles' numbers in original arrangements for finger-style guitarists at all levels. In standard notation and tablature, with tips on learning each arrangement. All the arrangements are by Eric Schoenberg.

The Beatles Twenty Greatest Hits is a matching portfolio to the twentieth anniversary album, issued in 1982. It includes 20 of their most successful hits in a piano/vocal arrangement with chord symbols and complete lyrics.

The Beatles: 1967-1970 contains music and lyrics to 27 Beatles' numbers.

The Concise Beatles Complete is an excellent addition to any Beatles library, a handsome publication issued in 1982 to coincide with the twentieth anniversary celebrations. It contains lyrics and music to all the songs written and recorded by the Fabs – 184 numbers! It has easy-to-read arrangements with chord symbols, plus a full discography detailing all singles, EPs and albums with date of release and lead singer and production credits.

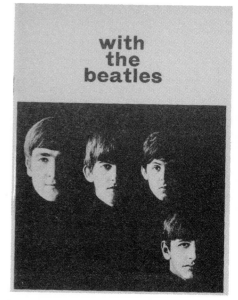

THE BEATLES MONTHLY

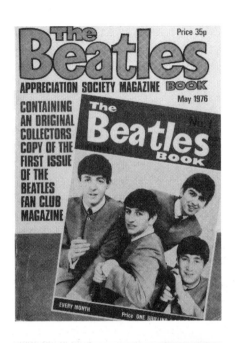

The Beatles

APPRECIATION SOCIETY MAGAZINE **BOOK**

Price 35p

May 1976

CONTAINING AN ORIGINAL COLLECTORS COPY OF THE FIRST ISSUE OF THE BEATLES FAN CLUB MAGAZINE

The Beatles Book

No. 1

EVERY MONTH   Price ONE SHILLING

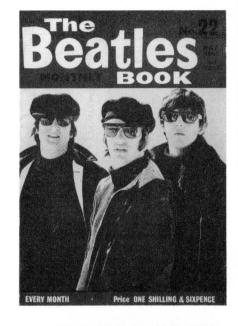

The Beatles BOOK

MONTHLY

No. 22

EVERY MONTH   Price ONE SHILLING & SIXPENCE

RECORD COLLECTOR

Sept. 1979
50p

For all serious collectors of :-
POP MEMORABILIA, FANPHALIA, POSTERS, NOSTALGIA, PHOTOS, RARE RECORDS ETC.

CONTAINING AN ORIGINAL COLLECTORS COPY OF THE 41st ISSUE OF THE BEATLES FAN CLUB MAGAZINE

The Beatles BOOK

MONTHLY

No. 41

GREAT NEW 'DRAW A

The Beatles BOOK

MONTHLY

OCTOBER 1982

FIRST NEW ISSUE

FREE POSTER OFFER

THE BEATLES MONTHLY BOOK

During the early months of 1963, when it was apparent that the Beatles were about to become the biggest stars of the British entertainments industry, a publisher named Sean O'Mahony approached Brian Epstein with a suggestion for a professional monthly magazine concerned with the Beatles activities. It would carry news and fan-club reports and would help to forge lines of communication between the group and their ever-growing army of fans.

Epstein agreed to the idea and arranged for O'Mahony to visit the group during a recording of *Saturday Club* at the BBC. Although the group didn't seem particularly enthusiastic, Epstein contacted the publisher a few days later and granted him the rights to produce an official monthly magazine, to be called *Beatles Monthly*. The first issue appeared in August 1963, at a modest cover price of 1/6d, and 80,000 copies were distributed. The magazine continued for 77 issues over a six-and-a-half-year period.

The group were concerned that their private lives should remain private and they requested the magazine not to photograph or write about their wives and girlfriends. O'Mahoney agreed to this, but later on – since the national press were covering the group's romantic affairs – *Beatles Monthly* began to introduce items on their wives and sweethearts.

The magazine's official photographer was Leslie Bryce; he was afforded an access to the group denied other photographers with the result that he took literally thousands of photographs of them. There were cartoons and sketches contributed by artist Bob Gibson and a small core of regular feature writers. The magazine was edited by' "Johnny Dean" – a pseudonym that O'Mahoney had decided upon. For various reasons, some of his regular writers also used pseudonyms. Tony Barrow, press officer to Nems Enterprises, wrote under the name Frederick James. Peter Jones, then editor of *Record Mirror* contributed pieces as Billy Shepherd. From the Beatles' own camp there were regular reports and occasional columns from Neil Aspinall and Mal Evans and photographs from Tony Bramwell.

The magazine thrived and was selling 350,000 copies at its peak. However, with issue No.77 dated December 1969, O'Mahoney decided to cease publication. In a lengthy editorial entitled "The End of an Era", he put forward several reasons for his decision: the difficulty of obtaining photographs and gaining access to the Beatles; the fact that they were all approaching their thirties; and their reluctance to maintain their group association and preference for being interviewed or photographed individually.

During the next six years, O'Mahoney received a considerable volume of mail from Beatle fans seeking back issues; he noted too that copies of *Beatles Monthly* were selling at outrageous prices to collectors, and decided to reprint the entire run of issues. The publication was relaunched in May 1976 under the title *The Beatles Appreciation Society Magazine Book.* George Harrison objected to this and unsuccessfully attempted to prevent publication. The entire run of issues continued until September 1982.

By that time, interest in the Beatles was still growing and O'Mahoney decided to begin a new series of magazines where the previous run had left off – using entirely new material. He had presented 1,000 photographs in the original 77-issue run, but still had over 4,000 unused photographs in the file. His new series, entitled *The Beatles Monthly Book,* was launched in October 1982.

Beatles Monthly used various editors during the reruns of the seventies, including Lorna Read and Pete Doggett. Many of its regular writers such as Mark Lewisohn, Tony Barrow, Peter Jones and myself continued to contribute to the new series.

Most back issues are still in print, and can be Beatles Monthly Book, 45 St Mary's Road, Ealing, London, W5 5RQ. When requesting current prices of back issues please write to the above address enclosing a stamped addressed envlope.

THE BEATLES MONTHLY

A CHECKLIST OF CONTENTS OF ALL 77 ISSUES

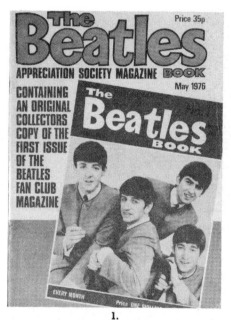

1.

The cover features the famous Dezo Hoffman picture of the Fab Four in grey collarless jackets. An editorial, fan-club newsletter, letters from Beatle people, 'Love Me Do' lyrics (this month's Beatle Song) and "Beatles News" are the regular features. Full-page introductory articles facing full-page photos of John, George, Paul, Ringo, Brian Epstein and George Martin are supplemented by a centre-page picture and a number of other photographs. Originally published in August 1963. The reprint, with eight additional pages of editorial, appeared in May 1976 and contained photographs of a bearded George Harrison, Paul on guitar, Ringo dressed as Klaatu (a character from *The Day the Earth Stood Still*), and John with Ann Murray, Harry Nilsson, Alice Cooper and Micky Dolenz. An introductory article outlined why the magazine was being reprinted.

2.

The cover shows all four playing table tennis. Features as before with 'Please Please Me' as song of the month. Billy Shepherd's *A Tale of Four Beatles* is serialised (the contents were compiled to form the first-ever Beatles paperback *The True Story of the Beatles*). There is an article on the Lennon/McCartney song-writing partnership, a centre pin-up of John and several other well-produced photographs in that style. The fan club newsletter prints a picture of little "Russell Beatle", Liverpool's youngest Beatle fan. Originally issued in September 1963 and reprinted in June 1976 with eight pages of additional material mainly comprising an article on Paul and the creation of Wings.

3.

The cover shows a wet foursome frolicking in the foam. Usual features with 'From Me to You' as the song of the month and Ringo as the centre-page pin-up. Special feature on road manager Neil Aspinall and many interesting photographs. First published in October 1963 and reprinted in July 1976 with eight extra pages, introducing a letter column and a feature by Johnny Dean on his first impressions of the group.

4.

A shot of a hotel bedroom is featured on the cover; 'There's a Place' is the featured song. Paul is the centre-page pin-up amid the usual features and a special piece by Helena Harding describing her feelings as a fan. The many pin-up shots include John in formal attire, imitating a waiter carrying a cuban-heeled boot on a salver; John wearing a false beard with his hand on Paul's head; and a shot of the group performing in the Cavern. The headings of the regular features are decorated with small sketches by Bob Gibson, who also illustrates the Billy Shepherd biographical series. First published in November 1963. An eight-page wrap-around section was published with the reprint in August 1976, featuring a photograph of John and Yoko and an article on "The Solo Lennon."

5.

The cover depicts the Beatles leaning over a balcony. In addition to the regular features, this Christmas issue introduces several offers for readers – including sets of black-and-white photographs, an official Beatles sweater and a 1964 Beatles calendar. The lyrics are from 'I Saw Her Standing There'; the centre-page pin-up is of George Harrison. There is an article by Raymond McGhee, on the Beatles' early days in Liverpool and a feature on fan-club secretaries Anne Collingham and Bettina Rose. Each issue usually features about 13 full-page photographs; the ones here include the Fab Four hoisting

Liverpool comedian Ken Dodd on to their shoulders; John with a fake beetle on his shirt; the group in their fan club HQ with Anne, Bettina and Paul holding up a Popeye mask. First published in December 1963 and reprinted in September 1976 with an eight-page extra section featuring a round-up of George's solo career, Beatle photo offers and a letters page.

6.

The setting for this cover is a theatre; John, Paul and George hold their guitars, with a pensive Ringo in the seat in front of them. The issue contains the usual features, with 'She Loves You' as the featured song and a bespectacled John as the centrefold. There is a report by Frederick James on the various rumours that abound about the group. Full-page photos include the Beatles displaying their silver disc awards; Paul with a false beard (and John attaching a match to it); Paul wearing a deerstalker and George signing autographs. Originally published in January 1964 and reprinted in October 1976, featuring an update of Ringo's career and a column of personal ads.

7.

The boys are shown smiling on the cover, and the featured lyrics are 'PS I Love You'. The centre-page pin-up is of Ringo seated at his drums; other photographs of an onstage gig at Wimbledon Palais during the Beatles' Southern fan club appearance, and various autograph sessions with their fans. A special report by Frederick James on their Christmas show at the Finsbury Park Astoria includes several photo-graphs and a full-cast pose. There is a short article by June Meredith on their forthcoming Paris appearance. Originally published in February 1964. Reprint issued in November 1976; the featured article was entitled "The Truth About Those Early Beatle Recordings", with a Peter Kaye photograph of the Beatles aboard a Liverpool ship. The credits in the reprinted version acknowledge Leslie Bryce as official photographer: he is uncredited in the original editions.

8.

The cover shows John, Paul, and George in a Paris street, and the issue has detailed coverage of their Paris stint with many photographs and a lengthy report by Billy Shepherd. 'All My Loving' is the featured song, and Paul is the centre-page pin-up. New offer from the fan club is an official Beatles badge – at only 3/6d. There is a short article by Dorene Hannah, entitled "How Different From the Cavern Days", and a general article by Frederick James, "Why the Beatles?" Also a full-page ad for a new *Gerry and the Pacemakers* magazine. Originally published in March 1964 and reprinted in December 1976 with "The Beatles Now", an update on their individual activities, as the main feature.

9.

The cover shows the Beatles with an American cop, Paul awkwardly holding his gun and the other three pressing their fingers in their ears. There are the usual features, with 'I Want To Hold Your Hand' as the featured song and George as the centrefold. Most of the pictures are of their American tour and are supplemented by a large feature covering the trip, entitled "What Happened in America". Billy Shepherd's *The True Story of the Beatles* receives its first ad airing. Published in April 1964. Reprinted in January 1977. The eight-page wrap-around features an article on the albums *Wings Over America* and *Thirty-Three & ⅓*.

10.

The cover picture was taken on the film set of *A Hard Day's Night*. Usual features with 'This Boy' as the featured song. The majority of photo-graphs and editorial matter concern the filming of *A Hard Day's Night* and include photographs of John wrist-wrestling with Norman Rossington, a centre-page of John and Paul with a clapper-board and a shot of the boys with Wilfred Brambell, Morecambe and Wise and the former Miss World, Rosemarie Franklin. Billy Shepherd reports at length on the filming in a piece entitled "Beatlescope". The issue was published in May 1964 and reprinted in February 1977. The eight-page extra is a report on Wings' world tour, with pictures of Paul and Linda.

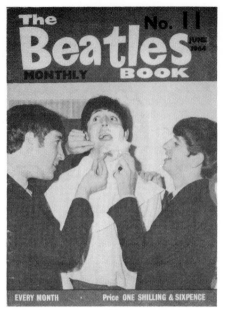

11.

On the cover, John and Ringo are shaving an alarmed-looking Paul – Ringo applies the soap and John wields the razor. The issue is filled with photographs and reports from the *Hard Day's Night* set. The featured song is 'Can't Buy Me Love'; the pin-up is of George and Ringo. There are several articles: a fan offering called simply "I Visited the Beatles on the Set", a piece by Billy Shepherd entitled "Filming with the Boys in a Hard Day's Night" and an article about Jerry Lee Lewis – "Thank You Beatles Says Jerry Lee Lewis" – in which one of the Beatles' rock idols enthuses over their success. First published in June 1964; the reprint appeared in March 1977. The eight-page extra contains an article on the Cavern by Terry Morgan and a photograph of the boys performing there; other pictures include a bearded Ringo and George and a back cover of John and Yoko.

12.

The cover shows John at the piano, wearing his jacket with the velvet collar. The featured song is 'Hold Me Tight', the centre-page pin-up is of Paul. Billy Shepherd reports on the "Beatles on Holiday"; and "Following the Beatles" details their tour of Denmark, Holland, Hong Kong, Australia and New Zealand. One of the new features is a pen-pal column. On the fan-club page there is a photograph of John with relatives taken in Rock Ferry in 1949 when he was eight and a half. Other shots include Paul salting a big cheese, Ringo drinking tea, John and George aboard a barge in Amsterdam, George trying on a pair of Dutch clogs, and the four of them

judging a competition. Published in July 1964, it was reprinted in April 1977. The eight pages of additional material include a feature on the "The Beatles' Hamburg Days" written by Iain Hines, a former member of the Jets (the first British band to go to Hamburg) who knew them very well during their early German trips. Pictures include John and Yoko looking at one another and George at the mike.

13.

A bespectacled Paul stares pensively from the cover. 'You Can't Do That' is the featured song, and John the centre-page pin-up. Items on the news page include Paul's purchase of Drake's Drum for his father, details of the cars owned by each of the Beatles and forthcoming dates. There is an interview with Paul by Frederick James, a piece about film-making by Billy Shepherd and quotes from the critics on *A Hard Day's Night.* Once again there are many pictures, mostly snaps of the four in Australia and New Zealand. First published in August 1964, reprinted in May 1977 – the eight-page extra features the second part of Iain Hines' Hamburg recollections.

14.

Ringo in a stetson hat peers from the cover. Inside, the Beatles are shown with various people, including Mal Evans, Leslie Bryce, Dusty Springfield, Billy J.Kramer and Henry Cooper. Featured song is 'I Call Your Name' the centrefold is George on the telephone. Among the contents is an article by Leslie Bryce on photographing the Beatles, a Ringo interview by

Frederick James, and an article by fan Irene Snidall on their show at the City Hall, Sheffield, entitled "A Day To Remember". Originally published in September 1964. The extra pages in the reprint of June 1977 contain part three of Iain Hines' Hamburg report.

15.

A smiling George graces the cover, with Ringo as the centrefold and 'Do You Want to Know a Secret' as the featured song. Frederick James reviews Brian Epstein's book *A Cellarful of Noise* and interviews John. Informal pictures of a recording session are followed by a report on the session. Frederick James writes another "rumour-busting" article, Billy Shepherd and Johnny Dean begin their serialisation of the Beatles story in "Behind the Spotlight", and there is a report on the group's American trip. First published in October 1964. The reprint of July 1977 contains reviews of the *Star Club Tapes* and *Live at the Hollywood Bowl* albums.

16.

The cover shows Paul and Ringo posing with a tambourine. The centre spread features Paul; 'Little Child' as song of the month. An on-the-spot report of the Beatles filming *Shindig* with Jack Good is followed by two pages of pictures of the event, including the finale with the Karl Denver Trio, Lyn Cornell and Sounds Incorporated. Competition winner Valerie Lloyd pictured with the Fab Four at the Gaumont, Wolverhampton, reports on her prize in "My Meetles with the Beatles". Usual features are supplemented by an article on George by Frederick James. First published in November 1964 and reprinted in August 1977 with an article on Hamburg and a picture-story of Arthur Dooley's "Beatle Street" sculpture (mounted on the wall in Mathew Street, opposite the former Cavern site).

17.

Portraits of all four grace the cover; John beams from the centrefold. Song of the month is 'If I Fell'. "Beatle News" features their cars again and a telegram Ringo received from Burt Lancaster concerning some guns the movie actor had promised him. There are also pictures of the group having breakfast and tucking into a meal in their dressing room. There is a page with nine small pictures of George opposite a short item called "The Faces of George" and a picture spread of the group on stage. "Outspoken But Charming" is the title of a feature by fan Diana Vero. First published in December 1964. Reprinted in September 1977; the additional pages are dominated by a lengthy article on "The Hamburg Tapes" by Iain Hines who is the first person to give credit to the man who actually made the tapes – that is, Adrian Barber *not* Kingsize Taylor.

18.

John and George appear on the cover, George in the centrefold. Song of the month is 'And I Love Her'. Photographs include Paul smoking, John dunking a biscuit in a cup of tea, all four wearing plastic beards, Ringo on the telephone, and John and Ringo cleaning their Chelsea boots. In a piece called "George Harrison's Hand", George is pictured having his palm read by Eva Petulengro, the Romany clairvoyant, who predicts a long life, success in the arts and good health. Mal Evans poses beside a bust of Napoleon, and on the opposite page is an article covering his association with the Beatles. "The Faces of Paul" continues the series of nine thumbnail pictures and a brief article; "Beatle News" reveals that the Fab Four bought Neil Aspinall a 2.4 litre grey Jaguar for Christmas. Originally published in January 1965, and reprinted in October 1977 with eight pages of extra features, including a large article and photograph of John and Yoko as well as an enlarged letters page. The back cover picture is of Paul and Linda.

19.

The cover shows Paul with handfuls, and a mouthful, of maracas. The centrefold is Ringo; the featured song is 'I Should Have Known Better'. This issue's main theme is the Beatles' Christmas Show at the Odeon, Hammersmith and there are many photographs of the event as well as a report. Frederick James begins a new series entitled "Beatles Talk" with a John and George interview; "The Faces of John" comprises nine small pictures and commentary, while Billy Shepherd and Johnny Dean continue their "Behind the Spotlight" series. Photographs include the boys rehearsing with producer Peter Yolland, Ringo studying the script with the Abominable Snowman (Jimmy Savile), George talking to Freddie Garrity (of Freddie and the Dreamers), Ringo holding up an oil portrait of himself, John in a furry costume, and Paul holding a phone to his ear (one of the stock poses featured in *Beatles Monthly*). Issued February 1965 and reprinted in November 1977 with a round-up of Paul's career during the previous two years, a picture of Wings in the Virgin Islands and a back cover of Ringo with his children.

20.

The cover sports portraits of George and Ringo, the centrefold is Paul and the featured song is 'Things We Said Today'. Frederick James interviews Paul and Ringo for "Beatles Talk", there is a large list of all the overseas fan clubs, and an appalling drawing of John at St Moritz. "The Faces of Ringo" continues the series; photographs include George blowing up a balloon, George with Jimmy Savile in the DJ's Rolls

Royce, Ringo tinkering with the engine of his Facel Vega, Ringo and Maureen signing the wedding register and the Fab Four in a bizarre four-man sweater knitted by Swedish fans. Issued in March 1965 and reprinted in December 1977 with additional material covering the *Ringo the 4th* album and a piece by Iain Hines, on Hamburg souvenirs. The back cover is of John and Yoko alighting from a coach.

21.

The cover features portraits of John and Paul. The centrefold is of John, the featured song is 'I'll Cry Instead'. The newsletter is decorated with a photograph of the fan club in Monmouth Street and there is a feature on the club – "The Writing on the Wall" – by Anne Collingham, who is also pictured. "Northern Songs Ltd" is a feature, written by Peter Jones, on Dick James and the publishing company; there are pictures of James with George and George Martin. "Beatles Tuning Up" is a photospread of the Four horsing around in the recording studios; other shots include John signing autographs outside Abbey Road and various pictures taken inside a studio. Originally published in April 1965 and reprinted in January 1978 with a lengthy feature entitled "Collecting Beatles Items" and an early Star Club hand-out picture of Tony Sheridan. The back cover is of George in check trousers playing a guitar.

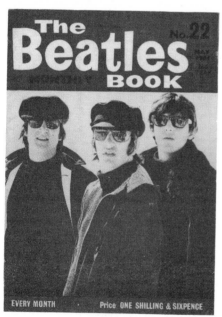

22.

The cover shows John, Ringo and Paul on location during the filming of *Help!* The centrefold is George, the featured song is 'I'm Happy

Just to Dance With You'. The main theme of the issue is the filming of *Help!* and most of the issue's illustrations show the boys on location. There is also a picture of Mal Evans smeared with grease for his scene in *Help!* "Beatles Talk" covers George and Ringo, and Norman Smith, the Beatles recording engineer, "Talks About Balancing the Beatles". First published in May 1965 and reprinted in February 1978 with an article entitled "Getting Up to Date on John, George and Ringo". The back cover is of Paul and his brother Mike McGear.

23.

The cover shows George wearing a stylish band uniform and clashing a pair of cymbals. Ringo is the centrefold, pictured lighting a cigarette (another stock shot); the featured song is 'Tell Me Why'. "Beatles Talk" covers Paul and John and "Behind the Spotlight" continues its marathon run. The Beatles pen-pals column now occupies a complete page; Norman Smith (called Normal Smith by John) presses on with his series about the boys in the studio. Pictures include John and a sewing machine, Ringo at the piano, Paul peering from behind a double bass, Paul on the telephone, Mal with Ringo and John in Austria, Dick Lester mapping out a film scene for Paul, George with a camera and Paul playing guitar on Salisbury Plain with an armoured tank in the background. First published in June 1965, reprinted in March 1978. The additional eight pages contain the usual editorial comment, personal ads, new letters and a feature by Rosie Horide on the *London Town* album, with a pic of Paul, Linda and Denny Laine in the 'Mull of Kintyre' TV promo. New back cover shows Ringo arriving at an airport with the words "First Class" stamped on his forehead.

24.

The cover features a portrait of Paul, who is also the centrefold pin-up. The lyrics are from the song 'Ticket to Ride' and the pen-pals section now takes up two whole pages. The majority of the pictures have been taken on location: Ringo playing drums on Salisbury Plain, Austrian snow sequences, shots with Eleanor Bron and Mal Evans and pictures of them in cars. The Beatles fan club list has also taken up a full page and "Beatles Talk" is conducted with all four members of the band. Originally published in July 1965. Reprinted in April 1978, with Rosie Horide's feature "Will the Beatles Re-Form", illustrated with a 1964 shot from the *Ready, Steady, Go* TV show. The back cover is of John, Yoko and Mal Evans.

25.

The cover portrait is of Ringo, the centrefold of George, 'She's a Woman' is the featured song. One of the most interesting series so far – the Beatles' childhood days – begins in this issue. The first is on "Young John" and he is pictured aged ten, when he attended Dovedale Road School. He is also photographed riding a bike at the age of eight and throwing a ball in his Aunt Mimi's garden. "Beatles Talk" is conducted with all four Beatles and Chris Denning contributes "A DJs View of the Beatles". Pictures include shots from *Help!* with Paul and Peter Asher, Ringo and George eating and the group receiving their golden award from the Japanese publication *Music Life*. First published in August 1965 and reprinted in May 1978.

26.

The cover features John smiling, in a checked hat with Ringo on the back cover. The centrefold is a pin-up of John; articles include "Beatles Talk" by Frederick James and "At the Première" by Elizabeth Sacks, a report on the première of *Help!* at the London Pavilion. "Young George" is the second in the childhood series. There are two pages of pictures from the Beatles' appearance in Blackpool with Mike and Bernie Winters; and other shots include Ringo chatting with George at the ABC, Blackpool, Paul straightening his tie, a young George rehearsing at home in Liverpool, Paul and George with Brian Epstein, Paul on the telephone, Mal Evans in *Help!* and various other shots, taken at Blackpool. Featured single is 'I Feel Fine'. Originally published in September 1965, it was reprinted in June 1978 with eight extra pages – including a review of *London Town* by Mark Lewisohn, and letters and personal ads.

27.

The cover features George at the wheel of his car. The centrefold is of Ringo puffing at a cigarette. Featured song is 'You've Got to Hide Your Love Away'. "Young Paul" is the third in the childhood series, featuring pictures of Paul and his brother Mike, as children on a hillside. There is a lengthy "American Tour Report" by Frederick James; "Beatles News" details the Beatles' meeting with Elvis and the birth of Zak Starkey. Photos include George smoking, Mal adjusting John's collar, Ringo with two giant Beatle dolls, rehearsals with Ed Sullivan, relaxing backstage at Shea Stadium, their London Palladium appearance, George signing an autograph and a picture of their American touring team (which includes press officer Tony Barrow). Originally published in October 1965 and reprinted in July 1978.

28.

The cover shows Paul with his Pentax. The centrefold is John, featured song is 'Yesterday'. In a popularity poll readers vote 'Yesterday' their Number One album track and 'Help!' the best Beatle song ever. Bernice Young, President of their US fan club reports on "The Beatles in New York", and Kathy Lewis, a Liverpool fan, discusses their Casbah residency in "The Beatles in 1961". The "Young Ringo" feature includes a picture of him in fancy-dress at a Dingle street party and one with Rory Storm and the Hurricanes. Photographs include John in a deerstalker, Paul taking photographs, John playing guitar, and backstage shots from their American trip. Originally published in November 1965 and reprinted in August 1978.

29.

John gazes from the cover of this Christmas issue; Paul is the featured pin-up, 'You're Going to Lose That Girl' the song of the month. An ad for a Beatles Christmas annual (published by the magazine) will become a future collectors' item. The main feature covers the Granada TV recording of the "Lennon & McCartney" programme, and includes pictures from the set. Other shots of the Beatles toying with various musical instruments, George and Paul on stage during their 1963 Christmas show, a Peter Kaye picture taken at the Tower Ballroom in New Brighton, Ringo behind the wheel of his car (another stock pose), and the group receiving their MBE's at Buckingham Palace. "Beatle Talk" continues, as does "Behind the Spotlight". Published in December 1965, and reprinted in September 1978, the extra pages contain part one of my feature, "The Beatles' Liverpool Days" – I am pictured presenting them with their first-ever award, the Mersey Beat Shield. The back cover features George with Olivia and his daughter Dhani.

30.

The cover is of the Fab Four – Ringo putting sugar in his tea. The centrefold is John, featured song is 'I'm Down'. An overseas song poll votes 'I Want to Hold Your Hand' the "Best Song Ever", and 'Yesterday' the best *Help!* album song. Freda Kelly of the Liverpool fan club, and pictured here with Ringo and Maureen, relates her experiences. Frederick James writes "Behind the Headlines". The standard features now take up most of the magazine: the editorial, fan club newsletter, two pages of letters, "Behind the Spotlight" series, two pages of pen pal addresses and "Beatle News". Photographs include Ringo with kettle, in a kitchen (followed by a sequence of full-page shots of the Fabs making tea), studio shots, the Beatles relaxing at dinner with the Moody Blues, in a car, with Bruno

Coquatrix (owner of the Paris Olympia), in the recording studio and playing cards with Mal and Neil. First published in January 1966, reprinted in October 1978. The extra pages continue my Liverpool recollections, with photographs of the Swinging Blue Jeans, Billy J.Kramer and the Searchers. The back cover features Paul.

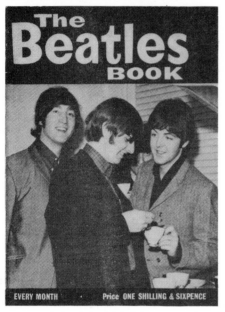

31.

The cover shows George with a white cat. The centrefold is Ringo, featured song 'Drive My Car'. Frederick James conducts his "Beatles Talk" with George and Paul, Freda discusses the Liverpool fan club and a double-page photographic spread shows the Beatles playing billiards with the Moody Blues – using the wrong end of the cues. Other photographs include Ringo playing a guitar, George with his white cat, onstage shots from a Sheffield Gaumont performance, Murray the K. on a train, all four at a press conference with Brian Sommerville, with Liverpool comedian Jimmy Tarbuck and swimming in a pool. Originally published in February 1966 and reprinted in November 1978, the extra contents include a report by Peter Jones of his first Beatles interview, with a picture of him talking to Ringo and George. The back cover features Ringo with a beard and top hat.

32.

A bespectacled Paul stares owlishly from the cover; George is the centrefold, 'I'm Looking Through You' the featured song. "Beatle Talk" is conducted with Ringo and John; Freda continues the Liverpool fan club story; two pages of pictures are devoted to George and Pattie's press reception – they show the smiling couple, Pattie displaying her gold wedding-ring. Other photos include John on drums, George and Paul playing guitars, recording studio shots and various behind-the-stage scenes from *A Hard Day's Night* and a 1964 *Ready, Steady, Go!* appearance. First published in March 1966 and reprinted in December 1978. The main new feature is by Peter Jones, covering "The Beatles Christmas Concert" of 1963. Back cover shot is of all four staring into the camera with puzzled expressions.

33.

The cover shows Ringo sipping tea. The centrefold is Paul and featured song is 'Nowhere Man'. Freda continues with part four of her Liverpool fan-club reminiscences and Neil Aspinall debuts with his own column. "Beatles Talk" is conducted with Paul and John; an ad displays the cover of a special edition of *The Beatles Book* containing 64 pages of photographs from the first six issues. Photos include more shots from *A Hard Day's Night;* George in a Mongolian lamb coat, smoking a cigarette; George, John and Ringo watching TV; a maniac Paul at a control panel, a pensive John; and shots from the Shea Stadium concert. Originally published in April 1966, reprinted in January 1979. The extra pages contain a feature I wrote entitled "The Unique Humour of the Beatles", with a picture of them wearing false beards and spectacles. The new back cover is a pose of all four, smiling.

34.

The cover is a standard pose of the Fab Four. John is the centrefold, the featured song 'Norwegian Wood'. "Neil's Column" is again included. The entire contents comprise regular features; for the first time there is no material other than the standard fan-club page, editorial, "Beatles News", and "Beatles Talk", "Behind the Spotlight", letters and pen-pal pages. Photographs include George holding up a giant-sized light bulb; the Four with an award from *Harper's* magazine; Paul at the wheel of John's Rolls; and more shots from *A Hard Day's Night*. First published in May 1966 and reprinted in February 1979, the extra contents mainly comprise a feature by Peter Jones on 'Love Me Do', with Paul grinning on the back cover.

35.

George, wearing granny-glasses, beams from the cover; Ringo graces the centrefold and 'Run For Your Life' is the featured song. The only item other than the regular features is "The Paperback Writer Session", with photographs taken during the song's recording. "Beatles Talk" features Paul and George, and "Beatle News" sports such headings as "Chauffeur Confusion",

"The Truth About Paul's Tooth", "Manila Visit", "TV Dates", "Germany in June" and "Fantastic Demand for Tokyo Tickets". Photographs in this issue include Paul on guitar with headphones and spectacles, and the Beatles in an open car during their Australian tour, with Jimmy Nichol in Holland and in the studio with George Martin. Originally published in June 1966, and reprinted March 1979 with a feature on 'Please Please Me' by Peter Jones. Also pictures taken with George Martin when they received their first gold disc, and a shot of George with Barry Sheene and Dave Cash. The back cover shows a smiling, bearded Ringo with a cigarette.

36.

Paul in pensive mood graces the cover; George stares from the centrefold. The featured song is 'Paperback Writer', and this time the original words as written by Paul on the back of a photograph are reproduced. There is a special report by Sue Mautner on their visit to Chiswick House (where they filmed a promo film of 'Rain'), entitled "The Invasion of a Stately Home". Iain Hines contributes part one of a series: "Their First Visit to Hamburg". "Ringocyclististics" is a two-page picture special of Ringo riding his fold-away bike. There are also photographs from *A Hard Day's Night*, from their trip to Australia and New Zealand and of them eating in the back seat of an Austin Princess. Originally published in July 1966, it was reprinted in April 1979; the new main feature is a review of the *George Harrison* album by Mark Lewisohn. Back cover is of a bespectacled John.

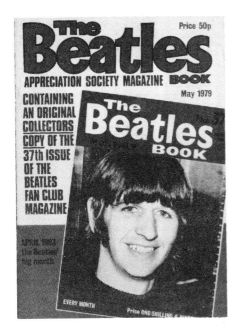

37.

Ringo, similing, on the cover; Paul on the telephone in the centrefold, 'Rain' as the featured song. "Triumphant Return!" recounts their trip to Germany and appropriately precedes part two of Iain Hines' Hamburg report. Frederick James talks to all four Beatles in "Beatle Talk", Billy Shepherd and Johnny Dean are up to August 1964 in the "Behind the Spotlight" series. There are half-a-dozen photographs from the Munich trip; also pictures of Brian Epstein and John and the hotel in Tremsbuttel where they stayed, George with his E-type Jag, a shot of the Beatles being interviewed at London Airport with Cliff Bennett and at a press conference. First printed 1966, reprinted in May 1979; the new main feature by Peter Jones covers the month "April 1963'" and includes a photograph of the Beatles with Gerry Marsden. The back cover is of George, with curly hair and moustache.

38.

The cover shows John in granny sun-glasses. Centrefold of Ringo, featured song 'If I Needed Someone'. Special interview with John, "I Don't Like Anything Different or Unusual", is the highlight of this issue. Iain Hines completes his Hamburg report. "Beatle News" details John's film début' in *How I Won the War*. Photographs include Ringo, George and Paul walking downstairs at the Schloss Hotel in Tremsbuttel; John in lotus pose; Paul taking a photograph; horseplay in a swimming-pool; all four on the American tour, on stage; Ringo in dark glasses, sporting a rifle and, in less threatening mood, hoeing the garden. First published in September 1966 and reprinted in June 1979, the extra copy includes a feature I wrote entitled "What the Beatles Didn't Mean to Say", concerning the hidden meanings in their songs. Back cover features Paul and Linda.

39.

On the cover, George looking suitably cool in a pin-stripe suit. John is the centrefold, 'Eleanor Rigby' song of the month. The magazine contains all the regular features in addition to "I've Thrown Away 30 Songs" – the main feature on George – and "US Notes". Pictures include a family shot of Ringo, Maureen and Zak at home, John having his hair cut for *How I Won the War,* Paul at the piano, Paul and John in sun-glasses, Mal Evans with Neil Aspinall in America, Ringo being interviewed, George with a camera and John, George and Paul eating. Originally published in October 1966 and reprinted in July 1979. The main new feature is a Rosie Horide review of *Back to the Egg*, with a picture of the Wings line-up (containing Steve Holly and Lawrence Juber). The back cover is a close-up of a bearded Ringo.

40

On the cover, Paul stares into the camera; George graces the centrefold. The song lyrics are from 'Yellow Submarine', sharing the page (the fashion since issue 33) with a photo – this time of Ringo in his garden. There is an ad for the 1966 Christmas Extra of *The Beatles Book*. The main feature is an interview with Paul entitled "We Can't Please Everyone". Shodhan Batt contributes "By George a Beatle Is in India", illustrated with a picture of Pattie and George during their Indian visit. The *Revolver* poll results indicate that 'Here, There and Everywhere' was the favourite track with readers; the news page announces that Paul will write a film score for "All in Good Time" (which became *The Family Way*). Photographs include the Beatles receiving their *Melody Maker* award from Johnny Mathis, Ringo sitting on a stone lion in the grounds of his home, Ringo and George eating, John in his Private Gripweed attire in *How I Won the War* and with Dick Lester, being interviewed about the film. The issue first appeared in November 1966 and was reprinted in August 1979. I wrote the main feature in the reprint – "The Beatles' Liverpool" – describing their home town and offering a "Beatle Walk" guide around the city. The back cover features John autographing a copy of *In His Own Write*.

41

The first issue in which *The Beatles Book* has been incorporated with a brand new magazine, *Record Collector*. The original copy sports a cover of Ringo. The centrefold is Paul and the month's lyrics are 'Here, There and Everywhere'. The main feature is an interview with Ringo entitled "They Won't Let Us Join the Golf Club". Regular features comprise the remainder of the contents. Photos include Paul playing a strange musical instrument called a tubon, Ringo holding a rifle aloft, Ringo in a hospital bed after his tonsilectomy, the group at the 1964 Christmas show and George pouring milk into his tea. Originally published in December 1966, and reprinted in September 1979 with 16 additional pages (due to the inclusion of the new magazine). A feature by David Hughes is entitled "Collecting Rare Records" and illustrated with photographs of David Bowie, Marc Bolan and the Who. There is an article on "Elvis Presley's Most Valuable Records" by Peter Jones with a picture of Elvis holding Stella Stevens; and a price index to the "Top 50 Rare Records". The personal ads now fill two pages and there is a three-page feature that I wrote on Stuart Sutcliffe. The back cover is of George Harrison.

John looking puzzled on the cover; Ringo smoking a cigarette is the pin-up. Song of the month is 'For No One', bordered by pictures of Paul and John in Eskimo suits from their 1964 Christmas show. Main feature is called "Visiting George"; it tells of his bungalow in Esher and pictures him in an 007 sweatshirt. "Neil's Column" has been replaced by "Mal's Page" – otherwise all the usual features remain. Photographs include Mal lighting Paul's cigarette, Ringo with a gramophone horn, Paul playing guitar at the Cavern, John reading his book (and Ringo indicating that it stinks), backstage shots from their 1964 Christmas show and shots of John in his top hat and uniform as usher to the Gentlemen's loo in the *Not Only, But Also* BBC TV show. First published in January 1967; reprinted as *Record Collector/The Beatles Book* in October 1979. New material includes an article on "Bootlegs" by Arian Sole and one on "Motown for Collectors" by Trevor and Clemency Little, a list of rare Motown singles, a "Top 50 Rare Records" list and Peter Jones' "How the Beatles Sold Sgt Pepper" feature. For the first time a non-Beatle graces the back cover: it is Mick Jagger.

43.

George indulges in a wet shave on the cover; John is the centrefold, 'I'm Only Sleeping' the featured song. "Visiting Paul" describes Paul's new house in St John's Wood, although the photograph is of George at his Esher home (posing in front of a mosaic of one of John's drawings). The winners of the ninth *Beatles Book* competition are announced, with a two-page spread reproducing the top three drawings. A full-page list of fan-club secretaries is opposite a picture of George in a wicker chair; other photographs include a rare shot of the original five Beatles on stage at the Top Ten club in Hamburg; another shot of George shaving; Ringo drinking a half of bitter; Brian Epstein with Ringo and Maureen, and Paul with George Martin. Originally published in February 1967; reissued November 1979, this *Record Collector/Beatles Book* magazine has 32 extra pages (the same number of pages as the reprint they enclose). There is an article on "Buddy Holly's Rare Misses" by Peter Jones, together with a Holly discography; "How I Became a Motown Collector" by Trevor Little and a Rare Motown Albums list; "Who and High Numbers Rarities" by J.E.Tubb; "The Valuable London Label" by David Hughes; and the "Top 100 Rare Records Listing". Beatle material comprises "My Beatles Collection" by Mark Lewisohn, a new regular column by Mark called "Beatles '79", a short obituary on Jimmy McCulloch and a feature on Liverpool's Magical Mystery Store. The back cover is a portrait of Elvis.

44.

Cover features Paul with a moustache – if you look closely you can see it has been touched up by an artist. The centre-page pin-up is George with a beard, also retouched; the featured song is 'Doctor Robert'. "Neil's Column" returns. The main feature is "Visiting Ringo" with a picture of him outside his Weybridge mansion, as well as some interior shots. Two pages are devoted to the runners-up in the "Draw a Beatle" competition. The "Beatles Talk" and "Behind the Spotlight" series continue. Photographs include John as Private Gripweed; several pictures from *Help!*; George and Patti in India, and Ringo smoking a cigarette. First published in March 1967, it was reprinted as *Beatles Book/Record Collector* in December 1979. The 32 pages of additional material contain "David Bowie's Early Releases" by Peter Jones, a Bowie discography, "Led Zeppelin's Recording History" by Gary Cooper, a Led Zeppelin discography, "Coloured Vinyl Records" by Rosie Horide, an article on the Vintage Record Centre and four pages of "Top 150 Rare Records". Beatle material includes "Beatles '79", a review of "Beatlemania" by Lorna Read and "Apple Mysteries" by Richard Nuzum. The back cover is an action shot of Marc Bolan.

45.

Ringo grinning on the cover, Paul playing the piano in the centrefold. Featured song is 'Good Day Sunshine'. There is a double-page picture of John superimposed before the gates to Strawberry Fields. All the usual features, as well as "Why Haven't the Beatles Fixed Another Con-cert Tour?" by Frederick James; "Recording: Why It Takes So Long Now" by Mal and Neil (first of a new series by the pair), and a news page with the information that Ringo is building his own Beatles Museum. Photographs include George with Ravi Shankar's brother, John and Ringo lighting cigarettes, Mal with John, David Crosby of the Byrds at a recording session, Pattie Boyd with her hair short, George and John talking to George Martin, and a double-page picture of the Fab Four with Neil and Mal. First published in April 1967, it was reprinted as *Beatles Book/Record Collector* in January 1980. The 32 extra pages include "Eddie Cochrane's Original US Singles" by Peter Jones; "Marc Bolan's Album Discography"; "The Stones' Live Albums" by Adrian Sole; and "Top 200 Rare Records". Beatle material includes "Beatles '80" and the first part of my feature, "The Beatles' London". Back cover is a shot of Mick Jagger and Keith Richard.

46.

The cover features John with a "Sword Swallower" badge on his scarf. Centre page is of Ringo, and the featured song is 'We Can Work It Out'. Frederick James asks "Why Did They Grow Moustaches?"; Neil pens "The First Official Mal Evans Story". A Johnny Dean piece on Paul completes the material, apart from the regular features. Pictures include shots of George with Ravi Shankar's brother, a bus in Penny Lane, Ringo at the piano, Paul and George Martin, Ringo in his garden with a rifle, George outside his Esher home, and several studio shots. First published in May 1967, and reprinted as *Beatles Book/Record Collector* in February 1980. The extra 30 pages contain "Cliff Richard's Early Discs" by Peter Jones, "Bob Dylan Oddities" by Dean Smith, a "Grease Records" article, "Top 250 Rare Records," and an ad announcing that – as from next issue – *Beatles Book/Record Collector* will become separate publications. Beatle material includes "Beatles '80" and the second part of my feature, "The Beatles' London." The back cover is of David Bowie at the mike.

47.

The first-ever *Beatles Book* colour cover, with a wraparound photograph of all four dressed in their Sgt Pepper outfits. The centre-page shot is John with moustache in hat and granny glasses. For the first time there is no featured song. "Sgt Pepper" by Mal and Neil covers the album session of their most famous LP; "How Was the New Album Cover Taken" completes the non-regular material. Photographs include the set for the Sgt. Pepper sleeve and several other colourful shots from the Pepper picture sessions, with the boys in uniform. There are several piano shots: John at the keys, Paul and Ringo tickling the ivories and Paul at the keyboard (watched by Dick James). Published in June 1964, the reissue in March 1980 has 16 pages of extra material. The main feature is the first part of "A Complete Catalogue of the Beatles' UK Radio Broadcasts" by Mark Lewisohn, who also contributes an enlarged "Beatles '80".

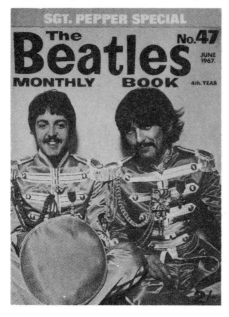

48.

Cover of a smiling Ringo wearing headphones; the centre page also features headphones – this time on George. Song of the month is 'Taxman'. Mal contributes "Paul and Mal in the States". "Paul's TV Statement" is a transcript of the interview Paul gave on ITN (discussing his mention in a *Life* magazine interview that he took drugs. Fan items include "My Point of View" by Ann Green, and "A Chance in a Million" by Julie Hunger. DJ Kenny Everett contributes a piece entitled "Beatles Dinner Party". Photographs include John and George playing harmonicas (said to be the longest harmonicas in the world), Paul – aged 24 – cutting his birthday cake, Paul and John in Paris in 1964, the group sitting with Mike and Bernie Winters on a Blackpool TV show, and George drinking tea (wearing a sweater with "Stamp Out the Beatles" on it). There is also a picture of George taken by Kenny Everett. Issued in July 1967, the magazine was reprinted in April 1980. The 16 pages of extra material include the second part of Mark Lewisohn's mammoth UK radio catalogue and "Beatles '80" – there are pictures of the Fabs with Ken Dodd, and one of Ringo with Kenny Ball. The back cover is of Paul.

49.

The cover features George, the centre page Paul; 'Got to Get You into My Life' is the featured song. Mal and Neil document the recording of the famous 'All You Need Is Love' session; Frederick James asks "Is Sgt Pepper too Advanced for the Average Pop Fan to Appreciate?" Photos include the "Our World" TV show, John at the piano; John, George and Paul in Hyde Park and by the Serpentine; Ringo at the organ; and all four, during their first US tour, being approached through the waves by two girls in swimsuits. First published in August 1967 and reprinted in May 1980.. Additional material includes "The Beatles' Early Tours" by Peter Jones, "Beatles '80" by Mark Lewisohn, and a column by me – covering films, fanzines, a quiz and errors in Beatle books. The back cover shows Ringo on drums.

50.

The cover shows a proud John with son Julian. Ringo is the pin-up; there are no song lyrics. Main feature, heavily pictorial, covers "How I Won the War?"; this is followed by "Our Visit to Greece" by Mal and Neil. A brief article describes a party at the "in" London club, the Speakeasy, attended by the Beatles. Photos include Paul smoking, John on drums, Paul with headphones, John watching the Fool paint his piano with a psychedelic design, some shots in the park (taken by Mal Evans), and one of Ringo, Maureen and Zak. First published in September 1967, and reprinted in June 1980. Reprint features "An Early Interview With the Beatles" by Peter Jones, "The Beatles UK TV Appearances" by Mark Lewisohn, "Beatles '80", and my own column – headed by the MBE story. Back cover is an early shot of George with guitar.

51.

Paul adorns the cover, and a Bob Gibson sketch of John the centre spread. No featured song. A two-page tribute to Brian Epstein includes quotes from various journalists, Cilla Black, John and Ringo. John comments: "Brian has died only in body and his spirit will always be working with us. His power and force were everything and his power and force linger on. When we were on the right track he knew it, and when we were on the wrong track he told us and he was usually right." There is a "John at Home" feature with photographs and an article on "George's California Trip" by Neil Aspinall. Photographs include John on a rocking horse with Julian, an early Cavern picture of George and Paul, John and Ringo smoking and Ringo tapping a tambourine. First published in October 1967, it was reprinted in July 1980. The 16 additional pages contain a review of *McCartney II* by Mark Lewishohn, a report on the Utrecht Beatles

Convention, an interview with Paul by Suzi Grant, "Beatles '80", and a piece I wrote called "Beatles Hits by Others". The back cover features John with Brian Matthews.

52.

On the cover, in profile, is John sporting his "eggman" skullcap from *Magical Mystery Tour;* there is a pensive Paul on the back cover and a moustachioed George in the centre pages. Most of the photos were taken during the filming of *Magical Mystery Tour,* though there are some of John and Julian in the "John at Home" feature. In addition to the usual features there are four separate reports on "The Magical Mystery Tour" by fan club secretaries Freda Kelly, Jeni Crowley, Barbara King and Sylvia Nightingale. Also an abbreviated transcript of a discussion with John and George on meditation, taken from BBC TV's *The Frost Programme.* First published in November 1967, and reprinted in August 1980 with 16 additional pages. Included is "The People Behind the Beatles", by Peter Jones, about people like Tony Barrow, Pete Best, Mal Evans, Terry Doran, Bobby Brown, Alistair Taylor and Tony Bramwell, who were associated with the Beatles from their early days. "Beatles '80", as well as letters, personal ads and some filler items of mine complete the issue – with Paul and Linda pictured on the back cover.

53.

The cover is a colour shot from *Magical Mystery Tour:* Paul dressed as a wizard. The centre page, also in colour, is of all four in their TV film; the song of the month is 'Hello, Goodbye'. The main feature is a report on *Magical Mystery Tour* by Mal and Neil; "The Mystery, Partly Explained" is by Frederick James. Almost all the photographs have been taken on location during the *Mystery Tour* filming, and include Paul in army uniform, the entire cast outside the Atlantic Hotel, Newquay, Paul with some female air cadets, Paul wearing a fish mask and George dressed as a wizard. Published in December 1967, reprinted in September 1980. Additional contents include a feature on their 1963 stage shows by Peter Jones and "Beatles '80" by Mark Lewisohn. I provided an obituary on Bert Kaempfert and some filler material. The back cover is of Ringo.

54.

The cover shows Ringo and Eva Aulin during the filming of *Candy.* Centre page is a Bob Gibson cartoon of Paul; there is no featured song. "How the Magical EPs Were Made" covers the recording of the Christmas record and the *Magical Mystry Tour* soundtrack. "Ringo in Rome" is a report by Mal Evans on the filming of *Candy,* with a shot of Ringo and Eva (in a miniskirt); "Apple Opens" is a feature on the Apple shop in Baker Street. Photos include the group horsing around at the Saville Theatre during the filming of a *Hello, Goodbye* promo film; George on drums; John in a bath chair with Julian; and scenes from *Magical Mystery Tour.* Orginally published in January 1968, the reprint appeared in October 1980. The 16 extra pages feature an article about the group's immense fan following written by Johnny Dean and Peter Jones, entitled "Beatle People". Also "Beatles '80" and a column of mine with various news items.

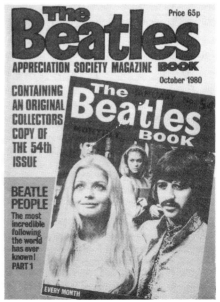

55.

George graces the cover, John the centrefold. "Beatles Have a Ball in Fancy Dress" is the main feature, with photographs. Maureen is dressed as a squaw, Ringo as a Regency buck; Paul and Jane as a Pearly King and Queen; John as a Rocker with Cynthia in an evening gown; and George as a Cavalier, Patti as an Eastern Princess. Part two of "Ringo in Rome" includes several photographs taken during the filming of *Candy;* "Beatle News" reports that George has written his first film score, for *Wonderwall.* Photographs include members of the group with fan-club organisers, Paul – in 1962 – with his father and brother Mike, George chatting to Spencer Davis. Published in February 1968, and reissued in November 1980, the 16 extra pages contain part two of the Dean/Jones "Beatle People", and "Beatles '80". The back cover is of John as Gripweed in *How I Won the War.*

56.

The cover shows John wearing granny glasses, the centre pin-up shows Paul. Articles include "Recording in India", a report on George's trip to Bombay written by Mal Evans; "A Beatles Report From Australia" by Terry Kilmartin; "Some Beatle Singles Are No Longer Obtainable" by Frederick James; and "George Harrison: Record Producer". There is also a cartoon quiz, illustrated by Bob Gibson. Photographs include Ringo with Vic Lewis of Nems; Paul Ringo and John reading the script of *Yellow Submarine;* recording-session shots; Paul chatting to actor Harry Corbett at a *Cilla* TV show rehearsal and Paul with a miniskirted Cilla Black. First published in March 1968, it was reprinted in December 1980. The extra pages feature "The Beatles Christmas Fan Club Discs" by their former press officer, Tony Barrow, as well as "Beatles '80" and a review of *Double Fantasy* by Peter Doggett. The back cover pictures Paul.

57.

Paul is the cover star, Ringo is the centre pin-up. "Ringo: What Will He Do Next?" features photographs of him with Cilla Black on her TV show. Readers Mary Abbott and Charlene Bass contribute the lyrics to "A Tribute to Beatle John" – to be sung to the tune of 'Big Bad John'; Mal Evans and Neil Aspinall report on the "New Single Sessions" – the recordings of 'Lady Madonna', 'The Inner Light' and 'Across the Universe'. There is a short feature on Apple. Photographs of Mal clowning it up while Paul plays guitar, the group at their recording sessions, at early theatre shows, and with Spike Milligan and George Martin at EMI Studios. Published in April 1968 and reissued in January 1981; a special tribute to John Lennon contains quotes from Cynthia, Ringo, Paul, George, George Martin, Aunt Mimi, Jimmy Tarbuck and many others. There is also the first part of Tony Barrow's three-part series on Brian Epstein. The back cover features Ringo.

58.

The cover is a colour shot of Paul and Jane Asher; the back cover portrays George and Beach Boy Mike Love. Both pictures, and the centre-page colour spread, were taken in India at the Maharishi's Meditation Academy. 14 black-and-white pictures were also taken in India; Mal Evans reports on the trip in the first of a two-part article. "First Full-Length Biography of the Beatles" is about the Hunter Davies book; the rest of the contents include "Behind the Spotlight" and the usual features – letters, "Beatle News" and pen pal page. First issued in May 1968, reissued in February 1981. Additional pages feature "The John Lennon I Knew" by Tony Barrow, "Beatles '81", personal ads, readers' letters and a back-page, black-and-white picture of John holding a Gold Disc of 'I Want to Hold Your Hand".

59.

The colour cover shows a clean-shaven Ringo, the back cover a colour shot of John; centre page is a colour pin-up of George. As well as part two of Mal Evans' series "Beatles in India", Hunter Davies – author of the official Beatles biography – has penned "Encyclo(Beatle)pedia", a short Beatle quiz. Photos in this issue include several shots from India, George Martin clowning in the studios, the group arriving by boat for a *Thank Your Lucky Stars* appearance, Paul with Dusty Springfield, an early Cavern picture of them with Gene Vincent and a Cavern stage shot taken by Peter Kaye. First issued in June 1968; reprinted in March 1981. The additional pages contain part two of "The Brian Epstein Story" by Tony Barrow, "Beatles '81" and "Hear the Beatles Tell All", a review of an interview album by Peter Doggett. The back cover features George in his car.

60.

The cover is a colour shot of George and Patti; the back cover, also in colour, of Ringo astride a stone lion at his Weybridge home; centre-page colour pin-up of John. "Revolution Report", by Frederick James, details the making of their new single; "Paul Started It All" is a piece by Hunter Davies; the wedding of Paul's brother, merits a two-page picture special – with Paul and Jane in all three shots. Other photographs include the opening party at the Apple Tailoring shop with various friends and celebrities present, Brian Epstein talking to George and Paul, Paul at the

Albert Memorial, George and Patti in the King's Road. Published in July 1968, and reprinted in April 1981. The extra pages feature part three of "The Brian Epstein Story" by Tony Barrow, "Beatles '81" and "The McCartney Interviews", a review of the interview album by Peter Doggett. The back cover is of Paul.

61.

An uncharacteristic colour shot of Paul, smiling from the cover; John in granny glasses, also in colour, on the back cover. The pin-up shows a clean-shaven Ringo beside his garden pond. Features include "With Paul to Hollywood" – Tony Bramwell's first contribution to the magazine – and "Ringo and George in California", by Mal Evans. There is a double-page ad for the Hunter Davies book. Pictures of Paul with Apple Records boss Ron Kass in Hollywood, George playing guitar, the four in 1963 on a lilo in a swimming-pool, Paul signing autographs, and Paul, George and Ringo with a life-size cut-out of John from *Yellow Submarine*. Originally published in August 1968, and reprinted in May 1981, the extra pages feature a review I wrote of Philip Norman's book *Shout!*, as well as two other pieces of mine: "The Day Ringo Almost Died" and "Beatle Tributes, Spoofs & Novelty Discs". There are two pages of "Beatles '81" by Mark Lewisohn; and Ringo on the back cover.

62.

A close-cropped John in granny glasses adorns the cover; back page features John and Yoko, George, Patti and Paul; centrefold pin-up shows the Four among some foliage – all in colour.

"The Eighteenth Single", by Mal Evans, is a report of a recording session; there is a feature on the "Yellow Submarine Premier", with Photographs; and the announcement of a new photo service from the official fan club. Pictures include Paul with Derek Taylor and Dennis O'Dell, the Beatles and their wives attending the *Yellow Submarine* première and recording session shots. First published in September 1968, and reissued in June 1981, the extra pages feature "The Beatles and the Press" by Tony Barrow, "Beatles '81", and a two-page picture spread of Ringo's wedding to actress Barbara Bach. Back cover features an early photograph of George, in collarless jacket, playing guitar.

63.

The colour cover shows Ringo in yellow shirt and blue jacket; the back cover, also colour, features the four on a park bench, centre colour spread of Paul. Fully illustrated main article – "The Fifth Beatle Gets Married" – reports on the wedding between Neil Aspinall and Suzy Ornstein; also in this issue is "Mal's Dairy", a feature by Frederick James entitled "John and Yoko Talk About Art and Vibrations", and lyrics to 'Hey Jude' and 'Revolution'. Photos include Paul and his dog Martha, shots taken around the London docks during the making of a promo film, and Paul playing acoustic guitar. First published in October 1968 and reissued in July 1981, with further reviews, by Tony Barrow and Johnny Dean, on the *Shout!* book. Also "Beatles '81", and reviews of the McCartney film *Rockshow* and George's new album *Somewhere in England*. The back cover is an early picture of John playing harmonica.

64.

A colour shot of Paul on the cover; the back cover colour shot – slightly out of focus – of all four; full-length colour centrefold of Ringo. Main feature is "Thirty New Beatle Grooves on Double Disc Album" by Mal Evans; there is a track-by-track coment on *The Beatles* double LP, and a Frederick James article entitled "Tracks You've Never Heard". News, letters, fan-club reports and an editorial complete the issue. There are 18 black-and-white shots, mainly taken during their album sessions, one of John and Paul with Yoko. First published in November 1968; reissued in August 1981, with "A Tale of Two Conventions" Mark Lewisohn's reports on Beatle conventions – "Beatles '81", "Quotes Quiz", a review I wrote of Ringo's *Caveman* as well as letters and small ads.

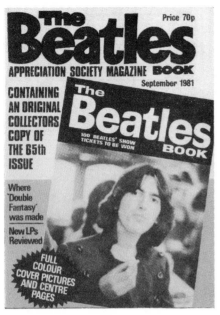

The Beatles

Price 70p

APPRECIATION SOCIETY MAGAZINE **BOOK**

September 1981

CONTAINING AN ORIGINAL COLLECTORS COPY OF THE 65th ISSUE

The **Beatles** *BOOK*

100 BEATLES' SNOW TICKETS TO BE WON

Where 'Double Fantasy' was made

New LPs Reviewed

FULL COLOUR COVER PICTURES AND CENTRE PAGES

65.

The colour cover shows George nibbling at food and wearing a fashionable brown overcoat, and the back cover the group performing in a studio; centrefold pin-up of them all in action. There is an article "What You Would Like the Boys to Do in '69", by Frederick James; and a general feature entitled "First Live Performance for Over Two Years". Regular items include the fan-club newsletter, letters, pen-pals page and two pages of "Beatle News". John Kelly and Tony Bramwell took photographs throughout the issue. First published in December 1968, and reprinted in September 1981, with 16 additional pages. The extra material includes Mark Lewisohn's report on his visit to New York's Record Plant where John Lennon had been recording shortly before he died. Mark Lewisohn also reviews *The Beatles: Early Years* (two albums which are really a repackaging of the Beatles' Hamburg tapes). "Too Biased Against Paul" is an article by Colleen Flanagan on Philip Norman's book *Shout!* Letters and personal ads complete the issue; back cover of Ringo with his Pentax.

66.

The colour cover shows Ringo, in a purple frilly shirt, playing drums in the studio with headphones on; the back cover is of the group during a break in rehearsals; colour centrefold of all four outside what looks like a television station. In "New Year's Day", Frederick James discusses events on that day over the various years of the Fabs' early career. "George's US Visit" is Mal Evan's report on George's trip to the United

States in the company of Jackie Lomax. Freda Kelly discusses a set of six pictures on offer from the fan club. "Beatle News" (Australian TV commissions a feature-length film from John and Yoko, John performs in *Rock 'n' Roll Circus),* letters, list of fan-club secretaries, pen-pals column; fan-club news and editorial complete the issue. There are 20 black-and-white pictures, mainly taken by John Kelly and Tony Bramwell, several from the Beatles' Christmas show in Hammersmith; close-ups of John, Paul and George; and Paul and Mary Hopkin discussing a song. First published in January 1969, reprinted in October 1981. The 16 additional pages feature "With a Little Help From Their Friends", by Tony Barrow, which is about people who worked for the Fab Four. "Beatles '81" by Mark Lewisohn and letters and personal ads complete the issue; the back cover shows George playing guitar.

67.

The colour cover is a close-up of a green-hatted, bespectacled John; the back cover of Ringo – with an Eastern stringed instrument – in a hotel room. The centrefold features Paul, with headphones, singing and playing piano in a recording studio. Frederick James writes about Freda Kelly and the Liverpool fan-club in "A Return Visit"; another lengthy feature is "Your Album Queries Answered by Mal Evans". There are some short items penned by readers; the editorial, fan-club news, pen-pal page, letters and "Beatle News" complete the issue. Other photographs include George Martin at the piano, Ringo in a trilby, George with Dusty Springfield and a scene from the set of *Help!* First published in February 1969 and reprinted in November 1981. Extra pages contain a lead feature on "Paul McCartney: Composer/Artist", my review of Paul's new book, part two of "With a Little Help From Their Friends" by Tony Barrow, "Beatles '81" and personal ads and letters. The back cover shows a smiling Paul on guitar.

68.

The colour cover has a close-up of George, in a blue shirt, playing guitar; the back cover Paul with a beard, wearing a yellow shirt and blue pullover and singing into a mike. The centrefold is a colour shot of a studio interior, with Paul at the mike (as back cover), George with guitar (as front cover), and John talking to Yoko – while a photographer snaps them in conversation. The main feature is "Mal's Diary": a lengthy item by Mal Evans relating various anecdotes. Frederick James contributes "Two Portraits of George", also the subject of Billy Shepherd's "The Helpful Beatle". Letters, news, and pen-pals and fan-club pages complete the text. There are 19 black-and-white pictures that include Paul with

Linda's six-year-old daughter Heather, John and Keith Richard playing in the Stones' *Rock 'n' Roll Circus,* and Yoko and Linda together. First published in March 1969 and reprinted in December 1981. The 16 additional pages feature "John in His Own Quotes" by Peter Jones, "Beatles '81" by Mark Lewisohn, a review of the world première of the *Lennon* play by Tony Barrow, letters, personal ads and a back cover of the Fab Four in their collarless jackets.

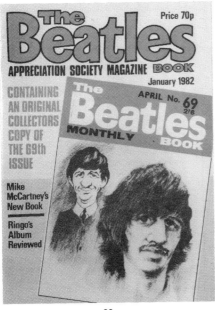

69.

The black-and-white cover features a portrait and caricature of Ringo – the subject of the front and back cover. Main feature is "When Did You Switch On?" an uncredited piece about their early career. Frederick James contributes "Two Portraits of Ringo", also the subject of "He's a Sensitive Soul" by Billy Shepherd. Editorial, fan-club reports, letters, pen-pals and "Beatle News" complete the text. There are 17 black-and-white shots, including three of Linda and Paul at their wedding, and some of Ringo at his Weybridge home. First published in April 1969 and reprinted in January 1982, with 16 additional pages. Tony Barrow reports on the launch party for Mike McCartney's book *Thank U Very Much;* Lorna Reed reviews the book. Peter Doggett assesses Ringo's album *Stop and Smell the Roses,* and also reviews John Blake's *All You Needed Was Love* and Bob Woffinden's *The Beatles Apart.* "Beatles '82" by Mark Lewisohn, letters and classified ads complete the issue. The back cover shows John playing guitar.

70.

Portrait and caricature of John on the cover; close-up shot of Paul on the back; Ringo as the centrefold. The main feature, "When Did You Switch On?" continues to uncover aspects of the Beatles' early career. "Two Portraits of John" by Frederick James, is complemented by a Billy Shepherd article. Editorial, fan-club news, pen-pals, letters and news complete the text. There are 18 interior photos, pictures of George with Joe Cocker, The Beatles on stage, meeting Princess Margaret, with Morecambe and Wise, and making their *Juke Box Jury* appearance. Originally published in May 1969; reprinted in January 1979. The extra pages contain Lorna Read's interview with Mike McCartney, "Beatles Memorabilia" by Mark Baker, an article about Sotheby's first rock 'n' roll auction, "Beatles '82" by Mark Lewisohn, letters and ads. The back cover features a smiling Ringo.

71.

Drawing by Bob Gibson on the cover of Paul as he looked in 1969, with an early sixties caricature of him in the background. Centrefold of all four; back cover of a bearded, bespectacled John. "So Many Are McCartney's Ideas" is Frederick James' offering. There is another "When Did You Switch On?" feature, and a "Two Portraits" story on Paul, written by Billy Shepherd. Photographs of Paul with camera, several shots of John and Yoko (including ones of them in bed during their Bed-In campaign in Amsterdam), behind-the-scenes glimpses from *Help!* and the Beatles with George Martin in the studio. First published in June 1968, and reprinted in March 1982. The additional pages feature a piece I wrote with Tony Barrow entitled "The Truth Behind the Decca Audition", "Beatles '82" by Mark Lewisohn, reviews a *A Cellarful of Noise* and *I. Me. Mine,* letters and personal ads. The back cover shows George with moustache, a thick scarf wrapped around his neck.

72.

The cover shows the group on a boat called Fritz Otto Maria Anna; centrefold once again of all four; Ringo on the back cover. "Derek Taylor Makes a Radio Teleprinter Call From the QE2" is the main feature; "The Beatles Get Back" is Mal Evans' report on their *Let It Be* album session – news, pen-pals column, letters, fan-club news and editorial complete the issue. There are 18 black-and-white photographs, most of them taken during a boating session on the Thames. First published in July 1969, reprinted in April 1982. The additional material includes a feature on the Cavern by Tony Barrow, "Beatles '82" by Mark Lewisohn, "Beatles' Novelties and Oddities" by myself, as well as personal ads and letters. The back cover shows Paul playing a guitar.

73.

The cover features Paul, the centrefold a pin-up of John, heavily bearded; Ringo appears on the back cover. There is an article on the 'Get Back' recordings by Frederick James, "One Pair of Eyes" by Bill McAllister and a two-page club secretaries. More Bed-In shots of John and Yoko, pictures of Paul imitating Elvis, Paul with Mary Hopkin in the studio and Paul with George Martin. First published in August 1968 and reprinted in May 1982 with an article on Alistair Taylor by Tony Barrow, "Beatles 82" by Mark Lewisohn, a review of 'Ebony and Ivory' by Peter Doggett, and readers' letters and ads. The back cover shows John in granny glasses, and a young Julian in his lap.

74.

The cover shows a bearded John at the piano, holding a cigarette; Paul is on the back cover; and two pictures of Paul rubbing his eye make up the centrefold. "In the Studio" by Frederick James covers the Beatles' recent recording activities; "Eight Days in Montreal with John and Yoko" is a piece by fans Gail Renard and Thomas Schnurmacher. News, letters, pen-pals, fan-club news and editorial complete the issue, which has 16 interior pictures – some of John and Yoko during their Bed-In, the rest taken during a studio recording session with Linda McCartney and Maureen Starkey sitting in the background. First published in September 1969 and reprinted in June 1982 with 16 additional pages featuring "With the Beatles Again", the second part of Tony Barrow's interview with Alistair Taylor, "Beatles '82" by Mark Lewisohn, a review of *Tug of War* by Peter Doggett, as well as ads and letters. The back cover is of a bearded Ringo.

75.

Cover of the Fab Four, all but Paul sporting beards. Back cover of a hirsute George with members of the Hare Krishna sect; he also appears as the centrefold pin-up. Main feature is "George Introduces Hare Krishna"; this is followed by "One Pair of Eyes", by guest writer Steve Turner, who concludes: "I wrote this article because I felt there is not enough serious journalism written on the subject of the Beatles and their influence on contemporary culture." As well as the usual features, there is a report on the 1969 Isle of Wight Festival, at which Bob Dylan topped the bill. 18 black-and-white photographs, mainly of George with Hare Krishna members and Dylan at the Isle of Wight (with George, Ringo and Maureen as spectators). First published in October 1969, reprinted in July 1982. The 16 additional pages include my article "Where They Lived and Played", "Beatles '82" by Mark Lewisohn, Peter Doggett's review of

The Beatles Down Under album and book, and letters and classified ads. The back cover shows a bearded George.

76.

A clean-shaven Paul on the cover, a bearded John on the back with the Plastic Ono Band on their "Toronto Rock & Roll Revival" sweatshirts as the centrefold. The lead feature is "John & Yoko's Toronto Concert" by Mal Evans, followed by "The End of the Performing Beatles" and "Apple Businessmen". "Beatle News", pen-pals, letters, fan-club news and editorial complete the issue, which has 13 interior illustrations, mainly covering John's Toronto trip. First published in November 1969 and reprinted in August 1982. The additional material includes Mark Lewisohn's report on the 'Take It Away' video; also his "Beatles '82". *The Beatle Interviews* album is reviewed, as is *The Playboy Interviews with John Lennon and Yoko Ono* book – by Peter Doggett. Personal ads and letters complete the issue. The back cover features John in granny glasses.

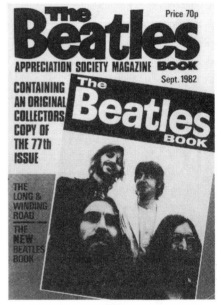

77.

The final issue has all four Beatles on both the front and back cover; Bob Gibson cartoons of John and Paul provide the centrefold. In "The End of an era", Sean O'Mahony outlines his reasons for discontinuing the series of books. There are two further cartoons – of George and Ringo – and an article by Billy Shepherd called "They Had to Change". Editorial, fan-club news, letters and pen-pal column complete the text; there are 11 interior pictures, mainly featuring

John in a Spanish-style black hat, George in a black stetson and Yoko with a bandanna across her forehead. First published in December 1969, and reprinted in September 1982. Additional pages contain "The New Beatles Book" (a description of Sean O'Mahony's aims for the new publication), "Beatles '82" by Mark Lewisohn, my review of Neville Stannard's book *The Long & Winding Road,* and letters and ads. Back cover of a cheerful Paul, toasting us with a cup of tea.

The Beatles Monthly Book continues to thrive, using the same format and layout as the original series – though the cover, back cover and centrefold are in colour. With the exception of the editorial and "Beatles '83" by Mark Lewisohn, the style of the publication is geared to covering, month-by-month, events from 20 years before. There is an almanac and news stories from the period, as well as articles written as if penned in the sixties. O'Mahoney continues to use the same pool of writers: Tony Barrow, Peter Jones, Mark Lewisohn, Peter Doggett and myself. About 25 black-and-white photographs are included in each issue.

Record Collector emerged as a separate entity with issue seven in March 1980, after readers had made known their preference that *The Beatles Monthly/Record Collector* should be split into two publications. The magazine thrived over the years, doubling the size of its pages to 11¾ x 8½" by July 1983. Most issues contain material of interest to Beatle fans – all are superbly illustrated with comparatively rare photographs. Here is a brief run down of Beatles, and Beatles-related, material contained in the first 50 issues:

7.

'US Beatles Memorabilia: Part One" – a short series written by Barb Fenick on collecting in America. She later penned the book *Collecting the Beatles.*

8.

'Where to Look for Beatles Memorabilia" – the second part of Barb Fenick's series, illustrated with photographs, and the reproduction of a John Lennon drawing taken from a London Palladium programme cover.

9.

'Beatles UK Singles Values" – an article by Johnny Dean on the group's British singles, together with a list of their current values, compiled by Mike Adams.

10.

"Beatles Facts: Sorting Out the Truth From the Fiction" by Peter Jones, discusses the number of inaccuracies that have appeared in various books on the Beatles.

11.

"Early Apple Records" – an article by Peter Mulholland on the early days of the Apple label, as well as an "Early Apple Discography".

12.

"Beatles UK LPs" by Johnny Dean and Peter Jones details "the albums the Beatles produced during their touring days"; also a "Complete Beatles UK LP Discography and Values" – researched by Mike Adams.

13.

"Beatlefest '80", Barb Fenick's report on an American Beatles' Convention.

15.

"John Lennon's Solo Rarities" – a lengthy feature on John's records written by Peter Doggett; also a "Complete John Lennon UK Discography With Values".

16.

Double-page Christmas competition in which readers are given the opportunity to win a set of six Beatle Fan Club Christmas discs.

17.

"Beatles UK Books & Magazines" – a report by David Hayles on the increasing value of collectable Beatles' publications.

18.

Results of the Beatles Christmas disc competition.

19.

"Paul McCartney's Solo Rarities" by Peter Doggett; also a "Paul McCartney UK Discography". Another feature by Doggett, this time on the Searchers – together with their discography.

22.

"The Beatles Decca Tapes: Why Haven't They Been Released?" by Peter Doggett.

25.

"Beatles Memorabilia", a guide to current values written by David Hayles. In "The Beatles Early Years" Peter Doggett reviews two albums featuring the Hamburg tapes.

29.

"Rare Recordings of Beatle Songs" details those Beatle songs recorded by other artists. Peter Doggett writes "The Songs the Beatles Gave Away" and a list is included; article and discography of the Mojos by Doggett.

30.

"Pop Memorabilia Under the Hammer!" – article by Lorna Read detailing the auction of Beatles' memorabilia at Sotheby's in December 1981.

32.

"George Harrison's Solo Rarities", by Peter Doggett, is complemented by a UK Discography. Gerry and the Pacemakers feature by Steve Scott, also with discography.

35.

"The Beatles' Unreleased Recordings" feature, by Peter Doggett, on the recordings still in the EMI vaults.

38.

"The Beatles Alternative Takes" is a guide to the different versions of Beatle songs officially available around the world – written by Nick Piercey.

40.

"The Swinging Blue Jeans" – a feature and discography by Peter Doggett.

41.

"The Beatles in Hamburg" by Peter Doggett outlines the history of the Tony Sheridan recording sessions made in 1961 and the 1962 Star Club sessions – also a listing of "The Beatles Hamburg Recordings".

42.

Feature on John and Yoko, by Peter Doggett, documenting "their guest appearances, outside productions, and other rarities by the Plastic Ono Band"; also a discography of "John Lennon's Guest Appearances". There is an article and discography on the Merseybeats, by Nigel Smithers.

43.

"Wings in Nashville" details the group's 1974 album recordings.

44.

In "The Get Back Sessions" Peter Doggett outlines "the confused history of the 1969 Beatles album that never reached the shops".

45.

"The Beatles EPs" – an article by Steve Scott, together with a discography of their UK EP releases.

46.

"The Apple Label" – a feature by Pete Doggett, complete with discography.

50.

"The Beatles and EMI Records" – an article about unreleased Beatle songs by Nick Piercey, taken from an interview with EMI's Mike Heatley.

BEATLE MAGAZINES

JAMMING!

40p
(U.S.$1·25)

THE BEATLES

Nº 13

SCRITTI POLITTI · BLUEBELLS PIRATE RADIO · POLAND POETRY

A NEW OPTIMISM FOR THE '80's

BEATLE MAGAZINES

Lee Curtis

The first regular reportage of the Beatles' activities began in July 1961 with the publication of *Mersey Beat*, the world's first alternative music paper. In issue No.1 I ran "On the Dubious Origins of Beatles", a Beatles' biography written by John Lennon. The second issue featured a front-cover story reporting on the group's first recordings in Germany and each issue was subsequently dominated by the group. The paper drew Brian Epstein's attention to the Beatles and he began submitting record reviews. Bob Wooler's famous article "Well Now – Dig This!" appeared in issue No.5. The group came top in the *Mersey Beat* poll, John Lennon began to write a regular column, "Beatcomber", and I wrote and serialised "The Beatles Story" and introduced a page of news, "The Mersey Beatle", each issue.

Initially no one else was interested in covering the Beatles' activities, not even the local evening paper the *Liverpool Echo*, but I began sending issues of *Mersey Beat* to various publications. The first paper to mention the Mersey scene was London's *Record Mirror*, which ran a small article reiviewing *Mersey Beat* in a tongue-in-cheek item, incredulous that so much was happening in Liverpool and drawing attention to the various colourful names of the groups and artists involved, in particular Ringo Starr. The writer, Peter Jones, later conducted the Fab Four's first interview with a national music paper (*Record Mirror*), and wrote regularly for *Beatles Monthly* under the name Billy Shepherd.

The first article on the Beatles to appear in a major national publication was an interview conducted by Maureen Cleave of London's *Evening Standard* in February 1963.

That year, other magazines and newspapers began to take note of the Beatles, and Sean O'Mahony launched *Beatles Monthly*. Sean also published the monthly magazine *Beat Instrumental*, which regularly featured the Beatles.

The major teen-magazine publishing house at the time was Fleetway Publications, whose output, with titles such as *Marilyn* and *Valentine*, was aimed at young girls. The advent of the Beatles and other Mersey groups inspired them to launch an ambitious, full-colour magazine in 1964 called *Fabulous*. For more than three years, this magazine produced numerous covers and large interior posters of the Beatles, with stories and special features on the band, reportage on other Mersey groups and picture spreads on the Beatles' wives and girlfriends such as Maureen Starkey and Jane Asher.

In 1964 I was contributing a weekly column on the Beatles and the Mersey scene to *Weekend* magazine and also to the Fleetway Publication *Marilyn*. I was also writing six pages of copy per issue for *Star Club News*, the German beat magazine launched by Manfred Weissleder of the Star Club. This contained information, news and photographs of all the bands appearing at the famous club. A new publication using the same title appeared in the eighties.

Around this time a number of nationally-circulated, family magazines in Britain also began to cover the new phenomenon of Beatlemania: *Reveille*, *Tit Bits* and *Today* magazine.

World Distributors began a series of handsomely produced, special issues devoted to the beat scene in 1963. The general title of the series was "Meet the..." and the most popular edition was *Meet the Beatles*, which sold a million copies. This was written by the Beatles' press agent Tony Barrow. Others in the series included *Meet Billy J.Kramer* and *Meet Gerry and the Pacemakers*. Another magazine published in 1963 was Pyx's *The Beatles*. This featured a number of colour shots of the Fab Four. Strangely enough, in 1982 a batch of several thousand copies were found in a warehouse where they had been dumped over 20 years before. The man who "found" them has since been offering them for sale at grossly inflated proces.

BEATLES

Words and pictures
compiled by SAM
LEACH

In 1964 another series of magazines, in a similar format to the "Meet the..." series appeared, entitled "On the Scene..." One of them, *On the Scene at the Cavern,* was credited to Alistair Griffin – a pseudonym for Tony Barrow. This was keenly sought after by collectors and was republished in April 1984 to coincide with the reopening of the Cavern club. *On the Scene at the Cavern* is available from the Cavern club itself or by mail order from Tony at 10 Buseph Drive, Torrisholme, Morecambe, Lancashire, LA4 6BQ (£3.00, including postage and packing).

In the mid sixties, Daily Mirror Publications issued some well produced magazines, one of the first being *The Beatles by Royal Command,* the colour cover of which featured Princess Margaret meeting the Beatles just after their Royal Variety Show performance. It contained over 30 photographs and was the first publication to concentrate on a specific show; similar comemmorative magazines were subsequently issued by a number of enterprising publishers.

One example is *The Beatles at Carnegie Hall,* issued in 1964 by Panther Pictorial at 2/6d. The text was written by Ralph Cosham and the publication contained 60 photographs of this Beatles' concert by United Press and the International Candid Camera team.

Pleased with the success of *The Beatles by Royal Command,* the *Daily Mirror* issued *The Beatles in America.* This was a pictorial souvenir of the boys' American trip with lots of black-and-white photographs by Robert Freeman; the front and back covers were in colour.

World Distributors issued a magazine with a similar layout called *Beatles on Broadway.* American fan Corrine Speziale lent me a copy of her American edition of this magazine, issued by the Whitman publishing company. It was written and compiled by Sam Leach, a Liverpool promoter who booked the Beatles for his venues. Over 20 years later, Sam issued another magazine, *Follow the Merseybeat Road.* The cover of *Beatles on Broadway* shows the Fab Fours' heads suspended above the Manhatten skyline. Photographs taken during the Beatles' American tour include shots of their arrival at Kennedy Airport; their press conference; the fans outside the Plaza Hotel; the boys in Central Park; appearing on the *Ed Sullivan Show;* visiting the Peppermint Lounge; receiving Gold Discs; travelling by train to Washington; appearing at the Washington Coliseum; appearing at a masked ball at the British Embassy; appearing at Carnegie Hall; relaxing in Miami; visiting Cassius Clay at his training camp; and returning to Heathrow Airport.

From time to time, British teen magazines produced special editions such as *Boyfriend's, Beatles in Sweden* and *Beatles in Paris* and *Pop Pic's Beatles Around the World.* The *Liverpool Echo* also brought out a special souvenir book *Around the World With the Beatles,* at Christmas 1964, priced at two shillings. Written by the papers senior journalist, George Harrison, this was a 32-page publication with four colour photographs, stories of the group's trips abroad and a large selection of early black-and-white pictures.

America, however, proved to be where Beatle magazines flourished. Various teen magazines produced special issues about the Fab Four: *Datebook* with *All About the Beatles; Teen Screen* with *John, Paul, George and Ringo; Dig* magazine with *Beatles Movie* and *Beatle Talk; Sixteen* magazine with *Sixteen's Beatle Movie: A Hard Day's Night, Sixteen's Beatle Movie: Help!; Sixteen's Beatles Complete Story from Birth to Now* and *Sixteen's Beatles Whole True Story;* and *Teen Talk* with *Teen Talk: the Beatles* and *Teen Talk: Picture Packed Edition.*

Among magazines published in the US in 1964 was *A Hard Day's Night,* billed as *The Official United Artists' Pictorial Souvenir Book.* It included background stories relating to the making of the film, many behind-the-scenes photographs and a foreword by the Beatles; *Best of the Beatles,* which featured a three-page colour pin-up and articles such as "63 Ways to Meet a Beatle", "What It's Like to Love a Beatle", "The Girl Who Stopped Paul's Marriage" and "Is Ringo Taken by Ann Margret?" This was published by MacFadden Bartell, who were also responsible for *Beatles Are Back* and *The Beatles Are Here.*

Magnum publications issued *Beatles Make a Movie* and other magazines included *Beatles Around the World* Nos 1 and 2 from Acme News Company; *Beatles Baby Family Album* from SMP Publishing; *Beatles USA* by Jamie Publications; *Beatles, Beatles, Beatles* by JLD Publishing; *Beatles: Fab Four Come Back* by Ideal Publications; *Beatles Meet Dave Clark 5* by Kahm Publications; *Beatles vs Dave Clark 5* by Tempest Publications; *Beatles Punch-Out Portraits* from Whitman Publishing; *Big Beatle Fun Kit* from Deirdre Publications; *Who Will Beat the Beatles* by Magnum Publications; *Beatle Hair Dos and Setting Patterns* by Dell Publishing; *The Original Beatles Book* Nos 1 and 2 by Peterson Publishing; a series of books on each individual Beatle from SMH Publications; *The Beatles Complete Life Stories* by Sunset Publications; *The Beatles Personality Annual* by Country Wide Publications; *The Fab Four Come Back* by Romance Publishing Corporation and *Real True Beatles* by Fawcett Publications, a magazine version of Michael Braun's book *Love Me Do,* and many more.

The trend continued in 1965, with numerous Beatle titles being published including *Star Time Presents the Beatles* by AAA Publishing, *Help!* by *Help* magazine and *The Beatles – Our Naughty Nights* by Reese Publishing.

During the rest of the decade fewer Beatle magazines were published. However *Beatles Monthly* produced some special Christmas magazines and the *Yellow Submarine* movie led to various magazine spin-offs including *The Official Yellow Submarine Magazine* from Pyramid Publications and *Teenset Yellow Submarine Special* (both 1968).

Magazines continued to be published in the seventies, despite the group's demise. Magnum issued *Beatles From the Beginning* in 1970, an Australian magazine, *Beatle Revival*, was published in 1976 and *Beatles Yesterday and Today* was issued by Countrywide Publications in 1975. Charlton Publications issued *Beatlemania: the Beatles from Liverpool to Legend* in 1979 and in Britain, Rainbow issued the lavishly produced *The Beatles: a Giant Scrapbook.*

A magazine that was reprinted several times was *Beatles Forever,* first published in 1975. This was a glossy magazine with 150 photographs and a 40-page photohistory, discography and filmography. Later editions included pieces on the stage review *Beatlemania* and the film *Sgt Pepper's Lonely Hearts Club Band.* The magazine was revamped and rush-released immediately following John's murder.

Two particular magazines of interest were *Paul McCartney Is Dead: The Great Hoax,* issued by Countrywide Publications in 1969 and *National Lampoon's* Beatle issue, published in October 1977.

The first was an issue completely devoted to the ridiculous rumours sparked off by an American DJ that Paul had been killed in a road accident and replaced by a double. The DJ sought to prove this by pointing out a number of 'clues' that, he alleged, had been included on Beatles' records. The cover announced: "Paul McCartney Dead: The Great Hoax. Born 1942. Died 1966?" The magazine included articles such as "Why Did the Beatles Keep Paul's Death a Secret?"; "Paul's Mysterious Double – Who Is He?"; "The Death Clues, How the Public Found Out"; and "The Beatles Death Curse".

The *National Lampoon* Beatle issue was a totally irreverent look at the Fab Four with a cover that showed them being flattened by a steamroller on the Abbey Road zebra crossing. There is a spoof item on the "Paul Is Dead" theme, but the humour in general is of a sniggeringly sexual nature and is more tasteless than amusing.

The publication of Beatle magazines over the years may be seen as having three high points. The first followed their initial American impact; the second was occasioned by John's death in 1980; and the third commemorated the group's twentieth anniversary.

The John Lennon magazines published in America included *The Beatles Forever* (reprinted with some updated information from Ed Naha); *Beatles Memory Book* and *John Lennon and the Beatles, a Special Tribute* from Harris Publications; *John Lennon: All You Need Is Love* from Charlton Publications; *A Tribute to John Lennon and the Beatles* from US magazine; *John Lennon 1940-1980* and *John Lennon: the Legend* from S. J. Publications; *John Lennon Tribute* from Woodhill Press; *John Lennon: a Memorial Album* from Friday Publishing Corporation; *The World of John Lennon and the Beatles* from Graybar Publications; *Lennon: a Memory* from David Zentner Publications; *John Lennon: a Man Who Cared* from Paradise Press; *Sixteen Magazine: Presents John Lennon and the Beatles, A Loving Tribute; Teen Bag's Tribute to John Lennon* and *Lennon Photo Special* from Sunshine Publications.

JOHN LENNON
BEATLES MEMORY BOOK

BEATLEMANIA!
A TRIBUTE TO THE FAB FOUR AND THEIR MUSIC

THE 60's REMEMBERED
For Those Who Lived It... And Those Who Are Too Young To Remember!

THE COLLECTOR'S
Complete Written History

THE EARLY YEARS 1959 to 1962

THE BREAK UP!

JOHN LENNON
TRIBUTE
35p
COLLECTORS' ISSUE

THE PREMIERE
MEMORIAL EDITION

THE BEATLES

THE STORY
OF THE BEATLES

JOHN LENNON &
The BEATLES
A SPECIAL TRIBUTE

BEATLEMANIA!
The End Of An Era

THE FAB FOUR
A Time For Love,
A Time For Tears

JOHN & PAUL
TOGETHER
THEIR SONGS--
FOREVER

THE BEATLES...
From The Beginning

JOHN
WE LOVE YOU
Goodbye
To
Yesterday

The Greatest Collection Of BEATLE PIX You'll Ever See... The Way They Really Were

Undoubtedly, the best American tribute was the special issue of *Rolling Stone* magazine, dated 22 January 1981. This featured the famous Annie Leibovitz colour photograph of a naked John entwined around a clothed Yoko on the cover. Articles included "Inside the Dakota" by Gregory Katz; "For the Record" and "Radio: Tribal Drum" by Chet Flippo; "Sharing the Grief", a photospread; "Britain's Finest Hour" by Jan Morris; "Yoko and John" by Susan Brownmiller; "Life and Life Only" by Greil Marcus; "Ghoulish Beatlemania" by Dave Marsh; "A Portfolio", including a number of colour shots by Annie Leibovitz; "A Conversation" by Jonathan Cott; "Lennon Remembers" by Jan S.Wenner; "John Lennon, 1940-1980", a chronology with comments by celebrities; "A Reminiscence" by David Geffen; "Lennon's Music: a Range of Genius" by Stephen Holden; "The Last Session" by Kurt Loder and a discography.

On the whole the British tribute magazines were far better than their American counterparts, which were, in general, rather shoddy publications, rushed out with indecent haste. The British magazines were printed on better quality paper, included superior photo sections and more carefully considered articles. *John Lennon: Working Class Hero* was a large-sized, 40-page magazine written by Tony Tyler and Roy Carr. Tyler contributed "John Lennon 1940-1980", a history of John's life and career, while Roy Carr provided "John Lennon: A chronology". Published by IPC Publications, the magazine featured 70 black-and-white and 12 colour photographs.

John Lennon: The Life and Legend was a lavish *Sunday Times* special tribute with 36 colour shots and over 50 black-and-white photographs. Features included: "Twist and Shout: the Early Days and the Beatles Years" by Hunter Davies; "A Fan's Lament" by Susan Hill; "Some Time in New York City: Lennon After the Beatles" by Richard Williams; "Thank You Very Much and I Hope I've Passed the Audition" by Paul Gambaccini and "Some Days in the Life", a chronology by Mark Lewisohn.

John Lennon: a Melody Maker Tribute was edited by Ray Coleman and included half-a-dozen colour pics and 80 black-and-white photographs. Articles included "From the Mersey to Manhatten" by Ray Coleman; "Music and Blood of the Beatles" by Tony Barrow; "The Dreamweaver Lives Forever" by Patrick Humphries; a discography; "The Immortal Poet of Mersey Beat" by myself; and "John Lennon, In His Own Words", a selection of personal quotes.

In October 1982 a handful of special Beatle issues were published for the group's twentieth anniversary. The trade magazines *Music Week* and *Record Business* both paid their tributes and a few one-off magazines appeared that reflected the increasingly informative approach of later publications about the group. For example, the American *All About the Beatles*, issued in 1965 contained over 100 pictures and 75 pages, but its articles bore such titles as "This Is Your Life – by the Beatles Themselves"; "Girls and the Beatles"; "A Week with the Beatles" and "Give Yourself a Beatle Bob". 1982's *Rock Legends: the Beatles*; however, was firmly in the tradition of new Beatle magazines, being informative and less fannish. Compiled by Mike Davies and John Tobler, the magazine was a comprehensive A to Z of facts about the Fab Four with 30 colour shots and 14 black-and-white photographs.

Another early eighties highlight in Beatle magazine publishing was the 1982 anniversary magazine *It Was Twenty Years Ago Today*, published by Colourgold, and written by myself. It contained 65 colour photographs and, following an editorial, the articles were: "John Lennon 1940-1980"; "Paul McCartney"; "George Harrison"; "Ringo Starr"; "A Day in the Life", highlights from their career; "Tell Me Why", a Beatlequiz; "The Lonely Hearts Club Band", an article on Beatlefandom and details of 50 fanzines; "Yesterday", the Beatles Museums; and "Paperback Writer", reviews of a selection of Beatle books.

The specialist collector was catered for by *Beatle City Magazine*, a 1984 publication produced by Ian Wallace of Liverpool's the Beatles Shop; it mainly comprises photos and lists of the memorabilia obtainable at the shop, with a double-page colour poster and snippets of general information.

Mention also ought to be made of *Jamming!* a fanzine primarily concentrating on the eighties pop scene. Enterprising editor Tony Fletcher managed to secure a lengthy interview with Paul, which he serialised in two issues. This beautifully produced magazine testifies to the continued interest in information on the former Beatles.

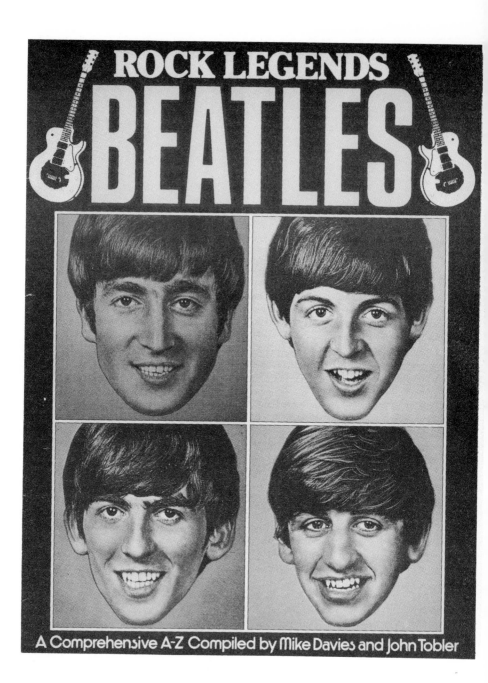

ROCK LEGENDS
BEATLES

A Comprehensive A-Z Compiled by Mike Davies and John Tobler

ANNIVERSARY

IT WAS 20 YEARS A

THE BEATLES IN PARTS

During the seventies, part works – expensively produced weekly magazines on a single subject that may be bound into a set of encyclopedias by the reader – became popular, especially in Britain, whence the idea originated. *The Story of Pop* was the first to cover the pop scene. Originally published in the early seventies by Phoebus Publishing, it proved so successful that a series of additional weekly parts was added to the original 26. The Beatles features were later gathered together in a hardbound volume, *The Beatles: the Fabulous Story of John, Paul, George and Ringo,* first published in 1975 and since reprinted.

Backtrack was an intriguing part work from Marshall Cavendish that attempted to cover the sixties. Unfortunately there was insufficient public interest to warrant completion of the series, which folded after four issues. I contributed several features on the beginnings of Mersey beat.

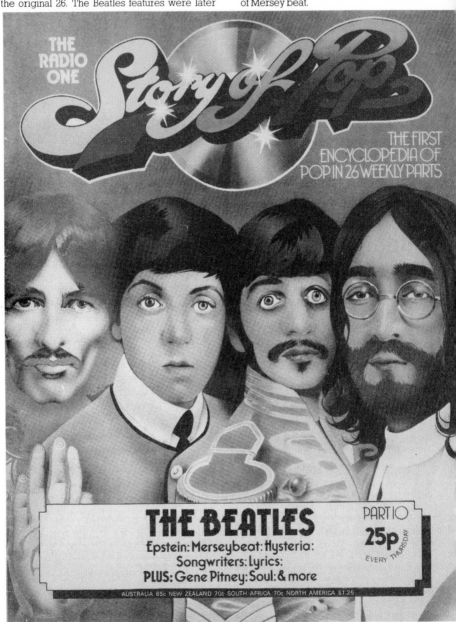

THE RADIO ONE

Story of Pop

THE FIRST ENCYCLOPEDIA OF POP IN 26 WEEKLY PARTS

THE BEATLES
Epstein: Merseybeat: Hysteria:
Songwriters: Lyrics:
PLUS: Gene Pitney: Soul: & more

PART 10
25p
EVERY THURSDAY

AUSTRALIA 65c NEW ZEALAND 70c SOUTH AFRICA 70c NORTH AMERICA $1.25

A Marshall Cavendish publication in 52 weekly parts

IR:90p UK:75p

Backtrack

PART 2
JANUARY-
FEBRUARY
1963

THE SCENE AND THE SOUNDS 1962-1972

SINGIN' THE BLUES

LITTLE MISS DYNAMITE

SHALL WE DANCE?

BEATLES BREAK THROUGH!

TOP 30 SINGLES

ROCK

The Beatles
1956-64

In 1982, Orbis Publishing began issuing *The History of Rock*, a massive review of the contemporary music scene from the early fifties to the eighties in over 120 parts. Three separate issues were devoted to the Beatles, and I contributed several features on the music scene in Liverpool in the early sixties.

London's Australasian Magazine

LAM

July 8-14 FREE

FLIGHT FREIGHT JOB MARKET

100th Issue

Kemsley Interviews
PAUL McCARTNEY

THE COMIC BOOK BEATLES

AT ONE TIME, LIVERPOOL WAS JUST A BIG PORT IN THE NORTH-WEST OF ENGLAND. A PLACE OF COMMERCE AND SHIP-BUILDING AND STAGE COMEDIANS.

THEN, ALMOST WITHOUT WARNING, THE ENTIRE IMAGE OF THE CITY CHANGED FOR EVER IN THE EYES OF THE WORLD..!

THEY WERE THE BEATLES... JOHN, PAUL, GEORGE AND RINGO. THE MOST DYNAMIC THING TO HAPPEN TO THE POP SCENE SINCE ELVIS PRESLEY.

♪ SHE LOVES YOU — YEAH, YEAH, YEAH... ♫

HISTORY WILL NEVER FORGET THEM. AND YET THEY WERE SUCH ORDINARY BOYS, FROM ORDINARY BACKGROUNDS.

JOHN'S STORY BEGAN AT THE HEIGHT OF AN AIR-RAID, ON THE NIGHT OF OCTOBER 9, 1940...

HEYY! WHAT ARE YOU DOING OUT? GET TO A SHELTER!

RUBBISH! MY SISTER'S HAD A BOY! A BEAUTIFUL BOY! I'M GOING TO TELL MY DAD!

MIMI STANLEY, JOHN LENNON'S AUNT. SHE WAS TO BRING HIM UP, IN THE COMFORTABLE SEMI-DETACHED HOME IN MENLOVE AVENUE, NEAR WOOLTON...

JOHN'S FATHER HAD LEFT, AND HIS MOTHER JULIA SAW HIM ONLY OCCASIONALLY.

AT FOUR, HE STARTED AT DOVEDALE PRIMARY SCHOOL, NOT FAR FROM A ROAD CALLED PENNY LANE...

HE WAS THERE AT THE SAME TIME AS GEORGE HARRISON, THOUGH GEORGE WAS TWO FORMS BELOW HIM...

DON'T KICK IT, HARRISON. JUST HAND IT TO US.

OKAY. HERE YOU GO.

THE COMIC BOOK BEATLES

Considering the number of magazines and books that have been pubished about the Beatles, comic strips about the group have been relatively rare. However the Beatles have been mentioned in various comics from time to time, most notably in Dell Comics' *Strange Tales,* No.130, March 1964. This issue featured a story entitled "Human Torch and the Thing Meet the Beatles". Dell also published a special Beatle comic in the autumn of 1964, named *The Beatles.* One of their "Dell Giant" series, this was a comic strip outlining the group's history to that date. There were also pin-up stories and some text on the individual members. In 1968 Gold Key Comics, published by the Western Publishing Company in the US, issued *Yellow Submarine,* which was the story of the film told in comic form.

The most interesting seventies comic-book venture concerning the Beatles was published in 1978 by Marvel Comics, one of the premier comic-book companies in the world. Unfortunately, the Marvel "Super Special", *The Beatles Story,* didn't quite live up to its promise.

Although Marvel have a reputation for producing comics with exciting visuals, the contributions of artists George Perez and Klaus Jenson to *The Beatles Story,* were somewhat crude and dated. Their illustrations seem to evoke the atmosphere of the forties rather than the sixties – for example Brian Epstein is shown, in Trilby and raincoat, stalking off into the rain like Dana Andrews at the end of some forties' mystery movie, despite the fact that hats had been out of fashion for men in Britain since the fifties. In addition, Liverpool's tiny Casbah club is depicted as a spacious night club, peopled by sophis-

ticated couples sitting at little round tables. In reality the cramped little cellar would have been packed, mainly with girls in their early teens. The Beatles themselves are shown using expensive equipment, whereas in those days, they didn't even have mike stands.

Perez and Jensen's story oversimplifies the Beatles' story, giving a false flavour to real events. For example, it appears as if the group first met Ringo Starr in Hamburg, whereas he had been a longstanding friend of theirs.

The Beatles are portrayed as a bunch of Cockneys in this comic, continually calling each other "mate", and using words like "ruddy" and "bloomin'". At one point Paul says: "This is ruddy insane, we're getting gongs!"; at another George says: "Stress doesn't bother me like it did before, mates"; and Ringo comments: "It'll tie in ruddy well with the TV taping, too".

No serious attempt has been made to capture the truth about the Beatles and their friends and associates, although clearly some picture research has been done.

Marvel's *The Beatles' Story* contains 39 pages of strip in colour, supplemented by several articles and photographs, including a pin-up poster, discography, filmography and group history.

The following year in the US the Pendulum "Illustrated Biography" series issued *Elvis Presley/the Beatles,* a comic book tracing the careers of both acts.

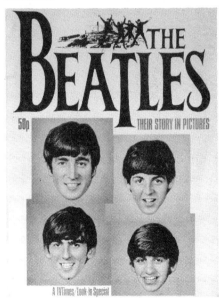

Perhaps the most significant strip devoted to the Beatles, however, appeared as a serial in the British teen paper *Look In* in 1981, under the name *The Beatles' Story.* The complete strip was published in April 1982 as a TV Times/Look In

Special. The strip was padded out with 13 photographs, three of which were in colour.

The strip's artist was Arthur Ranson and the text was written by Angus P. Allan. Ranson produced some lovely black-and-white drawings, based on well known Beatles' photographs. Unfortunately, the words that Allan put into the Beatles' mouths were not as accurately conceived as the illustrations, though their absurdity is, at times, extremely amusing.

On the night of 9 October 1940, against a sky lit by the flares of exploding bombs, an air-raid warden cries out to a hurrying woman: "Hey! What are you doing out? Get to a shelter!" The lady replies: "Rubbish! My sister's had a boy! A beautiful boy! I'm going to tell my Dad!" The boy is, of course, John Lennon.

Little John is later shown at Dovedale Primary School talking to another little toddler called George Harrison who is holding a ball. John says: "Don't kick it, Harrison. Just hand it to us." The smiling little boy replies: "Okay. Here you go." The next picture shows young Paul saying to George: "Come on, Harrison. Won't your Dad give us a ride in the cab?" George replies: "It's against the rules, McCartney. Even I can't get a go."

At another point in the story, a worried mum looks at a bedridden boy and says: "Don't worry, Ritchie. The Doctor's coming. . ." He replies: "It's – me stomach – Mam! It's – agony!"

These incidental gems alone are worth the price of the comic: events that probably never occured, with dialogue that was never uttered, all dramatically highlighted by exclamation and question marks. Reading the book, one might assume that it tells the Beatles' story as it happened, albeit in a simplified form – but in fact this strip is a pop-art creation in its own right.

A young John, enviously eyeing two Teddy Boys says: "I wouldn't half like some clothes like that, Mimi." His Auntie replies: "What? A lad who's going to Quarry Bank Grammar School?" She continues: "Done up like a yobo? Never! It's bad enough having to live, day in, day out, with those awful Elvis whatsit records of yours. You'll have to think again, John." A "thinks" bubble, inscribed "We'll see, Mimi. We'll see. . .", appears over John's little face. John is apparently gifted with second sight about his glorious future. When a schoolmaster at Quarry Bank says to him: "What's the matter with you, boy? Your work's a shambles. Don't you care about ANY-THING?" He glibly replies: "Can't help the way I'm made sir." The strip, rather than depict the heartaches and difficulties the boys faced in their early years, simply attempts to make the reader a co-conspirator in their seemingly irresistible rise to stardom.

There are nice little touches of accuracy, such as "The War Office" sign on the entrance to one of the rooms in Ye Cracke where John and Stu Sutcliffe are pictured. Yet these are offset by textual errors or at least chronic oversimplifications, as in the event leading to the "sacking" of Pete Best. George Martin complains to Brian Epstein that Pete's not a good drummer and Brian is worried because "Pete Best's a very popular boy". (In fact he was *the* most popular Beatle at the time.) Brian tells the boys and George says, in apparent alarm: "You mean we've got to sack him." In reality George was one of the members who most wanted Pete shoved out. Brian then informs Pete, who merely says: "Oohh! It's taken them two years to find out I'm not a good enough drummer!"

Thus in this comic-book version, even the most awkward moments in the Beatles' career are imbued with the sweetness and light of a fairy story. John phones Ringo, he joins them, leaving Rory Storm and the Hurricanes. Above a picture of a smiling Rory Storm appear the following words: "Like Pete Best, Rory Storm was philosophical about Ringo's transfer. . ." He says: "Good luck. From what I hear, those Beatles might be going places."

The real story is much more complex; Rory had initially visited Ringo's mother in order to persuade her to let Ringo go to Butlin's in Skegness as he was due to leave the Hurricanes to take up an apprenticeship. Rory then talked Ringo into staying with his group for the season. When the Beatles' offer came up, Rory explained to Brian Epstein that he and the Hurricanes needed Ringo to complete their season at Butlin's. Brian agreed, but Ringo refused to fulfill the remaining few weeks of engagements with the Hurricanes and walked out. Without their drummer, Rory and his band were sacked by Butlin's. Rory resented Ringo's behaviour and commented in *Mersey Beat:* "Now he's only a backing drummer, the Beatles front line is so good he doesn't have to do much. This is not the Ringo Starr who played with us."

A box states that after the Beatles had had a No. 1 with 'Please Please Me' and Gerry and the Pacemakers had hit the top with 'How Do You Do It?', "all sorts of Mersey groups began to record". The text goes on to mention acts such as Lee Curtis and Howie Casey and the Seniors. In fact, Howie and his band were the first Mersey beat group to make a record – prior to the Beatles. Lee Curtis also had had a record released (on Decca) before the Beatles. It is often forgotten that the Mersey scene was alive and flourishing years before the Beatles began making records. The text implies that the entire Liverpool scene grew up overnight as soon as the Beatles had entered the charts.

These criticisms aside, the strip remains very enjoyable entertainment and is well worth perusing.

BRIGITTE BARDOT WAS JOHN LENNON'S FAVOURITE ACTRESS. SHE WAS HIS "PERFECT IMAGE OF A WOMAN" SAID HIS FIRST WIFE CYNTHIA, WHO EMULATED THE FRENCH STAR'S DRESS SENSE AND HAIRSTYLE.

"ALL ABOUT THE BEATLES" WAS AN ALBUM OF RADIO INTERVIEWS CONDUCTED BY GEORGE'S SISTER LOUISE HARRISON CALDWELL. ISSUED IN 1965 ON REDCAR RECORDS IT CONSISTED OF EXCERPTS OF HER DISCUSSIONS ABOUT THE GROUP ON FIVE U.S. RADIO STATIONS.

AN EARLY PSEUDONYM FOR PAUL McCARTNEY WAS PAUL RAMON. HE HAS SINCE USED SEVERAL OTHERS, INCLUDING BERNARD WEBB (WHEN HE PENNED PETER & GORDON'S "WOMAN") AND APOLLO C. VERMOUTH (FOR HIS BONZO DOG DOO DAH BAND RECORDINGS).

THE BEATLES MADE THEIR CAVERN DEBUT ON MARCH 21-1961

THE CONCERT FOR BANGLA DESH WAS A 99 MINUTE COLOUR FILM PRODUCED BY GEORGE HARRISON & ALLEN KLEIN AND DIRECTED BY SAUL SWIMMER. RELEASED IN 1972, THE FILM COVERED THE SPECIAL MADISON SQUARE GARDEN CONCERT IN AID OF BANGLA DESH WHICH DREW AN AUDIENCE OF 40,000 PEOPLE ON AUGUST 1st, 1971. GEORGE, BACKED BY KLAUS VOORMAN, LEON RUSSELL AND ERIC CLAPTON, PERFORMED "WAH WAH", "MY SWEET LORD", "BEWARE OF DARKNESS" AND "WHILE MY GUITAR GENTLY WEEPS." RINGO STARR ALSO APPEARED AT THE CONCERT AND IS FILMED PERFORMING "IT DON'T COME EASY" AND "HERE COMES THE SUN." THE FILM ENDED WITH GEORGE'S RENDITION OF HIS OWN COMPOSITION "BANGLA DESH."

JOHNNY & THE MOONDOGS WAS A NAME USED BY JOHN, PAUL & GEORGE WHEN THEY ENTERED THE CARROLL LEVIS DISCOVERIES COMPETITION AT THE EMPIRE THEATRE, LIVERPOOL IN 1958. THEIR REPERTOIRE CONSISTED MAINLY OF BUDDY HOLLY NUMBERS AND ALTHOUGH THEY REACHED THE FINALS, THE COMPETITION WAS WON BY A GROUP CALLED THE GLADIATORS.

"BEATLE NUT" WAS AN ICE CREAM PRODUCED IN AMERICA IN 1964

AN AMERICAN SERIES OF CARTOONS OF THE BEATLES, COMPRISING 52 EPISODES, WAS FIRST SCREENED IN 1965. NO LIVERPOOL ACCENTS WERE USED AS IT WAS THOUGHT THAT THE AMERICAN PUBLIC WOULD NOT UNDERSTAND THEM.

CILLA BLACK HAD THE UNIQUE OPPORTUNITY OF RECORDING LENNON & McCARTNEY NUMBERS WHEN THE BEATLES WERE BECOMING THE MOST INFLUENTIAL GROUP IN THE WORLD. "LOVE OF THE LOVED" DIDN'T DO WELL FOR HER AND IT TOOK THE TALENTS OF TWO OTHER SONGWRITERS, BACHARACH & DAVID, TO PLACE HER HIGH IN THE BRITISH CHARTS WITH "ANYONE WHO HAD A HEART" AND "YOU'RE MY WORLD."

THERE WERE HUNDREDS OF BEATLE NOVELTY DISCS RANGING FROM THE BANAL TO THE BIZARRE, FROM "FRANKENSTEIN MEETS THE BEATLES" TO "TO KILL A BEATLE."

Two years ago I realised that despite having studied for so long at Liverpool College of Art and having received all the necessary diplomas, I had never put my training to use (I'd begun Mersey Beat while at college and have been writing about music ever since). In 1982 I decided to begin my own comic strip of the Beatles called "The Beatles File", which I hope will eventually become a daily comic strip in some enterprising newspaper!

THE WORLD OF BEATLEZINES

THE WORLD OF BEATLEZINES

Fanzines – limited-circulation publications run by enthusiasts to circulate information, provide news and to link up with people who share the same interests – are a unique form of communication. They are different from mainstream publications in that they are generally run at a loss and rarely at a profit and have different aims. They range from simple, duplicated newssheets to immaculately produced magazines. Beatle fanzines come in all shapes and sizes, each one having a "personality" of its own. They range from Club Sandwich, the glossy full-colour publication produced by the Wings Fun Club, to the modest but vital, duplicated production the *McCartney Observer*. For some reason, many fanzines have adopted the size and format of *Beatles Monthly*, as if their aim were to emulate that worthy and professional publication.

Beatle fanzines really took off in the seventies, although there were several in existence in the sixties. The number of fanzines has increased in recent years and in the early eighties there were no less than 80 different Beatle fan mags world-wide. Many fall by the wayside, some survive for a number of years and then mysteriously disappear; this may be due to what the sci-fi fanzines call GAFIA (Gone Away From It All), a state in which a formerly active fan ceases to put out his publication for various reasons, ranging from loss of interest to change of address. Something of this kind must have happened to *Strawberry Fields Forever,* one of the most prominent of the American fanzines of the seventies, run by a fan called Joe Pope. Another first-class British fan magazine, *Come Together,* edited by Carl Dunkley, has also not appeared in print since 1982. It had a clear layout, superb photographic reproduction, stiff covers, and informative articles from a number of top-rank contributors that included David Hayles, Richard Buskin and Steve Baker. The last issue was No.13, published in newspaper tabloid size, although the heavy quality of the paper was far superior to usual newspaper-style production. The cover featured a large photograph of Paul, some record reviews and an editorial from Carl, which ended: "We can look forward to a brighter future." Page two provided a lengthy review of *Take It Away* by Richard Buskin, and further record reviews by J.Murray; page three comprised a complete John Lennon discography; and the fourth and final page included news, a crossword and book and record reviews.

Yoko Only is a fan club devoted to Yoko, situated at 61 Middle Drive, Toms River, NJ 08753, USA. There is also a fan club for Mike McCartney called Gear Box; and for fans seeking Beatle-loving pen pals, there is Apple's Kin, run by Katie Collard of 1751 N.Grand W. No.73, Springfield IL 62702, USA. *Yesterday* is the title of the magazine produced by the Beatles Fan Club of Austria from Prehausergasse 2, 1130 Wien, Austria and *Beat Land* is produced by the West Midland Beatles Club, c/o J.R.Smith, 98 Glenpark Road, Alum Rock, Birmingham, B8 3QN.

I have selected a number of fanzines that I receive regularly and regard as among the most durable. All of them are worth supporting and I suggest that you initially send a stamped addressed envelope (or International Reply Coupon for overseas enquiries) when you write for information requesting subscription fees.

There are fanzines in almost every Western country, and new ones are appearing even as I write. For any future editions of *Paperback Writers,* I would appreciate information and sample copies of any fanzines not featured in this section of the book.

The fanzines reviewed are:

BEATLES VISIE

THE FAB FOUR PUBLICATION

FROM ME TO YOU

THE WRITE THING

BEATLEFAN

LIVE

BEATLES VIDEO NEWSLETTER

REVOLVER

THE HARRISON ALLIANCE

INSTANT KARMA

RAM ON!

BEATLES NOW

CLUB SANDWICH

RINGO

CAVERN MECCA

MAXWELL'S SILVER HAMMER

DARK HORSE

MY SWEET LADY JANE

BEATLES BEAT

BEATLES UNLIMITED

GOOD DAY SUNSHINE

THE McCARTNEY OBSERVER

TOMORROW NEVER KNOWS

Beatles Visie

14

THE FAN MAGAZINES

BEATLES VISIE

Johnny te Lintelo, the Dutch Beatles Fan Club, PO Box 1464, 1000 BL Amsterdam, the Netherlands
This is the official magazine of the Dutch Beatles Fan Club, founded by Har von Fulpen on 10 November 1963 with official permission from the Beatles and EMI Records. Its editor, Johnny te Lintelo, comments: "Since that date we've been active in many ways. Our fan club magazine was our most important activity and it changed three times during the next 20 years. From November 1963, until February 1970, it was called *Chains*. It then became an irregular newsletter appearing from September 1970 until April 1976. It then became a magazine until December 1979. In March 1980, the new fan club magazine *Beatle Visie* was launched and this appears four times a year in March, June, September and December."

The club is the longest-lasting Beatle fan club of all and their magazine, therefore, was the first Beatle fanzine ever published. The club has issued numerous posters, calendars and printed merchandise, and organised several popular conventions.

If we take Issue No. 14 of *Beatles Visie* as a fair sample, it has a green card cover in the popular *Beatles Monthly* size, with a drawn heading and a photo of the Fab Four beneath it. There are approximately 24 illustrations and the contents include an editorial, fan-club information, a Beatles puzzle, a report on a Wings trip to Switzerland, reviews of 17 records, general Beatle news, a report on the Amsterdam Convention, an article on Ringo's "Scouse the Mouse" project; part 13 of "The Beatles Story"; a comic strip illustrating 'She's Leaving Home' and several smaller articles.

THE FAB FOUR

NUMÉRO DOUBLE 23 et 24 - octobre 1982 - 9ᵉ ANNÉE - PUBLICATION

THE FAB FOUR PUBLICATION

Le Club des 4 de Liverpool, 43 bis, Boulevard Henri IV, 75004 Paris, France

Jacques Volcouve began his organisation in the early seventies. He comments: "In 1972 a French radio station, Europe No.1, began a translation of "The Beatles Story" series, which had originally been made by the BBC. When I started listening to the programme I was delighted but I felt that a number of mistakes had crept into the story and went to see the journalist who adapted it into French. He checked and discovered that everything I told him was accurate. We then worked together and developed the original story from a twelve-hour programme to one which lasted for sixteen hours. It was broadcast three times between 1972 and 1973.

"We received thirteen thousand letters and suddenly realised that the Beatles were more popular in France than when they were still together. I wanted to start something more important than a fan club: a kind of press agency and information centre dealing with the career of the Beatles and also their solo work. There were so many mistakes being printed about them that I started Le Club des 4 de Liverpool with the magazine *The Fab Four Publication.*" The aim: "To try to explain the social and musical impact of the Beatles as a group and individually."

The size and thickness of this publication has varied, but the quality of the printing has always been first class. It is printed on glossy paper similar to *Beatles Monthly.* The double issue No.22/23 features 64 pages and 59 photographs, some of them printed across two pages. The cover design depicts the heads of the four in their Sgt. Pepper days, and the cover photo shows John with his outstretched arms, wearing his "Eggman" hat by the side of his psychedelic Rolls. There are numerous photos from the set of *Magical Mystery Tour,* showing the boys in their fancy-dress costumes for the Royal Lancaster Hotel party; chatting with 73-year-old Soho character, Bill Davies; Paul in the garden of his London house, playing with his sheepdog Martha; and Yoko outlining her plans for Strawberry Fields in Central Park. There is an editorial; an article on Strawberry Fields; "The Four Magicians", a piece about the *Magical Mystery Tour* film; a review of the songs from *Magical Mystery Tour* and a discography.

FROM ME TO YOU: Das Magazin Uber Die Beatles
Peter Schuster, Postfach 555, 6430 Bed Hersfeld, West Germany

Glossy magazine in German that contains an English section and is edited by Peter Schuster, who was born in March 1963 and didn't really become interested in the Beatles until the early seventies. He began publishing *From Me to You* in July 1978, when still at school.

Taking No.13, published in July 1981, as a sample issue, it has a blue cover, with a black-and-white photograph of George inserted in the centre. The 28-page issue contains 20 interior photos and the poster from *Caveman* as the backcover. It is in the popular *Beatles Monthly* size and the articles include "Ringo and Barbara," with details of their wedding; reviews of the film *Caveman* and the LP *Somewhere in England;* book reviews and several pages of news items. The English insert is eight pages long, printed on blue paper and contains news stories illustrated with two photographs.

THE WRITE THING
Barb Fenick, 3310 Roosevelt Ct, Minneapolis, MN 55418, USA

Barb Fenick is one of America's leading Beatle fans and has been publishing *The Write Thing* since 1973. She is also author of the book *Collecting the Beatles* and the fanzine mirrors her interest in memorabilia. It has a membership of over 2,000 readers throughout the world, in 48 states in the US, in Canada, Mexico, Central and South America, Australia, New Zealand, Japan and Britain. Barb comments: "Our members range in age from eight years old to folk in their fifties and we have one family of two generations enrolled as members. The average age of our readers these days is the early twenties, surprising when you consider these fans were only two or three years old when the Beatles first burst into fame in the early sixties. Once the majority of Beatle fans were young girls only, today it is even, with perhaps the males taking a bit of a lead as more and more young men get into the collecting side of fandom."

Barb began her first Beatle fan club in 1967. "I first began it as a hobby, just to unite my friends and penpals. But from word-of-mouth and a few ads in the Teen mags, it grew to about 300 in 1968. At that time the 'independent' fan clubs (as they were called then), really proliferated. At one point there were nearly 200 of them in the US alone. While Beatles Ltd was doing an excellent job in Britain, the Stateside branch had floundered under mismanagement, so there was a need for individuals to run their own organisations. Of course, the inevitable happened: Beatles USA Ltd reorganised itself and tried to pull together all of the 'unofficial' branches. It became almost a pitched battle with fan against fan as some clubs were absorbed into the 'official chapter' status, others folded under pressure and a few, like my own 'Beatles Rule' club, stubbornly continued as an independent, which was supposed to be illegal. I felt I was doing just fine without any supervision and my members agreed.

"Today, there are only a few fan clubs around but they are better organised, and thus more efficient in handling a large number of fans all over the world."

Taking Issue No.36 of *The Write Thing*, dated March/April 1982, as a sample, it is a large-sized, stapled magazine of 28 pages, packed with information and photographs. The photographs, in particular, are well researched; there are over 30 of them in this issue, which displays a portrait of George and a shot of Paul playing guitar on the cover. Contents include an editorial; a sales page with offers of photos, records, books and magazines; letters; convention news; "December 8th" (an article on Yoko on the anniversary of John's death); "Collector's Column" – an essential source of information for the collector; "Collecting Video," details of Beatles' videos; "Collecting the Beatles," a feature on collecting by Barb; contests; small ads; fan directory; reviews; a feature on Ringo; stories of close encounters with Paul and Mike McCartney by Gloria Rossie and Debbie Gendler; publishing news, book reviews and general news stories.

The Write Thing is probably the best choice of fanzine for a fan who wants to collect Beatles' memorabilia as its information is helpful, informative and knowledgeable.

143

BEATLEFAN
William P.King, The Goody Press, PO Box 33515,
Decatur, GA 30033, USA

Bill King is the music/radio editor of the *Atlanta Constitution,* a major morning daily newspaper, and his wife Leslie is editor of a national magazine for salespeople. They started *Beatlefan* in October 1978, with the first issue appearing in December 1978. They considered that most of the existing fanzines at the time "were run by fan clubs, by amateurs with rather poor reproduction and articles consisting mainly of gushy accounts of near-miss encounters with the Fab Four and lots of unsubstantiated rumours." Bill commented: "Since in my capacity as a music editor I deal with all the major record companies (and have interviewed one Beatle – George Harrison in '76), I had access to all the latest hard news about the group. And as a dedicated follower of the band since 1964 and a veteran collector, I had the background. Being professional journalists, we felt we could combine our interests – Beatles and publishing – into a Beatles fanzine like no other. We also determined it should be run like any professional publication – with display advertising (an innovation in Beatles fanzines) and with regular deadlines, an area in which the other fanzines were very weak. We have never missed an issue since we started and come out regularly every two months.

"We are the biggest US Beatle publication in terms of editorial volume. We run it as a business but it is, of course, not yet a profitable venture. We underwrite the expenses because we enjoy putting it out."

Taking issue No.2, Vol.3, as an example, *Beatlefan* features an excellent black-ink drawing of John Lennon by Jaimie Sustaita on its cover; page two features the first page of "Beatlenews Roundup", which is crammed with news items concerning the activities of individual Beatles. There is an editorial letter from Bill King, then a five-page transcript of a John Lennon/Yoko Ono interview conducted at the Dakota Bulding on 8 December 1980, entitled "The Final Interview." "Some Outtakes From Beatles History" by Nicholas Schaffner details certain little-known facts about Beatle discs. "Collecting Beatles Picture Discs" follows, and an article called "Cavern Mecca Opens in Liverpool" concerns the opening of the Beatles Museum on 3 January 1981. "Fanscene", by myself covers news from the fan world and "Instant Memories Flooding Market" is a guide to the numerous publications issued as a tribute to John Lennon following his death. There is a review of Paul McCartney's *Rockshow* film and several further quotes about the Lennon killing and a "Lennon Discography." *Beatlefan* letters, record reviews and Beatle Bookshelf are regular items, as are the pen pals and classified ads pages. "Thingumybob" is a column by various contributors on Beatle subjects and "Beatles Almanack" is an occasional feature. Lou O'Neill Jr pens his impressions of a meeting with the Fabs in the "Meeting the Beatles" article, which is a regular feature.

ᵽeatlefan

Vol. 3   Box 33515, Decatur, GA 30033   No. 2

JOHN LENNON

Artwork by Jaime Sustaita.

The Final Interview

Conclusion Of The McCartney Interview	Nicholas Schaffner's Outtakes From Beatles History	Collecting Beatles Picture Discs

LIVE

Henrique Carballal Alvarez, Caixa Postal 24, 036 Tijuca, RJ, CEP 20. 650, Brazil

This Brazilian fanzine was launched in January 1977. Taking issue No.25 as an example, it is a 20-page foolscap magazine, duplicated, but with very clear reproduction. The cover is a photograph of John pulling on his tongue and is about the only illustration in the entire magazine. Since the publication is not in English, the observations I can make about its contents are limited, but it carries an editorial; an interview with Paul lifted from *The Musician: Player & Listener;* album, book, film and concert reviews; letter pages; a Beatles' Items for Sale column and classified ads.

BEATLES VIDEO NEWSLETTER

Gloria Patti and John Dobrydnio, 184 Emerson Street Springfield, Mass. 01118, USA

This bi-monthly newsletter was launched in May 1983 by two 22-year-old fans, Gloria Patti and John Dobrydnio, who explain: "We've been Beatle fans our whole lives. We're also collectors and since video has become so popular we've found Beatles video the most exciting thing to collect. When we realised that there was no fanzine devoted entirely to video we decided to start one." They intend to expand the size of their newsletter as their list of subscribers grows.

If we take issue No.2 as a sample, it has ten large pages and features eight photographs. Contents include a story on the making of *Princess Daisy* with Ringo and Barbara; an article on the career of Richard Lester; a review of the video tape of the 1966 concerts at the Budokan Hall in Tokyo; news of the Johnny Carson movie of John and Yoko's life together; advice on trading videos, as well as letters, news items and classified ads.

REVOLVER
Gwyn Jenkins, 37 Hare Hill Close, Pyrford, Woking, Surrey, GU22 8UH

This enterprising publication was launched by Gwyn Jenkins in 1982, when he was just 16 years old. He comments: "On a rainy day in August '82 I was bored, so I wrote, designed and produced the first issue. *Revolver's* original intention was to be an outlet for opinions by fans from Woking Sixth Form College and to keep them informed of the latest news, thus the fanzine was originally entitled "The Beatles Unofficial Fan Club Magazine." After starting at Woking College, I showed the issue to Beatle pal Alistair Morton, who was impressed with it. Alistair insisted that I show it to Beatle freaks Rob Turner and Phil Wood, who we had met at college. We came to the unanimous conclusion that the fanzine should be produced for college Beatle fans every month. The magazine continued to be a regular event, with students contributing in addition to regulars Rob, Phil and Ali. The magazine was expanding rapidly and in the third issue an old friend, Paul Wightman, began contributing regularly. Paul has consequently designed the headings and logos for the magazine. After the Christmas issue we decided to change our name and style, because we were gaining readership outside the college. *Revolver* in its present form was born in January 1983, and continued to expand, gaining more readers all the time. In Issue Seven we changed from a monthly to a bi-monthly fanzine."

Issue No.9 features Paul and George on the cover. The contents are printed in litho from handwritten material, nicely drawn in a plain, bold style and illustrations average about ten per issue. Following the editorial there is a feature on Paul's singles; a report on a visit to Friar Park in Henley; reviews of 'From Me to You', *The Beatles' Black Album; Live at Washington Colliseum; John Lennon Telecasts; Wings Over Wembley '79* and *John, Paul, George, Ringo and Bert.* There are news items and an article on John's experimental albums *Two Virgins* and *Life With the Lions.*

The Harrison Alliance

THE HARRISON ALLIANCE

Patti Murawski, 67 Cypress Street, Bristol, CT
06010, USA

This magazine was originally launched in 1972 by Pamela Elijah of Goshen, Indiana, USA. Pamela was the former Vice President of the Official George Harrison Chapter of the Official Beatles (USA) Fan Club prior to its closing. Patti Murawski had written a few articles for the early issues and when Pamela decided to give up directing the magazine in 1974, Patti was asked if she would agree to continue with the publication. She then took charge in April 1974, her first project being the production of issue No.13 in June of that year.

Patti has a degree in English and a career in the graphic arts/printing/publishing industry. Her assistant and Vice President of the club is Jennie Swenton. Patti comments: "The Harrison Alliance is a grassroots organisation. Like the *McCartney Observer* and *With a Little Help From My Friends,* THA's foundation was built on popular support of the Beatles by First Generation fans. We listen to our membership and try to provide a cross-section of the features that are in demand. Jennie and I see *THA* as a society of George fans trying to catch glimpses of George-the-human-being, through his art, through interviews, through his past with the Beatles etc. I feel there is a place for both our kind of organisation and the collector's/commercial/consumer-oriented fanzines. We have a personal and human interest in George that most commercial and collector's magazines tend to shun. We are not so much interested in the trivia (though we do include it) as we are in George's thoughts, emotions and beliefs, hence the transcripts of interviews and the personal encounter

articles (one feature that is in constant demand). We try to provide material that many of our members would not normally have seen in their part of the world (we have members in 14 countries, but our membership is largely American). We also include news columns concerning the other three members of the Beatles.

"We sometimes find issues are difficult to fill, however, with a staff of only two volunteers (Jennie and myself). We do have one correspondent, Kris Spackman, who writes a column on Ringo for us on a regular basis, but as far as actual production and organisational duties, it is just Jennie and myself. Time was, we could put out a bi-monthly magazine. Over the past few years we have only been managing an average of four issues a year."

Issue No.48 of *The Harrison Alliance* has an editorial by Patti on George's record releases, while "Read All About It" covers news on George and is illustrated by a drawing which George originally contributed to Derek Taylor's book *Fifty Years Adrift (In an Open-Necked Shirt).* There is a reproduction of a *Sun* newspaper article "I'm George, Not a Beatle" and a lengthy section "Good Morning Australia," which is the transcript of his Australian television interview in March 1982. "Dakota Territory" is Jennie Swenton's coverage of Yoko Ono news and she also covers McCartney information in "Get Your Wings." "Starr Gazing," by Kris Spackman, concerns recent events in the life and career of Ringo. The publication is well produced and contains two pages of information on obtaining various Beatle photographs.

"Peace is a very good thing, and so is salmon when it's smoked."
Sean Ono Lennon

INSTANT KARMA
Marsha Ewing, PO Box 256, Sault Ste. Mre. Michigan 49783, USA

This magazine was launched in December 1981 by Marsha Ewing, who comments: "It was an effort on my part to get in touch with other John Lennon admirers who were as devastated by his death as I was. Also, after subscribing to a few other fanzines, I felt that there was a need for a magazine that shifted the emphasis from Paul to John and Yoko. I have always respected and admired Yoko and felt she was receiving very little respect from the more Beatle-oriented fanzines. With a background in writing and a huge stock of Beatle articles and photos from 1964 onwards, I decided that I could put together a decent fanzine for John and Yoko fans to enjoy.

"Instant Karma is not an authoritative source for Beatle trivia, chronological information, facts and figures. We are a more personal, member-oriented fanzine. I started the fanzine to get in touch with other people's feelings, and it turns out that other fans' feelings are what members are most interested in. I feature an editorial page, which I either write myself or open up to a member each issue. We also delve into people's thoughts and feelings in a regular feature called 'Mind Games'. It's one of the most popular features that we have. I also use Instant Karma for a handgun control vehicle each issue, with 'Season That Never Passes.' One poem (and sometimes two if I'm playing catch-up) is featured each issue, along with lots of news, especially news about Yoko, 'The Ballad of John & Yoko,' members' articles (I rely on members to supply me with any collected info, reviews etc) and as often as possible, fan meetings with Yoko/Beatles.

"I am the sole editor, but do get input from regular correspondents in England, Japan, Ireland and Belgium, with special mention to Tony Gorse in England. It's mostly a one-person effort from the standpoint of layout, typing, arranging and finally mailing. We switched from xeroxing to professional printing at the onset of 1983 and our issues have generally averaged between 40 to 60 pages, although we did once have a 96-page issue."

A typical example of Instant Karma is Issue No. 10 which was a cover shot of Sean Ono Lennon on Yoko's knee, smiling and giving the "Victory V" sign, below which is printed his quote: "Peace is a very good thing, and so is salmon when it's smoked." Following the editorial there are poems by Dorothy Hatchett and Michelle Dwoskin; "Straight Talk" is the readers' letters section, which contains viewpoints about the books The Love You Make and John Lennon – A Family Album. "Instant News" is a comprehensive news section, followed by "News From England", compiled by Tony Gorse. The centrepage is a shot of Yoko, Sean and staff at New Year 1981. "New York Adventure" is a close encounter account by some fans who met Yoko and Sean near Central Park. Tom Ewing interviews John Green, a former Tarot reader for the Lennons and author of Dakota Days. "Crime: Japan Vs the U.S." reveals that Yoko's brother-in-law pleaded with her to return to Japan following John's murder and that the US has 10 times more murders and 25 times the amount of rapes as Japan. There is a transcript of an interview with Yoko conducted by Paul Cook of London's Capital Radio. "Mind Games" is a section in which readers comment on a particular issue and the subject is: "Why the deep sense of loss shown world-wide at John's death. . .continues even today." "Fixing a Hole – The Video Trader" concerns video information and "How I Write a Hit Song by Paul McCartney" has been adapted from a conversation Paul had with George Martin. "Secrets of a Starminder: The Truth About Paul McCartney's Drug Bust" is the final article before the small ads and pen pals section. The 64 pages contain a great deal of reading material and almost 50 illustrations.

RAM ON!
David Dunn, 14 Clincarthill Road, Rutherglen, Glasgow, G73 2LG

Soft Touch was a fanzine launched in March 1981 by C.McMillan. His part-time assistant Dave Dunn took over the publication after issue No.4. Dave, a Scottish student, initially ran a George Harrison fanzine, but comments: "Unfortunately, it only lasted fourteen issues due to a lack of interest in George Harrison." He immediately launched a new bi-monthly fanzine called *Ram On*, aimed at Paul McCartney/Beatle fans. The fanzine then became incorporated in the Paul McCartney Fan Club of Scotland, which also runs conventions and Beatle discos.

Issue No.6 features Paul in a sweatshirt playing guitar. There is an editorial page followed by reprints of an article covering John and Yoko's astrological signs; a page of Macca photos; information on Derek Taylor's *Fifty Years Adrift (In an Open-Necked Shirt)*; a range of reprints of newspaper articles covering Mike McGear's book; the cover story from the *Scottish Evening Times* announcing John's murder; and Beatle quotes. Other items include a review of *Gone Troppo* and a Mersey Beatle convention, news and information on obtaining Beatles' records. There are approximately 40 photographs in the 34-page issue.

BEATLES NOW
Roger Akehurst, PO Box 307, Walthamstow, London, E17 4LL

A bi-monthly glossy magazine, basically the same size as *Beatles Monthly*, that includes colour photographs. It was launched by Roger in January 1982. He'd originally had the idea of producing a Beatle magazine on his return from a convention in Liverpool in the seventies. Aided by assistant editor David J.Smith and an editorial staff that includes Stephen Baker, Daniel Beller, Steve Phillips and Mark Wallgren, Roger intends to continue to improve the publication and hopes to extend distribution to newspaper stands.

Issue No.7, dated July/September 1983, features a colour photograph of a bearded John, emerging from a doorway. The back cover is a colour shot of Paul. There is an editorial, followed by a column on Beatles' records by Mark Wallgren (author of *The Beatles on Record*). Dave Smith contributes two pages of news, and an intriguing article by John Squire, entitled "Lennon & the No.9 Connection," details John's obsession with the number 9 and its impact on his life. Readers' letters and "The Beatles Detective" precede a centre-page photo of Ringo, which is followed by a report on Beatlefest '83, "15 'New' Beatles Singles" by Mark Wallgren and a Beatleologist 1983 page, compiled by Terry Payne and Colin Jennings. The Beatleologist page is a well researched series of questions and answers pertaining to the Fab Four's life and career. Ads play a part in the visual appeal of *Beatles Now* and are also informative. Apart from the classified ads section, there are ads for Beatle books, the Abbey Road Studios and several fanzines. Artist Noel Bruan contributes an excellent sketch of John and Ringo, and approximately ten photographs illustrate the issue.

BEATLES NOW

15 UNPUBLISISED BEATLES SINGLES

NOT FOR SALE: THE 12" MOVIE MEDLEY

NEW YORK CONVENTION REPORT

ALL THE LATEST NEWS

WAS JOHN'S LIFE GOVERNED BY THE NUMBER NINE?

CLUB SANDWICH

Wings Fun Club, PO Box 4UP, London, W1A 4UP

This is the official magazine issued by MPL Communications, Paul's company; although aimed at fans, it is too professionally produced to qualify for the term fanzine. It is a giant-sized publication with superbly reproduced colour and black-and-white photographs, printed on coated art paper. *Club Sandwich* has been appearing regularly for several years and always contains exclusive stories and photographs of the McCartneys' world, including many shots from Linda and occasional news of the other ex-Beatles.

Issue No.28, published at Christmas 1982, is a typically lavish production. It is 24-pages in length and sports a colour cover featuring Paul, Linda, Ringo and Barbara in Victorian costume. Contents include a Christmas tree-shaped crossword; a column of news stories; a colour photo-spread of shots from the location filming of *Give My Regards to Broad Street;* "Twenty Years Ago," a tribute to the Beatles' anniversary, with a selection of pictures; "Looking Back on '82," a photo round-up of Paul's activities the previous year; "Listen to What the Fans Said," a letters' column; and a Linda McCartney Christmas recipe for cranberry sauce. The largest feature is entitled "Hollyday of a Lifetime" and covers the trip to Buddy Holly's home town of Lubbock, Texas, by two British winners of the "Buddy Holly Rock 'n' Roll Championship." "Meet Humphrey Ocean" is a feature about the musician/painter, who has published his drawings and paintings of the Wings' US tour of 1976 in a book, *The Ocean View;* several of his works are reproduced. There is a large pin-up colour photo of Paul and Michael Jackson, a full-page shot of Paul and Phil Everly and a humorous snap of Paul and Linda engaging in horseplay at the end of a recording session. "Hispano-Suiza" is a colour feature on the 1929 saloon car that Paul bought, now displayed at the National Motor Museum; the article includes a painting of the vehicle by Sandwich reader Stan Jones. Finally, the publication features a selection of interesting Christmas greetings from organisations connected with the McCartneys' various ventures.

**INSIDE
THIS HOLIDAY ISSUE**
PAUL'S NEW FILM
BEATLES ANNIVERSARY
BUDDY HOLLY PRIZEWINNERS
HUMPHREY OCEAN
REVIEW OF '82

WINGS FUN CLUB   1982 No. 28

Christmas Greetings to all Sandwich readers from Paul and Linda and Ringo and Barbara.

RINGO

Chris Daniels, The Ringo Starr Fan Club, 416 Chartridge Lane, Chesham, Bucks, HP5 2SJ

Chris launched the fan club in June 1981 and began to publish his glossy fanzine in 1982. There have been ten fanzines that have specialised in the activities of Ringo Starr; the most notable was probably *Our Starr Monthly*, published by Allen Seal of Louisiana in the US, a 12 page bi-monthly, which was originally launched in October 1974 but has now folded.

Beatles Unlimited also published a special *Starr Unlimited*, in December 1976. The entire issue was devoted to Ringo and included an exclusive interview between Ringo and Erik Bakker; a feature on his solo career between 1967 and 1976 by Hank Hager; a lengthy, track-by-track review of *Rotogravure*, with Ringo's own comments; an article on the different drum kits he's used over the years and a diary of his trip to Holland in October 1976.

The much-neglected Ringo, however, seems far more enthusiastic about a fanzine dedicated to him than the other ex-Beatles and he invited Chris to visit him in Ascot, so he could meet him and have a look at the first issue of Ringo.

Issue No.1 was a well-designed, glossy, professionally printed fanzine, approximately the same dimensions as *Beatles Monthly*, although much thinner at only twelve pages, six-and-half of which comprise photographs of Ringo. There is an editorial, a newsletter, a poem "Ode to Ringo Starr" by Kenny Surtees, a review of *Stop and Smell the Roses* by Mark Sandle, details of Reel Music and a Ringo competition. The magazine also advertises merchandise, available to club members, ranging from T-shirts to colour photographs.

CAVERN MECCA

Liz and Jim Hughes, Cavern Mecca, The Eleanor Centre, Mathew Street, Liverpool, L2 6RE

This quarterly is produced by the Beatle Information Centre run by Liz and Jim Hughes. *Cavern Mecca* is the only fanzine produced in Liverpool and Liz and Jim are among the Fab Four's most fervent champions. Liverpool has now awoken to the world-wide interest in the Beatles, but for several years Liz and Jim were unable to enlist the aid of the city's governing bodies; however they persevered and finally succeeded. One of their early ventures in the seventies was the setting up of the Magical Mystery Store which, following several address changes, eventually found a home at 18 Mathew Street under the name of Cavern Mecca. The couple's original concept of a shop grew to include a Beatles' museum and information centre. In the eighties Liz and Jim increased their workload by organising an annual "Mersey Beatle" convention at the Adelphi Hotel, now a regular and very welcome August Bank Holiday attraction on Merseyside. In March 1984, Cavern Mecca found a new home in the Eleanor Centre, also in Mathew Street, built above the site of the original Cavern Club itself. A more appropriate setting would be hard to imagine.

Liz and Jim are to be found at Cavern Mecca virtually every day and they are supported by enthusiastic helpers such as Connie O'Dell, Eddie Porter and Steve Phillips.

Issue No. 10, spring 1983, features a portrait of John on the cover and its 32 pages contain an editorial; news items; an article by Roger White on the Beatle City Exhibition; details and background to the Third Mersey Beat Extravaganza; Shaw Fulper-Smith's American column "Across the Universe"; Connie's "A Yank in the Pool" report, an American's eye view of the world of the Scouser (and Connie should know, she married one); Eddie Porter's "Eight Days a Week"; reproduction of rare newspaper features such as the November 1968 *Daily Express* feature on Stuart Sutcliffe, "A Beatle Who Walked Alone," and a *Daily Express* feature from 1964, one of the George Harrison reports ghosted by Derek Taylor. Members' letters and penpal pages complete the issue. This is the only fanzine to convey the "feel" of Liverpool and it is written with typical Scouse wit. Eddie's column, in particular, gives a fine sense of Liverpool as it is today, with news of local events and gossip from the folks who drop into the Centre.

FOR BILL xx

Liverpool's Original Beatle Information Centre

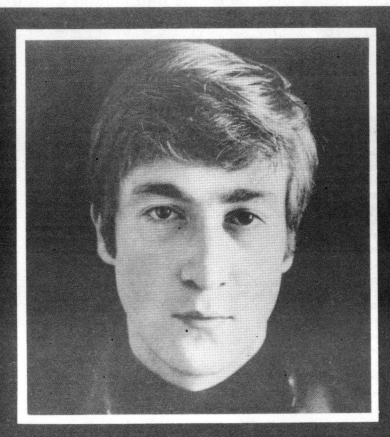

Open: Tuesday - Saturday 10 a.m. - 5.30 p.m.
FROM OCTOBER 1st TO MARCH 31st
Open: Monday - Saturday 10 a.m. - 5.30 p.m.
FROM APRIL 1st TO SEPTEMBER 30th

MAXWELL'S SILVER HAMMER

Allison Villone, 15 Rock Ridge Road, Larchmont, NY 10538, USA

A second-generation, bi-monthly fan magazine, first launched by Allison Villone when she was only 15. She first "discovered" the Beatles in 1978 when she heard 'Twist and Shout' on the radio and a few weeks later she bought the *Introducing the Beatles* album. She was only 12 at the time and couldn't afford any more records, but when she graduated from middle school that year, her father bought her seven Beatles' albums. During 1980 she saw *Beatlemania*, attended the New York Beatlefest and on 10 April decided to start her own fan club, *Maxwell's Silver Hammer*. She comments: "The basic difficulty in running a fanzine is the time element. You have work, school, lots of tasks to do, then you have to sit down at night and answer 17 letters! But I wouldn't give it up for the world. The pleasure of knowing how many Beatlemaniacs are around and active pays for the writer's cramp."

If we take the November 1980 issue of *Maxwell's Silver Hammer* as a sample, the cover shows a photograph of the Fab Four, without any titles or contents list. There is an editorial; "Working Class Heroes," a Beatles' solo news column; "Come Together," Beatles' news from around the world; "The Beatles Monument Campaign," an article about the efforts of dedicated fans in their campaign for a Beatles' statue to be erected in Liverpool; "Magical Mystery Tour," the story of Jim and Liz Hughes' original Beatles' souvenir shop; "Beatles Thesaurus," a series with definitions of various words and names associated with the Beatles – Butterfly Stompers, Bungalow Bill, Blue Meanies, Jeremy Boob and Billy Shears for example; "Your Mother Should Know," a quiz; and classified ads.

The major feature of the issue is a 15-page article "Whatever Happened to Baby Paul – The Paul-Is-Dead Story," an exhaustive investigation by Gene Dillenburg who nevertheless intimates that this massive item isn't the last word on the subject. He suggests that will be found in a book being prepared by "Paul Is Dead" expert Joel Glazier, who has been assisted in this work by Gene.

DARK HORSE

Joey Chadderton and Joe Clark, Dark Horse, 30 Woodlawn Street, West Haven, CT 06516, USA

A fan club for and about all four members of the Beatles (despite the title's strong association with George), launched in 1981 by Joey Chadderton and Joe Clark. The duo publish a newsletter of the same name that includes special columns such as "Spotlight," a focus on people who are or have been associated with the Beatles, like Phil Spector and Allan Williams. "Odds & Ends" (a page of up-to-date news), artwork, poetry, reviews and classified ads make up the regular contents.

Taking issue No.3 as a sample of this quarterly, the cover is printed on blue paper and features the sleeves of four albums: *The Best of George Harrison, Ringo, Abbey Road* and *Unfinished Music No.2*. The editorial is followed by a full-page drawing of John and an in-depth article entitled "The Story Behind the Bangla Desh Concert," illustrated with several photographs of George. There is a full-page drawing of Paul by Rick Adelkopf and a three-page transcript of an interview with Cynthia and Julian Lennon from the "Good Morning America" show, which is well illustrated. "Odds & Ends" is a news page and the regular "Spotlight" feature concerns Mick Fleetwood of Fleetwood Mac, his tenuous link with the Beatles being that he was once George's brother-in-law when he was married to Jenny Boyd (Patti's sister). A review of Mike McCartney's book, *Thank U Very Much*, by Lynn Szyszka is followed by two pages of ads for memorabilia and a classified ads page.

Dark

Issue #3
March-April-
May

Horse

LADY JANE

MY SWEET LADY JANE
Penny Lane, PO Box 1399, Campbell, CA 95008, USA

My Sweet Lady Jane is a fan club devoted to Jane Asher that was founded by Penny Lane. Penny comments: "I launched the fan club in January 1982 and to my knowledge it is the only fan club in existence for Ms Asher. It is international. I began the club for two reasons: one, because I have been a fan of Ms Asher's since 1965 and secondly, because there is a lack of 'adult', serious fanzines on the market. I am interested in the presentations of more serious themes as well as differing opinions. Those movies of Ms Asher's that are trash, such as *Deep End*, will receive the reviews they deserve and will not be glossed over because they appear in a fanzine. The response from the readers has been 100 percent supportive.

"Most of the members of *My Sweet Lady Jane* are first generation Beatle fans. Most of them are women. I am currently running the second of a two-part series on Maureen and a two-part piece on Yoko. The influence of the unfortunately called 'Beatle Women' has not received the attention it deserves and that is why I chose to examine Cynthia, Patti, Maureen and Yoko in some depth. I am interested in politics so we usually run some of Gerald Scarfe's cartoons in each issue."

Taking Issue No.2 as a sample, it has a portrait of a wide-eyed Jane on the cover. Page one contains an editorial; page two "Beauty of the Month," an article reprinted from a magazine circa 1971. The next two pages carry photos and information about Gerald Scarfe, including a photograph of Jane on the day she met her future husband; "Scarfe's Savage Satire" is a page featuring a drawing of Garrett Fitzgerald, with some information on Scarfe's inimitable style; "Bits and Pieces" is a column of news, and the following four pages contain reviews of the play *Before the Party*, which starred Jane and Michael Gough, together with a design by Scarfe. "Jane Wants To Make Us Laugh" is a feature about her sense of humour and "Jane Enjoys Creating a New Role" concerns her role in the TV series *Brideshead Revisited*. An article on Peter Asher is followed by a short piece on Peter and Gordon. A classified ads and letters page completes the issue, which contains 15 photographs and illustrations.

Beatles Beat #2.

BEATLES BEAT
Royce Hurt, 702 South Main Street, Ripley, Mississippi 38663, USA

This bi-monthly fanzine was launched in early 1983 by 19-year-old Royce Hurt. Royce plans to increase the number of its pages to 40 and to include news, contests, reviews and an "oldies" section.

If we take issue No.2 as a sample, it is a special "all picture/all clipping" edition. There is a large centre-page poster of John and a number of full-page photographs of the Beatles, individually and as a group. There are clippings about Paul in prison in Japan; the naming of certain Liverpool streets after the Fab Four; reviews; lyrics to songs; personal stories and items about their love affairs; reproductions of longer articles, such as John's interview with Barbara Graustark; a piece about the *Beatlemania* movie; "What John & Cyn Fight About" and a piece on George called "And Quiet Flows the Ganges!"

161

beatles unlimited

BEATLES UNLIMITED
Erik Bakker, PO Box 602, 3430 AP, Nieuwegein, The Netherlands

This is one of the most durable of all Beatle fanzines, beautifully produced with a range of tinted covers. A fine selection of photographs and illustrations adds to its visual appeal, and the text is expertly compiled. The publication has been in existence for several years and has run to over 50 issues in addition to some special one-off publications such as *Starr Unlimited, Dig It, Beatles Concerted Efforts* and *Lots of Liverpool.*

The editorial staff comprises Joe Remmerswaal, Evert Vermeer and André Koolmees, with help from over a dozen assistants and correspondents, including Erik Bakker, René van Haalem and Michael Pope.

The Dutch *Beatles Werk Group* was formed in 1971 and the magazine was originally conceived in 1973 by Koos Janssen and Aad van Zilt, who headed the Werk Group. They'd already published 50 issues of their 52-page magazine *Beatles Werk Group,* which was in the Dutch language, and wanted to produce a magazine in English. They had some difficulties and Erik Bakker took over from them and launched the magazine in December 1974.

If we take issue No.42 as a sample, it has an orange-tinted portrait of Paul on the cover. There is an editorial followed by a five-page news section entitled "I Read the News Today Oh Boy. . .", comprising a few dozen news items, illustrated with a picture of Denny Laine in a plane cockpit, the Todd Rundgren album sleeve *Swing to the Right,* the cover of *The Long & Winding Road* book, a letter from Genesis Publications about *Fifty Years Adrift (In an Open-Necked Shirt),* a shot of Ringo and Lynd-

sey De Paul and the Mersey Beatle convention leaflet. "The Beatles Information Centre" follows – a column by Artillio Bergholtz containing information on new releases by Paul, John, George and Ringo. "The Beatles Reel Music" is a review by Michael Pope of the EMI compilation album, while "The 4 Gotten Most" is a feature on Merseybeat group the Fourmost, together with a discography, penned by Evert Vermeer. Evert also contributes the book reviews, which include *As I Write This Letter* and the Dutch publication *Beatles Dagboek* (published in Britain in 1983 as *The Beatles Illustrated Diary).* Jos Remmerswaal reports on the Sixth Annual Beatles Convention in Los Angeles and there is a report by Piotr Metz, called "Yoko 1981 in Budapest," about the trip Yoko and Sam Havadtoy made to Budapest, with a translation of excerpts of an interview she did with *Popular,* a Hungarian weekly publication. "Interesting Facts," compiled by Michael Pope, comprises several items of intriguing trivia and is followed by part 22 of the "Dig It" column, a collection of information and reviews of Beatle bootleg records. Some ads follow and the back page is a reproduction of the *New Musical Express* cover that featured an ad for 'Lady Madonna'.

GOOD DAY SUNSHINE
Charles F.Rosenay, Liverpool Productions, 397 Edgewood Avenue, New Haven, CT 06511, USA

This publication is issued by Liverpool Productions, a fan club run by enterprising Beatle-enthusiast Charles F.Rosenay. In addition to running the fan club and producing its bi-monthly magazine, Charles promotes the annual New England Beatles Convention and in 1983 organised the "Good Day Sunshine Magical Mystery Tour of England," which was featured in *The Sunday Times* colour magazine. He took over the fanzine from Rosita Rodriguez, who originally launched the publication. He then expanded it and also absorbed the fanzine *Here, There and Everywhere.* The large-sized issues are wrapped in tinted covers on semi-stiff card and are well illustrated.

If we take Issue No.17 as an example, the green-tinted cover features an ad for the Fifth New England Beatles Convention. Charles contributes an editorial, which is followed by three pages of letters, "Please Mr Postman." There are five pages of "Beatle News," with lengthy reports on the opening of Beatle City, the Sotheby's Auction, Julian Lennon's group Quasar and the escapades of Zak Starkey. May Pang is the subject of a four-page interview by Bill Last and her book *Loving John* is reviewed by Joel Glazier. John Dobrydnio Jr contributes an article on Beatle videos, as does Bill Last with his "The Last Word on Video." The next four pages are convention reports, with the accent on the

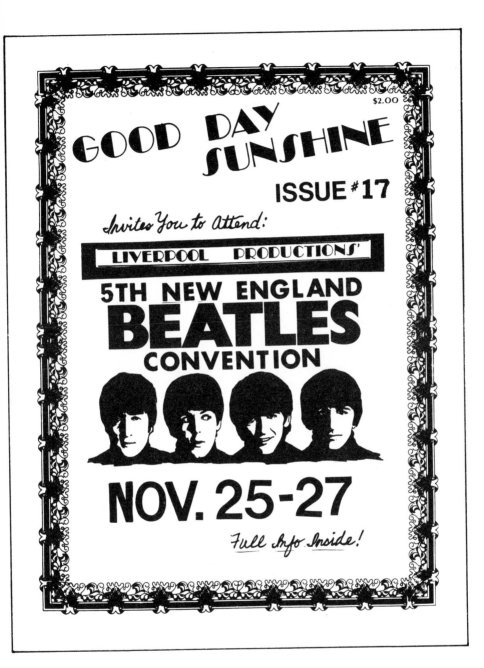

$2.00

GOOD DAY SUNSHINE

ISSUE #17

Invites You to Attend:

LIVERPOOL PRODUCTIONS'

5TH NEW ENGLAND BEATLES CONVENTION

NOV. 25-27

Full Info Inside!

1983 Mersey Beatle Convention in Liverpool. Seven pages are devoted to the "Magical Mystery Tour of England," the trip by 70 US fans between 23 and 31 August 1983, with day-by-day commentary and contributions from several of the fans who participated. Mark Wallgren and Tom Frangione review Ringo's album *Old Wave*.

There is a review of the stage show *Beatlemania* by Eugene Dillenberg and the book *Yesterday* by Mark Wallgren. "Off the Beaten Track" is a regular feature by Mike Streeto, who writes about Peter and Gordon in this issue. The inside back cover features the cartoon serial "The Baegles" by Jane Oliver and there is a large portrait of John on the back cover.

THE McCARTNEY OBSERVER

Doylene Kindsvater, 220 East 12th Street,
LaCrosse, KS 67548, USA

This is edited by Doylene Kindsvater, who comments: "I first started this particular publication in March 1977 after having worked as co-editor with Sarah Nolte on a publication called McCartney Ltd from 1972 to January 1977. McCartney Ltd was originally the Paul Chapter which was loosely operated under the Official Beatles Fan Club in NYC (later The Apple Tree). The Paul Chapter was run by a girl called Joanne Maggio, and Sarah was the last in line of Joanne's many vice-presidents. When the Official NY club disbanded Joanne gave the Paul Chapter to Sarah and she changed its name to McCartney Ltd. It was through my work with Sarah that I gained enough experience to start my own club and to know that I'd enjoy it in spite of the work and problems involved. It was easier for me to start a new club because I had a membership listing. My first step was to run off info sheets on my new club and mail it to each old member on that list. I also advertised in other existing fan clubs. I also had help from the beginning from my very good friends Marie Lacey (co-editor) and Susan DiLorenzo (assistant to editor). They both write columns, help type, provide negatives and so on. We also have a foreign correspondent, Moira Warren, who sends us a lot of information from Britain.

"We're not a business and we're not in operation to make money. We're a very small and, I hope, a very personal club. We simply want to bring news of Paul to the people who care most about him and give the members a chance to share their common interest. We do sell photos and from time to time special magazines or records that we're able to get duplicates of (no bootlegs or tapes)."

If we take issue No.19 as a sample, it has a cover photo of Paul from the *Tug Of War* sessions. The three news pages include photos of Paul and Linda at his brother's wedding and the couple with Yoko Ono. The editorial takes up a full page and there is a three-page interview with Paul, conducted by an EMI employee during the *Tug Of War* sessions. Mary Ann Dolphin reports on her meeting with Paul in Los Angeles and there is a four-page interview with Mike McCartney when he travelled to the US to promote his book. John Crichton supplies a poem about the book and there is a two-page feature on Jane Asher, "A Lady for All Seasons." "Meeting the Mass at Air" is another close encounter story by Isabella Gargiulo and there are two pages full of various photo offers.

/

THE McCARTNEY OBSERVER #19

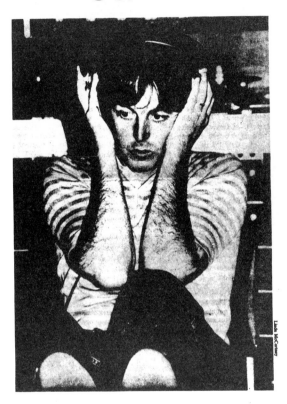

Linda McCartney

TOMORROW NEVER KNOWS

Issue 12   December 1983

35p

TOMORROW NEVER KNOWS

Simon Wordsworth and Andy Hayes, 86 Shoebury Road, Thorpe Bay, Essex

A modest, but worthwhile, publication run by two teenagers: Simon Wordsworth, who is studying catering and Andy Hayes, who is a drummer with a rock band. Andy has more spare time than Simon and handles all the typing and layout chores, but they share the writing and editing. The duo originally began the fanzine for themselves, before deciding to try for a wider audience. It's a loss-making operation at present, but the pair remain full of enthusiasm; they are assisted by various contributors, including Neil Hadley, Denis Lambilliotte and Stuart Payton.

Issue No.12 of the monthly publication, dated December 1983, has a set of early sixties' autographed pictures of each individual Beatle on the cover. Page two includes quiz and crossword answers from the previous issue and an "All Time Beatles Top 10", a readers' choice, compiled by Stuart. Page three features "The Beatles Pseudonyms," an article by Denis that stretches over two pages and is illustrated with a picture of Paul holding a Popeye mask. "With a Little Help From My Friends" is a two-page uncredited article listing the various musicians who have recorded with the ex-Beatles during the seventies; it includes pictures of Eric Clapton, Pete Townsend, Elton John and Marc Bolan. "Spicy Beatles Songs" is the next double-page item, a review of a bootleg album of that name by Neil. The fourth and final instalment of a series called "The Beatles on Video" is followed by various news items, a Ringo singles discography, a quiz, some further lists and a back cover photograph of Ringo playing guitar.

THE BEATLES IN EUROPE

IT ISN'T JUST ENGLAND AND AMERICA....

THE BEATLES HAVE TAKEN OVER THE WORLD!!!

THE BEATLES' FRENCH PUBLICATIONS

Beatlemania reached France in January 1964 when the group flew to Paris for a short season at the Olympia. Despite the fact that the language barrier resulted in the group being far more popular in English-speaking countries. There have been several French-language books published about the Fab Four, most of them translations from the English. I am grateful to Jacques Volcouve, president of the Le Club des 4 de Liverpool for much of the following information.

The first publication was issued at the beginning of 1964 and was a translation of John's book *In His Own Write*, entitled *En Flagrante Delire*. Volcouve comments: "The cover says 'Desperate try of translation'. They did succeed in recreating the Liverpudlian humour, but to really understand it you still need to have the English text also and compare them". Rachel Mizrahi was the translator; she was also involved in a new translation of the book, published after John's death.

Of *Les Beatles*, by Alain Dister, Volcouve says: "This is the one I always advise people to buy first, the new Beatles' fan who doesn't know too much about their story. There are some rare pictures in it, too, in contrast to *Les Beatles: Yesterday For Ever*. This book has a larger chapter on the early days in Liverpool and Hamburg."

Les Beatles: Yesterday For Ever was published by Rock Genius and Volcouve says: "It's OK for a Beatle beginner. It covers more of the break-up story than Dister's book, but most of the pictures come from *The True Story of the Beatles*, published by the Beatles Book Monthly.

Editions Elvill published *The Beatles*, a translation of Roy Carr and Tony Tyler's *The Beatles: An Illustrated Record*. "This was a translation of the first edition," comments Volcouve "and there is virtually no alteration from the English edition".

Solar were the publishers of *Les Beatles: Leur Biographie Officielle* by Hunter Davies. "This is a translation of the Hunter Davies official biography but a number of the pictures and documents which appeared in the English edition are missing from the French."

Les Beatles Chansons Illustrés, is both volumes of Alan Adridge's *The Beatles' Illustrated Lyrics* published with a French text.

The publishers Best issued *Lennon/McCartney* by Jacques Leblanc, of which Volcouve comments: "A beautiful book, but most of the photos are bootlegged from a fans collection and the guy who wrote it did not know anything about the Beatles and did not understand any of it. So you can imagine the amount of mistakes!"

Souvenirs des Beatles was published by Artefact and written by Har Van Fulpen. Volcouve says: "Another book from the guy from Holland.

Ninety per cent of the photographs are bootlegged from the Beatles Book Monthly and seventy per cent of the text is taken from the American book *A Day in the Life*.

Har Van Fulpen also wrote *John Lennon: 1940-1980*. Volcouve comments: "A translation from a Dutch book, written immediately after John's death by the ex-president of the Beatles' fan club in Holland. A very easy way to make money!"

John Lennon 1940-1980 is a French-language book published in Canada, a translation of Ed Naha's American paperback. Volcouve doesn't think much of it: "A lot of pictures, but not a good book."

Alain Moreau were the publishers of *Pour John Lennon* by Maurice Achard, of which Volcouve says: "A small book, no photos at all, but very, very good."

Les Beatles Yoko Ono et Moi is a translation of the Playboy interviews by David Sheff, published in France by Générique; *La Ballade de John & Yoko* is a translation of the *Rolling Stone* anthology *The Ballad of John & Yoko*. Says Volcouve: "There are some alterations. The cover and some pictures inside, but mainly the quality of the paper has been changed. *L'Hommage de la Bande Dessinée* is "An original tribute book containing articles, but mainly a comic book story. Some very nice drawings and the contributors are the best artists in France". The final book Jacques informs us of is a translation of *John Lennon in His Own Words*.

Volcouve has also provided his comments on a number of French magazines devoted to the Beatles. One of the earliest, *4 Garçons dans le Vent the Beatles*, he describes as: "A very rare magazine, published in 1964 when *A Hard Day's Night* came out in France"; *Surboum Beatles Special*, is "a translation from an English language magazine, circa 1964"; *Le Matin, Special Beatles*, "one of the best tributes produced in France. Some mistakes, still quite good"; *Juke Box, Beatle Box*, "an old Belgian magazine from the late sixties"; *John Lennon: 1940-1980*, "a French-Canadian magazine with 110 photos in its 48 pages"; *A la Mémoire de John Lennon*, "another Canadian magazine, with a special Beatles' calendar enclosed", *John Lennon: Poster Mag*, "Features a lot of pictures, but the text is awful"; *Salut! Numero Special John Lennon*, "a beautiful picture magazine in colour, but the text is awful"; *Edition Speciale John Lennon*, "A Belgian tribute magazine with an abundance of photographs, but a lot are printed two or three times on different pages and the text is unreadable"; *Podium: John Lennon la Vraie Fin des Beatles*, "This magazine was done in a night and contains a lot of pictures from my own collection. However, the text could have been better"; *La Vie et la Mort de John Lennon*, "Another Canadian magazine, includes four posters"; *Collection Hommages: the Beatles*, "A 1983

publication. It's awful. Poorly printed with very well-known photos and a lot of mistakes"; and *20 Ans Avec les Beatles*, "1983 Anniversary magazine. It is a translation from a German edition. A lot of photos both in black and white and colour, including many I've never seen before."

THE BEATLES' GERMAN PUBLICATIONS

When Hamburg's Star Club opened in 1962 with the Beatles topping the bill, the ceiling of the foyer was decorated with copies of *Mersey Beat*. Manfred Weissleder, the club's owner, took a particular interest in the publication and had large stocks of each issue for sale at the club. Later that year he asked me if I'd come and live in Hamburg and launch Germany's first beat-music newspaper for him. I declined his offer, but agreed to write a column for his publication.

Entitled *Star Club News*, it had a magazine-style format, colour photographs front and back and contained between 14 and 34 pages per issue. The Beatles were heavily featured, as were other Liverpool outfits such as the Searchers, Gerry and the Pacemakers and the Liverbirds. There were photo spreads, not only concerning the Star Club itself, but also Liverpool's Cavern; features on all the acts that appeared at the Star Club; and special picture spreads such as "Astrid & the Beatles", which covered photo sessions between Astrid Kirchnerr and the Beatles. *Star Club News* continued until 1966 when it was taken over by a major publishing group who incorporated it into a magazine called *O.K.* By this time, Germany's main music magazine, *Bravo*, had begun to cover the British music scene, thereby consolidating its position as Europe's most influential music publication.

The first German book to cover the Liverpool scene was *Beat in Liverpool*, published by Europaische Verlags Ansalt in Frankfurt in 1965. It was written by Jurgen Suss, Gerold Dommermuth and Hans Maier. The 196-page publication centred around a Liverpool band called the Clayton Squares and also contained a record by the group. Mike Evans, a member of the band (later to write *Nothing to Get Hung About* and *In the Footsteps of the Beatles*), wrote the book's introduction. There were numerous photographs of Liverpool in the sixties and a German text that described the Merseyside scene.

Paul List Verlag KB published *Die Wahre Geschichte der Beatles* in 1964. This was a German translation of Billy Shepherd's *The True Story of the Beatles;* during the same year, Lichtenberg Verlag Gmbh published *Die Beatles Kommen*, written by Dennis Bow and lavishly illustrated.

Hunter Davies' *The Beatles: The Authorised Biography* appeared in translation in 1968 under the title *Die Geschichte der Beatles;* and Deutscher Taschenbuch Verlag Gmbh published

The Beatles Songbook in 1971. This contained the lyrics of Beatles' songs in both English and German, with photographs and drawings.

In 1976 Cecilie Dressler Verlag published *Die Beatles* by Siegfried Niedergesass, a German-language book, with 168 pages of text and 91 black-and-white photographs.

A translation of Roy Carr and Tony Tyler's book *The Beatles Illustrated Record* was issued by Abi Melzer Productions Gmbh in 1977 as *The Beatles – Eine Illustrierte Dokumentation*. Another book by German writers was published the same year, *Die Beatles*, by Hans Rombeck and Wolfgang Neumann. 1978 saw the German-language edition of Anthony Fawcett's *One Day at a Time*, issued by Bastei-Lubbe Verlag as *John Lennon – Beatle, Kunstler, Provokateur;* also published that year was *The Beatage*, a lavishly illustrated book about beat groups in Germany in the sixties, with a complete chapter on the Beatles.

Paul McCartney und Wings by Klaus Dewes and Rudi Dertel was issued by Bastei-Lubbe Verlag in 1980 and the same year saw the publication of *Denny Laine's Guitarrenbuch* by Otto Maier Verlag. 1980 was the year when several John Lennon books were rush-released in Germany. They included *John Lennon – In Memoriam* by Peter Leukefeld, issued by Wilhelm Heyne Verlag. *The Playboy Report: Das War John Lennon (Alles über ihn und die Beatles)*, was issued by Moewig Verlag, credited to W.Spencer. Jan Wenner's *Rolling Stone* interview was published as *Lennon über Lennon: Abschied von den Beatles* and Andy Peebles' BBC interview was issued as *Lennon über Lennon: Leben in Amerika*, both from Rowohlt Taschenbuch Verlag Gmbh. *John Lennon im Spiegel der Weltpresse* from Argus Zeit-Doko contained 92 pages of newspaper cuttings about John's death from publications in England, America, Switzerland, Germany, Belgium, Holland, France and Austria. *John Lennon, Wie Er Sich Selbst Sah* was the German Translation of *"John Lennon in His Own Words"* and Bastei Lubbe Verlag, the publishers, also issued *Die Beatles Wie Sie Sich Selbst Sehen*, a translation of *The Beatles in Their Own Words*.

Star Club by Dieter Beckmann and Klaus Martens was issued by Rowohl Verlag, publishers of *The Beatage* and was another lavish photobook, 266 pages in length. Of the 500 black-and-white photographs, there were 21 shots of the Beatles included in a special chapter, which also contained reproductions of five of their original contracts.

Several of the photographs of the Beatles are quite rare; they include a shot of the group, with Stuart Sutcliffe and Pete Best, at the Indra Club; the band on stage at the Star Club; and at the Top Ten Club with Tony Sheridan. The book includes a reproduction of the 1962 Star Club poster announcing the Beatles' appearance at its opening.

One of the most ambitious German books, was *Das Album der Beatles* by M.Jurgs, H.H.Zeeman and D.Meyer. This was 383 pages in length and contained a fine selection of colour and black-and-white photographs, many of them previously unpublished or relatively rare.

In 1981, Wilhelm Heyne Verlag published *Paul McCartney und Wings* by Jochem Malms, and Rowohlt Taschenbuch Verlag Gmbh issued *John Lennon – In Seiner Eigenen Schreibe*, the German-language version of John's two books, *In His Own Write* and *A Spaniard in the Works*. Hunter Davies' book *Die Geschichte der Beatles* was also reissued by Droemer Knaur Verlag.

In 1982, *Shout, Die Wahre Geschichte der Beatles*, a 299-page translation of Philip Norman's biography, was published; the same year saw one of the most unusual German-language books of all, *John Lennon Hat Mir das Rauchen Verboten*, a novel by Karin Keppel (The title translates as "John Lennon Forbade Me To Smoke".) The author fantasised about the Beatles and wrote down her daydreams in a diary between the years 1965 and 1967. She has used the diaries as the basis for this romantic novel about a 13-year-old German girl called Grischka who becomes separated from her parents while on holiday in London and ends up as housekeeper for the Beatles. She is eventually adopted by John.

Although *Star Club News* became incorporated with *O.K.* magazine in the sixties, a new Star Club magazine was launched in Germany in the eighties. There was a special 48-page Beatle issue with over 100 photographs, many of them in full colour. There was an article about the origins of rock 'n' roll, with pictures of Elvis, Bill Haley, Chuck Berry, Jerry Lee Lewis – and John Lennon in 'Rocker' gear. The early days in Liverpool are covered, illustrated with shots of the individual Beatles as children and a photograph of an "under-16s" session at the Cavern. Next came a feature on their Hamburg days; the story of their first recordings; the birth of Beatlemania; the swinging sixties in London; a profile of Brian Epstein; their film career; Apple days; the break-up and a discography.

THE BEATLES' ITALIAN PUBLICATIONS

Rosario Grasso's *The Beatles in Italy* is a beautifully produced publication, with 320 giant-sized pages and hundreds of photographs. Rosario has one of the largest collections of Beatle memorabilia in Italy and the book reproduces many items from his collection.

The text is both in English and Italian. The volume is divided into three parts: The first section contains news and information on all the Beatles' Italian releases with photographs and translations in English of the complete text of the various record sleeves. The next section is

divided into 17 parts, each covering a different year, beginning with 1963. In addition to the reproduction of Italian Beatles' LP sleeves, there are comments on each release. The third section comprises several appendices with an alphabetical list of albums and songs, including records issued by Apple, Dark Horse and Ring O' Records. There is also information on Italian tours, film releases and books. Reproductions of film posters and drawings illustrate the text and a thorough index makes for easy reference. At the end of the book is a pictorial section displaying the covers of over 30 Italian magazines that featured cover stories of the Fab Four.

Rosario mentions ten Beatles' books, published in Italian, several of which are translations. They are: *Vivendo cantando* published by Longanesi in 1965 and reprinted in 1968; *I Beatles*, the Hunter Davies biography, printed by Longanesi in 1968; *Il Sottomarino Giallo* ("The Yellow Submarine"), published by Mondadori in 1969; the same publishers also issued *Il Libro delle Canzoni dei Beatles*", the Alan Aldridge book of the Beatles' illustrated lyrics; *The Beatles – 170 Songs* was issued by Fama in 1976; and an Italian version of the Beatles story, *La Storia dei Beatles*, by C. E. Sarino, was issued by AID in 1977. Roy Carr and Tony Tyler's *The Beatles Illustrated Record* was translated by Massimo Villa and published as *I Favolosi Beatles* by Sonzogno in 1979. Manuel Insolera penned *Paul McCartney*, published by Arcana in 1979 and Roberto Antoni was the author of *Il viaggio dei cuori solitari*, published by Formichière, also in 1979. The following year Gammalibri published *Beatles*, a book by Marco Pastonesi.

THE BEATLES AS LIVING LEGENDS

THE BEATLES AS LIVING LEGENDS

One of the most unusual publishing ventures of recent years is the launching, by Pierian Press in America, of a series of scholarly books about the lives and careers of the Beatles. As a result Pierian are assembling a growing library of superbly produced, hardbound books.

The company clearly believes that the Beatles are suitable subjects for a series of this kind, commenting: "The Beatles are the object of serious study in music and social history, a study perhaps unique in terms of it being directed at entertainment figures who are still living (and have many more years to go). The Beatles may be around when someday someone declares that all accumulated evidence indicates they never existed, almost like the study of Jesus."

For some time I have been corresponding with the company's Vice President, Tom Schultheiss, who is also the author of the book *A Day in the Life*. Tom gives this account of the birth and policy of Pierian Press: "The company is now about 14 years old. It began as a family business, the hobby of a friend of mine whom I first met in graduate library school at the University of Michigan. He decided he wanted to publish some reference books for libraries instead of just working in a library, and so the company was formed. After about two years of a basement operation, I became the first full-time salaried employee: he remained part-time, as did his wife (who is [now] sales manager). We set up offices in a small frame house in downtown Ann Arbor; we now occupy a twenty-five room, mock-Tudor mansion on the east side of Ann Arbor. The company remains relatively small – about 15 employees. I live in the mansion in about four rooms; the rest of the house is used as offices for the Press.

"For the first six years or so, we published nothing but library reference books, or books on library topics, plus we began many of the serials and quarterlies that we continue to publish – all aimed at the library market. All this began to change about seven years ago when Harry Castleman and Wally Podrazik offered me a book called *Not A Second Time* (the title then was a reflection that a group like the Beatles would never come around again, but also that the authors had done so much work that they never wanted to do it again.) They had been rejected by many, many publishers, but I saw the immediate value in the book, which became *All Together Now*, simply as a reference book on the Beatles, one which I knew libraries alone would be interested in. At that time, I was without knowledge of Beatle fandom, or the soon- to- be- resurgent interest in the Beatles typified by the Capitol re-releases in the States.

"So, *All Together Now* began as a reference book, which is basically what it remains and offers as its chief value (as opposed to something deliberately focused on the Beatle fan in a popular way). Soon it became apparent that the book would have a wider audience than our usual reference book, however. My conversations with Harry and Wally – the fact that a discography had never been done in this detail on the Beatles knocked me out to begin with – led me to believe that this was a book thousands of fans would want, not just libraries. When the first printing came off, I shipped copies to large New York publishers, offering up paperback rights. Within days I had five-digit offers from several publishers but decided that I as an individual and we as a company were really unequipped to handle a deal of this kind. We had no knowledge of what to ask for as an advance, what to get as a royalty. So we got ourselves an agent in New York to sell the book for us and the advance was three times as large as any we had previously received. Needless to say, the authors lost all interest in *not* having all this happen a second time and immediately began work on what soon became *The Beatles Again*.

"My own book *[A Day in the Life]* grew out of a gradual and continuing familiarity with Beatles' literature which came about as I worked on Harry and Wally's two books. I have a bachelor's degree in History and a master's degree in Library Science. At the time this all began, I had only about a half-dozen Beatle records and no interest in collecting any more. At the time I preferred Vivaldi. As I got familiar with all the Beatles' books, though, one thing stuck out like an elephant in a cornfield: despite all the books published, there was absolutely no comprehensive, fully reliable history or biography of the Beatles and the literature that did exist was full of uncaring mistakes made in the process of churning out books usually just to make quick money. (Not that we aren't interested in money; but you'll notice pictures, in our books, take second place to information and reference material, and we at least make the effort to try and correct and get things close to the truth). All of this is discussed at great length in the introduction to my book, *A Day in the Life*.

"There are of course mistakes in my book, many growing out of the fact that I found information in sources which was wrong to begin with. I never offered up *A Day in the Life* as the truth, or fact, or an almanack, or a diary, however. I offered it up as a record of the various histories, with all conflicting facts still conflicting, attempting to resolve what I could, point out errors, differences and discrepancies where I caught them, etc. Naturally I added mistakes of my own, but look to a day some

As I write this letter

An American Generation Remembers
The Beatles
by Marc A. Catone

To celebrate the 18th anniversary of The Beatles arrival in the U.S., Pierian Press will publish *As I Write This Letter* in February of 1982. Containing over 160 fan letters and 70 drawings by fan artists, an American generation finally gets to speak out on how The Fab Four has influenced their lives and society as a whole. Your favorite Beatles book is here at last!

254 pages   clothbound   8½X11" $17.50

" . . . the first changes The Beatles caused in my life were to increase my library and record collection slowly . . . and decrease the amount of money in my wallet quickly."

"As for their effect on society . . . it's obvious . . . we loved them."

"Thinking of a world without The Beatles, I see a generation of crewcutted boys still listening to The Four Seasons. Thank God for The Beatles."

"There are two kinds of musicians today. Those influenced by The Beatles and liars."

"I was thirteen when I first saw The Beatles on The Ed Sullivan Show . . . When they began to play, I actually fell backwards, feet in the air, I was so lost and desperately in love."

"They held us together through an exploding decade."

"All of The Beatles were so warm and friendly, I enjoyed their songs. This may sound weird, but I also liked the pants they wore. They looked so cute in those pants."

"My first impression of The Beatles was when I was about seven . . . I can remember thinking how nice it was of Paul to play his guitar in the other direction, so it would not hit into George. No one had ever told me that some people in this world were left handed."

"The Beatles were the greatest force in music since Bach. They still are."

"In sixth grade we were taught drug education and our teacher interpreted *Hey Jude* as a pro drug song . . . . I had always thought it was about love."

"I did everything I could that The Beatles might do. When I read that George Harrison practiced bad table manners, so did I."

"The Beatles served as our parents when our real parents lost their credibility . . . . They gave us a feeling of what success could be without selling out."

" . . . a neighbor returned home, clutching a jelly bean that Paul had thrown out the window. No matter how much I persuaded him, he wouldn't sell it . . . not even for a month's allowance of $5.00."

"Honesty is what The Beatles taught."

years hence when I can revise this (pointing out my previous mistakes, too) so that it becomes an ever more correct outline history of the Beatles.

"I had at first tried to interest Harry and Wally in doing *A Day in the Life* but when they refused – three times – I then decided to do it myself. My ultimate goal, as I said, is a revised book which offers a chronology that: 1) is close to the truth in terms of dates and events; 2) notes all discrepancies in books or magazines devoted to the Beatles; and 3) is the most accessible book about the Beatles to use because of very detailed indexing and source referencing. With that as a beginning, future writers will produce better history and biography, which is not my interest even though many have criticised my book because it doesn't resolve these problems. I don't want to resolve them! It's like complaining to someone who has just flown across the Pacific Ocean in a balloon that they are a failure because they haven't flown across the Atlantic Ocean.

Two more books are coming from Harry and Wally and from me: *The End of the Beatles* by Castleman and Podrazik and *In My Life: John, Paul, George & Ringo, Day-By-Day, 1971-1980* by myself. Eventually I hope not just to revise *A Day in the Life* but to merge the two books (years and years from now) so 1960 – 1980 is covered in one book. Eventually, too, all of Harry and Wally's three books will be merged into a mammoth discography.

"As for another of our books, *Things We Said Today*. This was offered to me soon after *All Together Now*. It is a computerized book. In other words, we have worked on it for over three years. The authors have listened to all the EMI/Capitol recordings both written and recorded by the Beatles (not including songs written but not recorded, or songs recorded but not written by them), and come up with what will be a classic and standard presentation of the lyrics for over 180 songs word-for-word as they are sung on the records. This is not a sheet music reprint, and when I say word for word I mean all the "yeahs" and "ohs" and "mmms" and backing vocals, and background talk. It took me over two years to secure all the publisher permissions to do this book, which has never been done before. This is not your average Beatle book, like *Illustrated Record*, but again a work of reference and scholarship (the book was done by the authors in a sociology department in a University as a study in popular culture).

"Personally, I think the book is a classic and a real event, not only in Beatles history but in the history of popular music: imagine, a concordance similar to those which are published for Shakespeare's works and the Bible!"

The books from Pierian Press, which include *All Together Now; The Beatles Again?; A Day in the Life; Things We Said Today; You Can't Do That; As I Write This Letter* and *The Literary Lennon,* have separate entries in the bibliography section. In addition, Pierian Press has other books that are either nearing completion or in the planning stages.

All Together Now is issued, as Tom mentioned, in an American paperback edition, but with the exception of that work and *A Day in the Life,* published in Britain in paperback form by Omnibus Press, the other books are available only in hardback directly from the publishers. As they are not to be found in bookshops, they are relatively rare and therefore quite invaluable additions to the bookshelves of a genuine Beatles fan. Copies can be obtained by writing directly to: Pierian Press, PO Box 1808, Ann Arbor, Mi 48106, USA.

Pierian Press is not the only publisher to make the decision to begin a "Beatles Library". Virgin Books in Britain, naturally pleased at the success of Neil Stannard's *The Long & Winding Road,* published a second volume by Neil entitled *The Beatles: Working Class Heroes* (Written in collaboration with John Tobler). These are part of a series of Beatle books of which this volume is but one. Further information on the Virgin Beatles Library can be obtained from Virgin Books at 61-63 Portobello Road, London, W11 3RR.

COLLECTING
THE BEATLES

BY BARBARA FENICK

Written by an experienced, knowledgeable Beatle fan, COLLECTING THE BEATLES is intended both as an introductory guide to collecting for neophyte fans & novice collectors, as well as a quick reference handbook for more practiced collectors and all who deal in Beatles memorabilia.

SECTIONS INCLUDE:

- A discussion of the origins, scope, limitations, and use of this guide

- An overview of the history of Beatles memorabilia, with commentary on the current collecting scene

- A look at counterfeit collectables, with tips on telling them from the genuine article

- The story behind Beatles' bootlegs, with advice on finding, evaluating, and buying them

- A thorough discussion of how and where to buy Beatles collectables, with practical tips on shopping, bidding and making the final purchase

- The price guide: broken into nine categories, it provides a check-list of current "going rate" prices for collectable Beatles albums, singles, EPs and other compact recordings, promotional records, bootlegs, novelties, books, magazines, pamphlets, programmes, and other memorabilia — over 800 items are listed!

- An exclusive appendix: a reprint of an official Nemperor Holdings internal document listing nearly 100 merchandising licenses granted during the 1963-64 era, with details on names of manufacturers, terms of licenses, and lists of products licensed

- Another special appendix: a listing of every Beatles-related item ever auctioned off at Sotheby Parke Bernet galleries in London (with asking prices and prices actually paid), together with a photographic reprint of 23 pages from the December 1981 auction, where over 120 one-of-a-kind Beatles items were offered for bid

An Introduction & Price Guide
to Fab Four Collectables,
Records & Memorabilia

Over 100 photographs (majority Full-page)
Approximately 200 pages
8½X11" Clothbound

Rock & Roll Reference Series, No.7

Individuals, $15.95; Institutions, $19.95
(Please do not order before June 1, 1982)

Individual orders must be prepaid.
PIERIAN PRESS P.O. BOX 1808 ANN ARBOR, MI 48106

INDEX

INDEX

The following publications are discussed in some
detail in
Paperback Writers:

A La Memoire de John Lennon, 171
Abbey Road, 66
Across the Universe, 46
Album der Beatles, Das, 174
All About the Beatles, 13
All About the Beatles (magazine), 123
All Night Stand, 80
All Together Now, 33, 177
All You Need Is Ears, 44
All You Need Is Love, 83
All You Needed Was Love: the Beatles After the
  Beatles, 53
Alvin Stardust, 85
Apple to the Core, 24
Around the World With the Beatles, 119
Art & the City, 82
As I Write This Letter, 63
As Time Goes By, 26, 75

Backtrack, 123
Ballad of John & Yoko, The, 65
Ballade de John & Yoko, La, 171
Beat in Liverpool, 173
Beatle Book, The, 13
Beatlefan, 144
Beatles Concert-ed Efforts, The, 43
Beatles: a Day in the Life, The, 45, 177
Beatles: Dezo Hoffman, The, 30
Beatles Discography, 33
Beatles Down Under, The, 66
Beatles — eine Illustrierte Dokumentation, The,
  173
Beatles' England, The, 62
Beatles: the Fabulous Story of John, Paul, George
  and Ringo, The, 28
Beatles for Classical Guitar, The, 90
Beatles for the Record, The, 56
Beatles Forever (magazine), 120
Beatles Forever, The, (Spence), 59
Beatles Get Back, The 22
Beatles: an Illustrated Diary, The, 72
Beatles Illustrated Lyrics, The, 22
Beatles Illustrated Lyrics: Volume Two, The, 23
Beatles Illustrated Record, The, 29
Beatles: an Illustrated Record, The, 38
Beatles in America, The, 119
Beatles in Italy, The, 174
Beatles in Their Own Words, The, 39
Beatles in Yellow Submarine, The, 21
Beatles: It Was Twenty Years Ago, The, 74

Beatles Ltd, 14
Beatles Lyrics Complete, The, 29
Beatles Lyrics Illustrated, The, 29
Beatle Madness, 40
Beatle Songs for the Recorder, 91
Beatles, The (Burt, Pascall), 73
Beatles, The (Clark), 55
Beatles, The (Colour Library Books), 74
Beatles, The (Harry), 75
Beatles, The (Parkinson, Cleave), 15
Beatles, The (Pirmangton), 28
Beatles, The (Pyx), 117
Beatles, The (Saroyan), 24
Beatles, The (Scaduto), 21
Beatles, The (Schaffner), 42
Beatles, The (Shinko Music Co.), 30
Beatles, The (Stokes), 49
Beatles A-Z, The (Friede, Titone, Weiner), 48
Beatles A to Z, The (Leppert), 34
Beatles Again, The, 36
Beatles Album File & Complete Discography, The,
  60
Beatles Apart, The, 54
Beatles at the Beeb, The, 59, 75
Beatles at Carnegie Hall, The, 119
Beatles: the Authorised Biography, The, 20, 38
Beatles Beat, 161
Beatles Big Note, 91
Beatles Book, The, 21
Beatles Bumper Songbook, The, 91
Beatles by Royal Command, The, 119
Beatles City Magazine, The, 123
Beatles Collection, The, 29
Beatles: a Collection, The, 63
Beatles Complete, The, 90
Beatles Monthly, 95
Beatles Monthly Book, The, 95
Beatles Movie Catalog, 43
Beatles National Lampoon, 120
Beatles 1967-1970, The
Beatles Now, 150
Beatles on Broadway, 119
Beatles on record, The, 60
Beatles Quiz Book, The, 15
Beatles Reader, The, 74
Beatles: the Real Story, The, 20
Beatles Records in Australia, The, 73
Beatles Singles Collection 1962-1970, The, 89
Beatles Songbook, The, 173
Beatles Story, (A Marvel Super Special), The, 131

NOT Linda's Pictures

With the Beatles: The Historic Photographs of Dezo Hoffmann
edited by Pearce Marchbank

Import $14.95

There's a 99% chance that *your* first look at the "lovable Mop-Tops" was a Dezo Hoffmann photo. Hoffmann, the photographer responsible for all the early Beatles promo shots, also scored some great behind-the-scenes pics during the crazed and zany years of Beatlemania. 200 of these photos—some whose negatives were never even printed up before—are gathered here, along with captions and anecdotes by the photographer, to create an important Beatles collector's item.

Or send for our brand-new catalog of over 300 best books on rock 'n' roll!!!

Free Rock Read button with every order!

Rock Read   799 Broadway   New York, N.Y. 10003

☐ **Yes,** please send me __ copies of *With the Beatles.* I am enclosing $14.95 + $1.00 shipping for each copy. (N.Y. residents please add sales tax.)

____ Send catalog

Amount enclosed $ _____ _____

Name _____

Address_____

City _____ State _____ Zip _____

Rock Read   799 Broadway   New York, N.Y. 10003   BF4

Beatles Story in Pictures, The, 131
Beatles: a Study in Sex, Drugs and Revolution, The, 21
Beatles Themes and Variations (series), 91
Beatles to Bacharach, 90
Beatles Trivia Quiz Book, The, 40
Beatles: 24 Posters, The, 70
Beatles Twenty Greatest Hits, The, 91
Beatles Unlimited, 162
Beatles Up to Date, The, 13
Beatles Video Newsletter, 146
Beatles Visie, 138
Beatles Who's Who, The, 67
Beatles: Words Without Music, The, 21
Beatles Years, The, 90
Beatles: Yesterday for Ever, Les, 171
Beatles: Yesterday . . . Today . . . Tomorrow, The, 27
Beatles: Yoko Ono et Moi, Les, 171
Behind the Beatles Songs, 39
Best of the Beatles, 119
Body Count, 26
Book of Lennon, The, 75
Boys From Liverpool: John, Paul, George, Ringo, The, 46
British Invasion, The, 86

Cavern Mecca, 156
Cellarful of Noise, A, 15, 56, 75
Celluloid Rock, 81
Chant and Be Happy, 85
Chase the Fade, 83
Club Sandwich, 152
Collecting the Beatles, 64
Collection Hommages: the Beatles, 171
Collection of Beatles Oldies, A, 91
Come Together, 137
Communism, Hypnotism and the Beatles, 18
Compleat Beatles, The, 51
Complete Beatles Lyrics, The, 64
Complete Beatles Quiz Book, The, 31
Complete Beatles US Record Price Guide, The, 70
Concise Beatles Complete, The, 91
Custard Stops at Hatfield: an Illustrated Biography, The, 84

Dakota Days, 69
Dark Horse, 158
Day the Music Died, The, 75
Dear Beatles, 16

Edition Spéciale John Lennon, 171
Encyclopedia of British Beat Groups and Solo Artists of the Sixties, 82
Encyclopedia of Rock, The, 81
En Flagrant Delire, 171

Essential Guide to Rock Records, The, 84
Every Little Thing: the Beatles on Record, 43

Fab Four Publication, The, 141
Fabulous, 117
Facts About a Pop Group, Featuring Wings, The, 35
Finger Picking Beatles, 91
First Book of Fifty Hit Songs by John Lennon and Paul McCartney, 90
Follow the Merseybeat Road, 72
4 Garçons dans le Vent, the Beatles, 171
From Me to You: das Magazin über die Beatles, 142

George Harrison Yesterday and Today, 36
Geschichte der Beatles, Die
Girl Who Sang With the Beatles, The, 23
Good Day Sunshine, 162
Grapefruit, 86
Great British, The, 81
Growing Up With the Beatles, 34
Guiness Book of 500 Number One Hits, The, 84
Guiness Book of Records, The, 82

Hands Across the Water: Wings Tour USA, 40
Hard Day's Night, A (Burke), 15
Hard Day's Night, A (DiFranco), 36
Hard Day's Night: the Official United Artists' Pictorial Souvenir Book, A, 119
Harrison Alliance, The, 148
Help! (Hine), 17
Help! (Random House), 17
Here Come the Beatles, 13
History of Rock, The, 123
Hommage de la Bande Dessinée, L., 171

I. Me. Mine, 47
Illustrated History of Rock Music, The, 81
Illustrated New Musical Express Encyclopedia of Rock, The, 81
In the Footsteps of the Beatles, 50
In His Own Write, 16
In His Own Write: the Lennon Play, 21
Instant Karma, 149
It's Easy to Play Beatles, 91
It Was Twenty Years Ago Today, 123

Jamming!, 123
John Lennon & the Beatles Forever, 55
John Lennon—Beatle, Kunstler, Provokateur, 173
John Lennon: Death of a Dream, 47
John Lennon: a Family Album, 70
John Lennon 4 Ever, 55
John Lennon Hat Mir das Rauchen Verboten, 174
John Lennon in His Own Words, 50
John Lennon: in My Life, 73

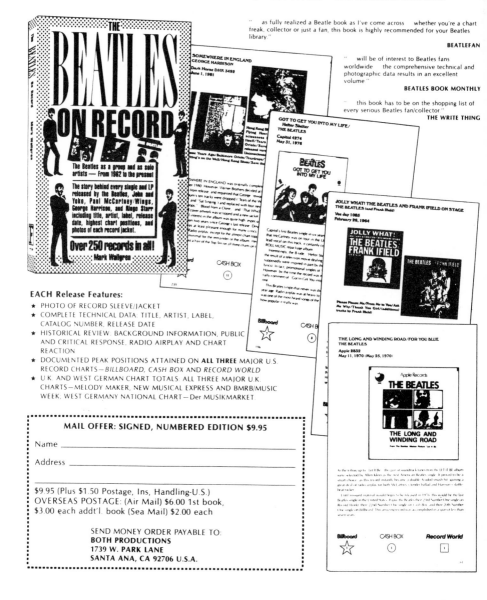
186

John Lennon: in Seiner Eigenen Schreibe, 174
John Lennon: the Life and the Legend, 123
John Lennon: a Melody Maker Tribute, 123
John Lennon: 1940-1980 (Connolly), 57
John Lennon: 1940-1980 (Schworck), 57
John Lennon: 1940-1980 (Van Fulpen), 171
John Lennon: One Day at a Time, 35
John Lennon 1940-1980: One Day at a Time, 47
John Lennon: a Personal Pictorial Diary, 57
John Lennon Story, The, (Swenson), 31
John Lennon Story, The (Swenson), 55
John Lennon: Summer of 1980, 70
John Lennon: Working Class Hero, 123
John Lennon's Secret, 62

Legacy of John Lennon, The, 63
Lennon Factor, The, 25
Lennon/McCartney, 171
Lennon and McCartney, 54
Lennon & McCartney: 50 Great Songs, 90
Lennon Remembers, 24
Lennon '69: Search for Liberation, 55
Lennon Tapes, The, 57
Lennon: Up Close & Personal, 49
Lennon: What Happened!, 49
Let's Go Down the Cavern, 70
Linda's Pictures, 32
Literary Lennon, The, 72
Live, 146
Liverpool 8, 59
Liverpool — the 60's, 74
Long & Winding Road, The, 61
Longest Cocktail Party, The, 25, 75
Lots of Liverpool, 61
Love Me Do: the Beatles Progress, 14
Love You Make, The, 68
Loving John, 69

McCartney Observer, 164
Making Music, 86
Man Who Gave the Beatles Away, The, 30
Marilyn, 117
Matin, Spécial Beatles, Le, 171
Maxwell's Silver Hammer, 158
Meet the Beatles, 117
Mersey Beat, 117, 173
Mersey Beat: the Beginnings of the Beatles, 37
Mersey Sound, The, 74
Murray the K Tell It Like It Is, Baby, 18
Music of the Beatles, The, 74
My Sweet Lady Jane, 160

New Volume, 74
1975 John Lennon Interview, The, 65
No One Waved Goodbye, 85

Ocean View, The, 68
Official Sgt. Pepper's Lonely Hearts Club Band
   Scrapbook, The, 41
On the Scene at the Cavern, 119
1,000 Beatles Facts (and a Little Hearsay), 37
Out of the Mouths of Beatles, 14
Oxtoby's Rockers, 79

PS We Love You, 67
Paperback Writer, 39
Paul McCartney, 71
Paul McCartney: a Biography in Words and
   Pictures, 36
Paul McCartney & Wings
Paul McCartney: Beatle With Wings, 41
Paul McCartney Composer/Artist, 52
Paul McCartney in His Own Words, 33
Paul McCartney Is Dead: the Great Hoax, 120
Paul McCartney Story, The, 28
Paul McCartney and Wings, (Jasper) 35
Paul McCartney & Wings (Pascall), 36
Paul McCartney und Wings, 173
Penguin John Lennon, The, 18
Playboy Interviews With John Lennon & Yoko
   Ono, The, 65
Phantasia, 85
Photographs, 66
Pocket Beatles Complete, 42
Podium: John Lennon la Vraie Fin des Beatles, 171
Pop From the Beginning, 80
Popular Voice (a Musical Record of the Sixties and
   Seventies), The, 82
Pour John Lennon, 171

Ram On!, 150
Record Collector, 113
Record Mirror, 117
Record Producers, The, 83
Revolver, 147
Ringo, 155
Ringo's Photo Album, 14
Road Goes on Forever, The, 83
Rock Dreams, 79
Rock Legends: the Beatles, 123
Rock 'n' Roll Times, 51
Rolling Stone, 122
Rolling Stone Rock 'n' Roll Reader, The, 80

Salut! Numero Special John Lennon
Sgt. Pepper's Lonely Hearts Club Band, 41
Shout! The True Story of the Beatles, 53
Songwriters, The, 81
Souvenirs des Beatles, 171
Spaniard in the Works, A, 18
Star Club News, 117, 173, 174
Stardust Memories, 74

**Merseybeat:
The Beginnings Of The
Beatles**

"...A marvellous momento of
Beatlemania, of the Mersey-
sound, the sound that changed
the course of popular music..."
MUSIC'SOUND

Merseybeat was the first
newspaper ever to feature The
Beatles. Each page of this
book is a facsimile
reproduction of highlights from
the original issues. Merseybeat founder and editor, Bill
Harry, has added a fascinating
introduction.

**How To Succeed In The
Music Business**
By Allan Dann & John
Underwood

"...a wealth of advice and
information for anyone wishing
to break into music..."
MUSIC WEEK

Wise Publications
255 x 180mm
88pp, illustrated
£2.95 softcover
ISBN 0 86001 454 1
AM 19977

Omnibus Press
325 x 240mm, 96pp
illustrated
£3.50 softcover
ISBN 0 86001 415 0
OP 40286

**The Country Music
Encyclopaedia**
By Melvin Shestack

"...hard to fault..."
NEW MUSICAL EXPRESS

The most thorough innovative
and ambitious book ever
written on country music. Fully
illustrated.

**The Folk Music
Encyclopaedia**
By Kristin Baggelaar
& Donald Milton

"...as fascinating as its
companion book on country
music...entertaining and
attractively produced with
numerous illustrations...A first
rate reference book to interest
every folk fan."
PAISLEY DAILY EXPRESS
"...an interesting and useful
reference book..."
NEW MUSICAL EXPRESS

Story of Pop, The, 123
Strawberry Fields Forever: John Lennon
    Remembered, 46
Surboum Beatles Special, 171

Thank U Very Much, 58
Things We Said Today, 45, 179
Tomorrow Never Knows, 167
Top Twenty, 80
Tribute to John Lennon: 1940-1980, A, 56
True Story of the Beatles, The, 13
20 Ans Avec les Beatles, 173
26 Days That Rocked the World, 40
Twilight of the Gods: the Beatles in Retrospect, 27
Twist of Lennon, A, 41

Up Against It: a Screenplay for the Beatles, 43
Up the Beatles Family Tree, 18

Valentine, 117

Wahre Geschichte der Beatles, Die, 173
Waiting for the Beatles, 75
We Love You Beatles, 23
Whatever Happened to . . . ?, 86
Wings, 36
With the Beatles, 68
Working Class Heroes, 71
Write Thing, The, 143
Writing Beatle: John Lennon, The, 20

Yellow Submarine Gift Book, The, 21
Yesterday: Photographs of the Beatles, 71
Yesterday Seems So Far Away: the Beatles
    Yesterday and Today, 36
You Can't Do That: Beatles Bootlegs and Novelty
    Discs, 55

LA BALLADE DE
JOHN & YOKO

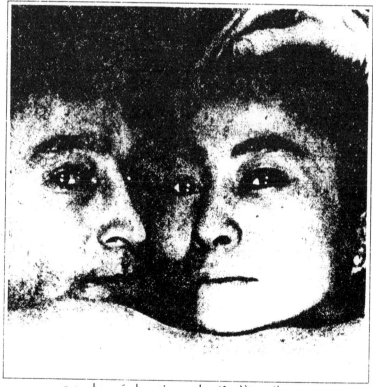

par la rédaction de *Rolling Stone*

DENOËL

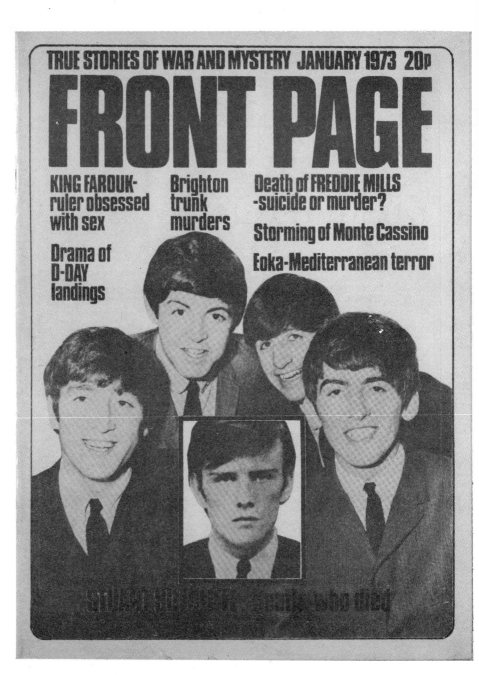

TRUE STORIES OF WAR AND MYSTERY JANUARY 1973 20p

FRONT PAGE

KING FAROUK- ruler obsessed with sex

Brighton trunk murders

Death of FREDDIE MILLS -suicide or murder?

Drama of D-DAY landings

Storming of Monte Cassino

Eoka-Mediterranean terror